Say It Ain't So, Joe!

Say It Ain't So, Joe!

The True Story of Shoeless Joe Jackson

SECOND REVISED EDITION

Donald Gropman

A CITADEL PRESS BOOK
PUBLISHED BY CAROL PUBLISHING GROUP

Carol Publishing Group Second Revised Edition 1999

A Citadel Press Book
Published by Carol Publishing Group
Citadel Press is a registered trademark of Carol Communications, Inc.

Editorial, sales and distribution, and rights and permissions inquiries
should be addressed to Carol Publishing Group, 120 Enterprise Avenue,
Secaucus, N.J. 07094.

In Canada: Canadian Manda Group, One Atlantic Avenue, Suite 105,
Toronto, Ontario M6K 3E7

Carol Publishing Group books may be purchased in bulk at special
discounts for sales promotion, fund-raising, or educational purposes.
Special editions can be created to specifications. For details, contact
Special Sales Department, Carol Publishing Group, 120 Enterprise
Avenue, Secaucus, N.J. 07094.

Manufactured in the United States of America
ISBN 0-8065-1336-5

10 9 8 7 6 5 4 3 2

Library of Congress Cataloging-in-Publication Data

Gropman, Donald.
    Say it ain't so, Joe! : the true story of Shoeless Joe Jackson /
by Donald Gropman.—Rev. ed.
        p. cm.
    "A Citadel Press book."
    1. Jackson, Joe, 1888-1951.   2. Baseball players—United
States—Biography.   I. Title.
    GV865.J29G76   1992
    796.357'092—dc20
        [B]   92-22172
                                                              CIP

Contents

Acknowledgments

IN THE COURSE of writing this book I received help from many people. One of the most important of these was Fred McAbee of Greenville, South Carolina, to whom I was referred when I blindly telephoned the Brandon Mill in search of someone who had known Joe Jackson personally or, at least, knew some things about him firsthand. Once a standout second baseman in the textile leagues, Fred now lives in retirement with his gracious wife, Corine, in one of the original mill houses which they bought several years ago when Brandon Mill, now owned by Abney Mills, sold off all its houses. Fred's house sits at the edge of the old Brandon ballgrounds, still laid out as a baseball diamond but in general disrepair.

I phoned Fred to introduce myself and enlist his help, but he interrupted before I could finish. Yes, he told me, he had indeed known Joe Jackson, but beyond that he knew some very old timers who had known Joe better. He even knew some men who had played mill ball with Joe back in 1907. Fred offered to help me in any way he could. All he wanted to know was the date on which I would arrive in Greenville.

When I finally did get to Greenville, Fred was true to his offer. Through his diligence and powers of persuasion, he located and introduced me to Mrs. Gertrude Jackson Trammell, Joe's younger sister. Gertrude patiently answered my questions about her brother and the entire Jackson family and also allowed me to study the set of scrapbooks on Joe's career, which had been compiled over a period of almost fifty years by her late sister-in-law, Katie Wynn Jackson. Gertrude, moreover, introduced me to her older sister, Mrs. Lula Jackson Ellis and to Lula's daughter, Mrs. Marguerite Ellis Hall, both of Savannah, Georgia. Lula, who died in December 1978, contributed a wealth of family history and detail. I am indebted to Joe's sisters and his niece for their cooperation. Without their assistance, this book would have lacked an important dimension.

Fred McAbee also introduced me to Jim McAllister, a columnist with the *Greenville News*. McAllister wrote a paragraph about my search for people who had known Joe Jackson and he included the name of the motel in which I was staying. Many people from the Greenville area telephoned to tell me what they knew about Joe. Between the people who responded to the McAllister column and the interviews arranged by Fred, I had more sources of information than I could handle. I am indebted to the following men and women for their willingness to share their recollections and for other acts of kindness and support: Joe Anders, Dora Bishop, Sue Bostic, Cole Brown, Ted Cabanis, Mr. and

Mrs. John T. Campbell, Hovey Cartee, Mr. and Mrs. E. P. Cashion, Norwood Cleveland, Mrs. Sarah Cole, Charles Davenport, William Denton, Ted Ellison, Mr. and Mrs. James Guy, Courtney Heath, Mrs. Helen House and her late husband, Harry House, Paul Humphries, Ray Jackson, Lloyd George McAbee, T. B. Ray, Aleck Mutt Rollins, Tina Rollins, Bobby Thompson, and Mr. and Mrs. Ed Young.

Other members of the Greenville community who provided valuable help include the Honorable Rex L. Carter, Speaker of the South Carolina House of Representatives; Yancey S. Gilkerson, president of the Textile Hall Corporation; staff members of the Greenville County Museum of Art, particularly director Jack A. Morris, Jr., his wife, Sylvia, and Edwin Ritts, Jr., chief curator; Charles Grubbs of the Greenville County Library; His Honor Max M. Heller, mayor of Greenville, and his secretary, Joan Stovall; and Mrs. Barbara L. Haynes of the Legislative Council of the General Assembly of South Carolina.

For the help they gave to the writing of this book, I am grateful to author Eliot Asinof; sportswriter and editor Furman Bisher; Judge Robert C. Cannon of the Circuit Court, Milwaukee, Wisconsin, who loaned me his copy of the three-volume transcripts of the bill of exceptions proposed on behalf of Joe Jackson by the judge's father, Raymond J. Cannon, who was Joe's attorney in his civil suit against Charles Comiskey in 1924; Bennett Curry of the Hillerich & Bradsby Company; sportswriter Dan Daniel; former major league third baseman Jumping Joe Dugan; author James T. Farrell; Mrs. Carol Haines of the Public Library, Brookline, Massachusetts; sportscaster Ernie Harwell; Clifford Kachline, historian at the National Baseball Library, operated by the National Baseball Hall of Fame and Museum, Inc.; William T. Loughman, member of the Society for American Baseball Research (SABR); sportscaster Ned Martin; Pete Palmer,

SABR member; John F. Redding, librarian at the National Baseball Library; Bob Richardson, SABR, member; historian Harold Seymour, whose multivolume work, *Baseball,* helped me to understand the context in which Joe Jackson's public career was enacted; Thomas P. Shea and Joseph E. Simenic, both SABR members; and Professor Ron Story of the history department at the University of Massachusetts.

I would also like to acknowledge the contributions made by people who have since died: Jack Graney and Ken Nash, former major-league teammates of Joe Jackson; Mrs. Eva Hollis, of Greenville, and her husband, the remarkable L. P. Hollis, who was in his nineties when he told me, with great clarity and detail, about the early days when the mills around Greenville were built and how he had been one of the men who first brought baseball to the mills.

During this project, I have worked with two editors. I would like to thank Llew Howland for giving me the opportunity to write this book and Bill Phillips for helping me to make it better.

My final note of thanks is to my children, Sonya and Adam, who offered encouragement and endured my preoccupation with good humor, and to my wife Gabrielle, who helped in more ways than I can say.

He was just a natural born baseball player, that's all there was to it.

— John Campbell, Monoghan Mill catcher

I've seen all the best players of the past twenty years and no one's been better than Joe. I never tired of watching him bat. It was a pleasure to see him swing and when he hit the ball there was a ring to it that pleased the ear.

— Eddie Collins, Hall of Fame second baseman

Joe Jackson hit the ball harder than any man that ever played in the big leagues, and I don't except Babe Ruth.

— Big Ed Walsh, Hall of Fame pitcher

I decided to pick out the greatest hitter to watch and study and Jackson was good enough for me.

— Babe Ruth, Hall of Fame outfielder

There was only one Jackson. There was only one Ruth. . . . Why compare them?

— Connie Mack, Hall of Fame manager

Preface to the Revised Edition

GOING BACK TO REVISE a book written almost fifteen years ago is a ticklish proposition; the longer you look at it, the more faults you see and the more changes you want to make. Before you know it, you've rewritten the whole thing. But that is not the task at hand. I have revised the original text for two reasons: to clarify Joe Jackson's role in the 1919 Black Sox scandal and to bring his legend up to date. The sections dealing with Joe Jackson's role in the Black Sox scandal have been completely rewritten to incorporate new materials. The last chapter, which covers the recent revival of Jackson's legend, is also new.

There was, however, much interesting and informative material that has become available in recent years, some of it discovered in the mid-1980's in a trunk in the attic of the undertaker who had buried Jackson in 1951, some released from the archives of a Chicago law firm. Many of these materials, including the full text of Jackson's 1920 testimony before the grand jury and correspondence sent to him by Baseball Commissioner Kenesaw Mountain Landis and White Sox owner Charles Comiskey, will be found in Appendices at the back of the book. These materials, presented with some commentary, will provide the reader with much of the documentation on which I have based my conclusions.

I am indebted to many people for fresh insights, materials, and suggestions. Among them are Stephen Adamson; Ray Allen, founder of the Joe Jackson Society; Attorney Thomas G. Cannon of the Milwaukee firm O'Neil, Cannon & Hollman, whose grandfather Ray represented Jackson in his 1924 civil suit against Charles Comiskey and the White Sox; baseball writer and historian Paul Green; baseball coach Lester Irwin, nephew of the late Katie Wynn Jackson; and Jean Vulf, whose assiduous research uncovered several key documents. I am particularly grateful to Attorney David B. Carlson of the Chicago law firm Rinella & Rinella, LTD. for allowing me to make use of his unpublished analysis of the Black Sox scandal, "Strike Four: Joe Jackson, the Black Sox, and the 1919 World Series."

The first edition of this book was published in 1979 and went out of print in the early 1980s. I would like to take this opportunity to thank Michael J. Fine, who, as president of Lynx Books, believed enough in this book to publish a paperback edition of the original version in 1988. When the Lynx edition appeared, public interest in Shoeless Joe, now seen more than ever as a classic and legendary scapegoat, was on the rise. The response to that edition, including numerous requests for more information about Jackson's role in 1919, eventually convinced me to undertake this revision.

A final note of gratitude to Chriss Fiebig and Richard Lips of Bamberg, Germany, who graciously allowed me use of their home and office, where these revisions were completed.

Introduction to the Revised Edition

EVERYBODY REMEMBERS Shoeless Joe Jackson, the greatest natural hitter the game of baseball has ever seen. As legend has it, he was discovered playing milltown ball in his stocking feet. In the second decade of this century, swinging Black Betsy, his famous homemade bat, he electrified the major leagues with his clutch slugging, bullet-like throws, and come-from-nowhere fielding.

But then, at the height of his career, he was disgraced and thrown out of organized baseball for his alleged role in fixing the 1919 World Series. The "Black Sox Scandal," as it has come to be called, involved eight members of the Chicago White Sox who were indicted for throwing the Series to the Cincinnati Reds.

The rise and fall of this great natural ballplayer—followed by his gutsy comeback as an aging star of semi-pro "outlaw" ball—has inspired numerous American writers ranging from Nelson Algren to William Kinsella. His life and legend infuse Joe Hardy ("Shoeless Joe from Hannibal, Mo.") in *Damn Yankees*, and Roy Hobbs, the hero of Bernard Malamud's *The Natural*, the character portrayed on screen a few years ago by Robert Redford. And he made another appearance in the movie *Field of Dreams*, based on Kinsella's novel *Shoeless Joe*. Whatever one thinks of his moral character, there is no doubt that he has become a unique figure in popular American mythology.

The most famous phrase to emerge from the Black Sox scandal, and perhaps from all of baseball, was the tearful question allegedly put to Shoeless Joe by a young fan: "Say it ain't so, Joe." But Joe did not say that it wasn't so. An illiterate country boy, he gave contradictory answers about his involvement in a gambling scheme. Although he denied that he threw any games, his major league career was over and he entered history as a personification of corruption.

That was over seventy years ago. Since then we have learned much about Jackson's real role in the Black Sox scandal, a good deal of it uncovered by Donald Gropman. This new edition of his groundbreaking Jackson biography contains information which strongly suggests that it wasn't so, or at the very least was not as bad as the powers of organized baseball have led us to believe.

Gropman's convincing account of the scandal—based on interviews, grand jury minutes, diaries and other new information—makes the 1919–1920 White Sox seem like the 1972–1974 White House. The White Sox cover-up was intended to protect club owner and president Charles Comiskey, much like the White House cover-up was intended to protect

President Nixon. The big difference is that the White Sox cover-up worked. And therein lies an interesting story about how much our legal system has changed for the better over the intervening half-century.

The facts, as they now have emerged, are as follows: Jackson was approached by a teammate and offered $10,000 to throw the World Series. He declined. A short time later the offer was renewed, this time for $20,000. Jackson refused again. This information, by the way, is from Jackson's own testimony before the Cook County Grand Jury, the very testimony that has, in garbled, twisted press accounts, been used as proof of Jackson's complicity. Furthermore, there is strong evidence that Jackson told one or more officials of the club before the Series began that a fix was in the making. He even asked to be benched for the Series to avoid any suspicion that he was involved, but his request was refused.

Several of Jackson's teammates did conspire to throw the Series, and the White Sox lost to the Reds, five games to three. Jackson, however, playing under the watchful eyes of club officials, was the star of the Series: he hit the only home run, fielded flawlessly, batted .375 to lead all players, and his twelve hits set a World Series record that stood for decades.

Like most of the known facts about the Jackson case, the event that is usually cited to prove his guilt has also been misrepresented. On the evening after the last game of the Series, one of Jackson's teammates came to his hotel room and offered him an envelope containing cash. Jackson refused to accept it, an argument ensued, and Jackson stormed out of his own room. His teammate, pitcher Lefty Williams, threw the envelope down and left. This version of the crucial event in Jackson's case was attested to, under oath, by the only two men who were there: Jackson and Williams. Their accounts agree. Jackson did not take the money, it was dumped on him.

Returning to his room, Jackson found the envelope and saw that it contained $5000 in cash. He put it in his pocket. The next morning he went to Comiskey's office at the ball park, but was told Comiskey would not see him. He waited an hour, then he left.

Comiskey, who at that very moment was in a secret meeting with two of the fixed players hearing the story of the scheme, chose a hypocritical course of action. While publicly proclaiming his commitment to "clean baseball," he privately spent the winter and almost all of the 1920 season denying the rumors that stubbornly clung to the 1919 Series and perpetrating a cover-up, in part to protect his valuable property, namely the guilty players. But in September of 1920, for reasons that had more to do with political in-fighting and greed than with "clean baseball," a grand jury was impanelled and the fix was exposed.

Now Comiskey's priority was to protect his own reputation. His best option was to feed the suspected players to the grand jury, but only after they had been counseled by Comiskey's own lawyer, Alfred Austrian. The point of this exercise seems to have been damage control—Comiskey would have looked bad if the public learned what he knew and when he knew it. Of the players fed to the grand jury, Jackson was the most problematic. He had been the only one to warn Comiskey *before* the Series began. If he told everything, Comiskey's self-proclaimed integrity would be impugned and he would be revealed as a hypocrite and perhaps worse.

Jackson was working under two misconceptions when he met with Austrian: he believed the truth would protect him and he believed Austrian was *his* lawyer. Neither belief was true. Jackson began by protesting his innocence, but in a session that lasted for several hours, Austrian finally convinced Jackson that the truth would not be believed by the grand jury. We do not know exactly what Austrian suggested to Jackson (while Austrian admitted under oath that he had kept notes on his pre-testimony meetings with the other players, he claimed he kept no notes during his session with Jackson), but we can make some logical deductions by analyzing the grand jury testimony Jackson subsequently gave. A careful reading of that testimony, reprinted in this book, reveals that Jackson told two diametrically opposed stories, one confessing his guilt and the other protesting his innocence. Logic leads us to believe the first story was probably Austrian's, the second Jackson's.

Gropman presents the intricate details of Jackson's case in his text. Suffice it to say that Jackson was eventually indicted, tried in criminal court, and found Not Guilty. Nevertheless, he was banished from organized baseball. That is when his love of the game led him to his second career in semi-pro "outlaw" ball.

In 1924, during a civil trial in which Jackson sued Comiskey for back wages on a three-year contract, the likely truth of how and why Jackson's name had been falsely implicated in the Black Sox scheme finally came to light. Sleepy Bill Burns, the fixer who put the players and the gamblers in touch with each other, testified under oath that he had *never talked to Jackson about the fix*. Instead, he took the word of Lefty Williams, who claimed he was empowered to speak for Jackson. And Williams himself, also under oath, swore he *never received Jackson's permission to use his name* with the fixers. This is perhaps the most compelling evidence we have, because it provides both motivation and means. The gamblers wanted a sure thing, and since Jackson was capable of going on a hitting streak that could carry the White Sox to victory despite the fix, they wanted Jackson in. So the fixed players, in the person of Williams, said he was. The means were equally simple: Williams and Burns both wanted the scheme to work, so one lied and the other took him at his word with no effort to substantiate his claim.

The outcome of the civil suit was ambiguous. The jury found in Jackson's favor, but the judge overruled the verdict. Nevertheless, it was the second jury to hear Jackson's story and find him innocent of culpable involvement in the Black Sox scandal. But the powers that be in organized baseball ignored the jury verdicts and refused to lift his life-time banishment.

Jackson received shoddy treatment, but this probably would not happen today. A modern-day Jackson would have his own lawyer from the very beginning. Nor would the shenanigans employed by Comiskey's lawyer be tolerated by the bar today. Most important, an honest prosecutor today generally seeks to follow the criminal trail to the top of the mountain. Convicting the Watergate burglars was not enough. The special prosecutor followed the trail to the attorney general and eventually to the president.

But in post-World War I Chicago, corruption tainted more than the White Sox. The entire city—judiciary and all— reeked with influence-peddling and power-brokering, and among the most influential brokers was Charles Comiskey.

It's therefore no surprise that Comiskey now holds an honored place in the Baseball Hall of Fame, while Shoeless Joe Jackson remains a scapegoat. Though both are now long dead, the true story deserves to be known. In the last years of his life, former baseball commissioner A.B. "Happy" Chandler got behind the efforts to clear Jackson's name. "I never in my life believed him to be guilty of a single thing," said the man who was privy to the secret files of the major leagues.

Baseball is a game of legends. Memories play as important a role as current events. If it "ain't so"—or even if it wasn't as bad as legend has it—big-league baseball should be big enough to admit it made a mistake about Shoeless Joe. Like any other institution, baseball can only be honest in the present if it is honest with its own past. And since baseball is still viewed by many as a metaphor for America itself, such an act of corrective justice would have meaning beyond baseball as a mere game. This book makes a well reasoned step in that direction.

—ALAN DERSHOWITZ
Professor, Harvard Law School

Introduction

THE TRAIL THAT LED me to Shoeless Joe Jackson began when my father arrived in America in 1909. He was six years old. His family settled in Boston, in a brick tenement section below Beacon Hill. One afternoon two years later some older boys took my father on a walk across Boston, all the way from the dense and immigrant West End to the more open land on the other side of the Fenway. They walked him to the Huntington Avenue Ballgrounds, home of the Boston Americans (Red Sox). They didn't have money to buy tickets so they watched the game from outside. At that time in his life my father was just starting to emerge from his boyish immigrant haze and in some sense he was at the Huntington Avenue Ballgrounds learning to be an American.

It was a hot, steamy Monday in August. The Boston team, struggling toward a fifth-place finish, was playing Cleveland. Nevertheless, there was a big weekday turnout of seven thousand fans in the ballgrounds and a couple of hundred kids outside. They had come to get a look at Shoeless Joe Jackson.

Joe Jackson was the talk of the major leagues in the summer of 1911. It was his first full season and he stood the fans on their heads everywhere he played. Coming into Boston that hot August he was hitting .397. He was in the middle of a great batting streak: between July 11 and August 26 he went to bat 147 times and got 68 hits. Over a span of thirty-seven games he batted .462.

My father and his friends took turns watching the game through the spaces between the fence slats. In the first inning Boston put a man on first. The next batter, shortstop Heinie Wagner, smashed a line drive toward right center field. The man on first held up a moment to see if the ball was catchable, and when it seemed that neither the center fielder nor Joe in right field could catch up with it, he started for second. But Joe raced after the ball, skimming smoothly over the green grass until he caught up with it at the center field fence. The base runner turned and made a frantic dash back to first base but Joe, with his back against the fence, fired a rifle shot to his first baseman, which seemed to come back in faster than the line drive had gone out. The runner was out by twenty or thirty feet. The crowd gasped, then gave Joe a mighty cheer.

Joe was the first man up for Cleveland in the second inning and the cheers followed him to the plate. My father, who hardly knew what it was all about, joined in the many-throated cry that rose up in the humid air over the old Huntington Avenue Ballgrounds: "Give 'em Black Betsy, Joe! Give 'em Black Betsy!" On the first pitch he hit a screaming line drive at shortstop Wagner. It was no more than five or six feet off the ground and the shortstop had a play on it, but it was hit so hard that he actually ducked out of the way. The kids watching from outside the fence joined in the cheers of amazement and satisfaction. Joe Jackson was doing all the things the crowd had come to see him do.

A generation later, when I was six years old, my father came home one evening with a flat cardboard box. It was for me. Inside was a baseball uniform, a glove, a bat, and a ball. The uniform was white with red trim. On summer evenings after supper I'd put it on and my father would lob soft pitches to me in our backyard.

As it had been for so many fathers and sons, baseball was a way of sharing experience between my father and me. It was not the only way, but at times it proved to be one of the easiest: a game of catch between the two of us or, later when I was bigger, a Sunday morning game of ball, the fathers against the boys. Other times he took me to see the Boston Braves or the Red Sox. But most frequent were the stories he told me, the anecdotes or bits and pieces about players he'd seen, or particular plays that had become fixed in his memory. That was how I heard about the first big-league game he ever saw. It was an important event in my father's life and his memory of it focused on the image of Joe Jackson.

Years later he still recalled that you didn't have to know anything at all about baseball to see that Joe Jackson was someone special. There was a beauty in him, even in the way he walked, that set him apart from other players. He walked like a big cat, my father thought, sure and graceful in his every move. He never forgot the way Joe Jackson walked.

Joe Jackson was not the only oldtime player my father told me about, but he was the only one who walked a special way, the only one who had a special bat like Black Betsy. So

Shoeless Joe stuck in my imagination. Sometimes when I was young I tried to conjure up an image of him throwing out a runner or gliding over the outfield grass in pursuit of a speeding ball. Then I forgot about him, or thought I did, but he remained a shadowy figure at the edge of my imagination.

At a barn sale in New Hampshire a few years ago I pulled an old magazine from the bottom of a box of books. It was a 1916 issue of *Baseball Magazine*, the "Joe Jackson Number." I held the magazine in my hand and studied the picture of Joe on the cover. A left-handed batter wearing a small black cap with the letter *C* on the peak was resting a dark bat on his left shoulder. It seemed he was supposed to be looking back at a pitcher, but his gaze was too high for that. In actuality, or so it seemed to me, he was looking out over the left center field fence. I fancied he was waiting for something, something that would float into view from the other side of the fence.

A sense of my childhood came over me as I recalled my father's story about the first big-league game he saw and the way Joe Jackson walked. Then I recalled some other things about Shoeless Joe, pieces of information which had lodged in my memory during the boyhood period when I'd read all the books about baseball I could find:

> —Shoeless Joe Jackson was the greatest natural hitter who ever lived. Even Ty Cobb said so, and Babe Ruth had copied his swing because it was the best he'd ever seen. Joe's career batting average of .356 is still the third highest of all time.
> —They called him Shoeless because that's the way he was playing when a major-league scout discovered him in the Carolina mountains. The nickname stuck because it fit this simple, uncomplicated country boy who couldn't read or write.
> —His natural physical abilities were unmatched, but he was

either stupid or cowardly or both. In his first full year in the majors he batted .408, but Ty Cobb either tricked or pressured Joe into a slump and came from behind to win the batting title.

—Joe Jackson was a crook. In 1919 he was one of the Chicago White Sox who threw the World Series to the Cincinnati Reds. When the scandal was revealed they called the guilty men the Black Sox. It seemed like the perfect name.

—When Joe walked down the courthouse steps after confessing his guilt to a grand jury, a little kid came up to him and said, "Say it ain't so, Joe." But it was so and they banished him for life. He walked down the courthouse stairs and disappeared from baseball forever.

I bought the old *Baseball Magazine* and read it. The author of the feature article about Joe had spent several weeks in Greenville, South Carolina, talking to Joe's family, friends, and former workmates in the Brandon Cotton Mill. He traced Joe's life from midcareer in the American League back through the cotton mill village where he'd grown up and all the way to the rural hills where he'd been born.

There were also many photographs. They were blurry by today's standards of reproduction, unclear around the edges of the figures and lacking sharp definition. But just because of those hazy qualities they seemed more real, more representative of their time and truer.

The lead photo of the article took up most of the first page and sat above the title: "The Man Who Might Have Been the Greatest Player in the Game." The picture is a montage. A studio portrait of Joe is superimposed on a frontal view of the Brandon Cotton Mill, where Joe went to work when he was six years old. His gigantic head seems to rise out of the roof of the six-hundred-foot-long building. His dark eyes, each as large as a mill window, gaze calmly back at the viewer.

As I read the article and studied the pictures I glimpsed an actual man named Joe Jackson who existed behind or beside a mythological character called Shoeless Joe. I wanted to learn more about him, and that is how I happened to write this book.

Say It Ain't So, Joe!

1

GREENVILLE SITS in the northwest corner of South Carolina, in the uplands where the hills rise to meet the Blue Ridge Mountains. In 1890, after a slow and steady growth since its founding before the Revolutionary War, the city had a population of 12,000. This number was increased on market days, when the farm families scattered through the countryside drove their wagons into town to sell their crops and buy supplies. But by 1905 Greenville was the urban center for a circling ring of thirteen cotton mills and their mill villages. The population of the city itself had grown to 15,000; the combined population of the mill villages approached 25,000.

Industrial development on such a large scale was something new in the South. A few scattered cotton mills had existed, but the South's major role had always been to grow the cotton and export it for manufacture somewhere else. Then the culmination of a long series of events — most notably the Civil War and the Reconstruction — created conditions in which the northern mill owners found it greatly to their advantage to expand into the South or to relocate there altogether. As investment capital and trainloads of dismantled looms and spinning frames flowed south, the sudden events which occurred in and around Greenville were repeated in many southern places.

First the investors bought land, often a bankrupt plantation, and quickly built modern cotton mills. The mills were made of brick and looked as if they were built to last forever. As soon as the mill itself was built, the rest of the mill village was built around it: rows of small wood-frame mill houses; a mill church; a mill store. When a mill village was complete, all that was needed were the people to work and live in it.

When the mill villages around Greenville were completed, the owners sent their recruiters through the South Carolina uplands, into the mountains of Tennessee and North Carolina and down into Georgia. Times were bad in the South, particularly in the rural areas, and the mill owners knew it. It was one of their chief reasons for moving south in the first place. Small landowners were losing their holdings all over the South and even tenant farmers and sharecroppers were being driven off the land by the economic conditions: raw cotton, the biggest cash crop, was selling at five cents a pound, a starvation price. The owners thought they would have an endless supply of inexpensive labor. In response to their recruiters' promises of steady work, steady wages, and low cost housing, whole families left the mountains and the farms and came down to the cotton mills. They were drawn in by the thousands. But once they got there the mill owners' problem was to hold them.

Life in the rural world of the southern uplands had done nothing to prepare the people for their sudden entry into the industrial world. Overnight, in the mill villages around Greenville, thousands of rural folks found themselves living a new life. Many of them — men, women, and small children — worked in the cotton mills, mills which hadn't even been there a year or two before. The mills were bigger and stronger than any buildings they'd ever seen and the noise inside of them was deafening. When the machines got going, the roar could be heard half a mile away in all directions.

The mill hands worked for seventy or more hours a week. In place of the mountain air they'd left behind, they breathed the lint-filled air of the mills. The lint they inhaled collected in their lungs; years later many of them developed emphysema and brown lung disease. Lint also clung to their clothes and hair and gave them their nickname: lintheads.

Mill life rarely matched the picture of it drawn by the recruiters, and many of the mill hands were disappointed. Some couldn't stand being shut up in the mill for twelve hours a day, others couldn't tolerate the lint in their lungs or the constant pounding of the machines. For these and other reasons many of the mill hands quit. Some returned to their homes in the countryside or up in the mountains, but for most there was no turning back. The best they could do was wander from mill to mill, dissatisfied and unable to find the life they wanted.

The constant turnover in the work force was a problem for the mill owners too. From their point of view it seemed that as soon as a new batch of spinners or weavers was trained, half of them left to go back home or moved on to another mill. The owners wanted a stable, permanent work force, and in the mills around Greenville they tried many things to hold the mill hands on the job.

The first thing they did was provide inexpensive housing. The mill houses usually had two to four rooms and were rented to the mill hands for fifty cents per room per month. Then they tried to help the mill hands acquire material things that would anchor them. Some mills arranged for families to buy furniture, musical instruments, and even cows on credit. These credit debts made it impossible for some mill hands to leave when they wanted to. In a few of the mill villages social services were offered: practical things such as homemaking, and entertainments such as community social-sings and movies. One mill even produced its own short film, on the evils of moving, which showed a mill family lose its belongings when the wagon moving it from one mill village to another tipped over. All the furniture fell off and was destroyed.

The mills tried many things to hold their workers but in the early years, when the mills were just starting, what worked the best was baseball.

The Civil War, which had helped to bring about the conditions in which the cotton mills could thrive in their new location, had, by coincidence, helped baseball to move south too. The game, which had evolved out of several older games, most of English origin, had its earliest popularity in the northeast corner of the country. By the middle of the nineteenth century baseball had begun to spread across the nation. This movement was advanced by the many northerners who reported to their Union Army units with bats and balls packed away among their field gear. They often played games in their own camps. Later, when many of them were captured, they played baseball to pass the dreary time in the prison camps. The prisoners played among themselves and sometimes teams of prisoners played teams of guards. When they played against the guards the prisoners frequently had to teach them the game first. In this way baseball entered many areas of the South. And when the mills appeared three or four decades later, the game was available.

The mill owners' choice of baseball as an activity that could generate a sense of community spirit had been a good one. Though it had not yet become popular in the rural southern uplands and was therefore relatively new to them, the mill hands took to it immediately. Their response exemplified the mood of the whole nation. As the contemporary journalist Will Irwin saw it, "Baseball had but to be seen by Americans to be loved."

The mill hands, players and fans alike, took up baseball so quickly and with such passion that the mill owners had little to do beyond organizing teams and setting up ballgrounds in each of the villages. The villagers, perhaps hungering for the sense of identity with place and the familiarity of local heroes, both of which they'd left behind in the hills and hollows of the uplands, adopted their new mill teams with an immediate loyalty. And since there was little else to compete for their attention, their ball team and its players were the favorite topics of conversation.

2

THE FIVE-STORIED front facade of the Brandon Cotton Mill sported over two hundred large windows, each of which looked out on the mill store, the mill church, small sections of the mill village, and the countryside beyond. Out in back, in a field between the rear of the mill and the first row of the largest section of mill houses, was the Brandon Mill Ballgrounds. The infield was trampled bare earth. The grass began in the outfield. The playing surface was rough and uneven; there was a dump at the farthest edge of center field.

One whole side of the diamond was bordered and dwarfed by the mill and between the mill and the diamond ran the tracks of a spur line, which curved gently away from the mill and disappeared from sight at the top of a small rise. When the sun was low in the sky the mill cast its shadow six hundred feet along the edge of the ballgrounds. Six hundred feet. Nobody ever hit a baseball that far at Brandon Mill or anyplace else, but local fans thought that if it was possible, their own Joe Jackson would be the man to do it.

Joe Jackson stepped to the plate batting cleanup in a big game against Monoghan Mill. Expectation rippled through the crowd. The small wooden grandstand behind home plate was packed with three or four hundred people, mostly men and boys. Here and there small clusters of women and girls stood out in their weekend wide-brimmed hats and long-sleeved, ankle-length dresses. From the festive Saturday afternoon grandstand crowd voices spun across the sparkling April air: "Give 'em Black Betsy, Joey! Give 'em Black Betsy!"

Black Betsy was Joe's baseball bat. She was thirty-six inches long and weighed about forty-eight ounces. But she was more than just a bat; she was Joe's talisman, his trademark, the handmade tool of his profession. She fit the grip of his big hands so perfectly and sliced through the air so smoothly when he cut loose at the plate that it seemed as if some of the sweeping power came from her, seemed as if Black Betsy was alive and eager to whack the baseball as it came whistling in over the plate.

The Monoghan catcher ambled out to talk to his pitcher. The one umpire, who covered the entire game from his position behind the pitcher, listened in, but there wasn't much to hear because there really wasn't much the catcher could say. All he could do was try to settle his pitcher's nerves. The Monoghan outfielders backed up as far as they could go.

Encouraging cheers from Joe's hometown fans poured out of the grandstand and were taken up by the even larger crowds gathered outside of the ropes strung along the foul lines. Everyone in Brandon knew Joe Jackson; he was the most spectacular baseball player they'd ever seen. His fellow villagers had been watching his progress for five or six years, ever since he was thirteen years old and the men who played on the Brandon Mill team had come to ask his mother if he could join them.

Joe acknowledged the cheers with a slight smile, hefted Black Betsy onto his left shoulder, and scraped a solid footing in the left-handed batter's box. The catcher squatted down behind him, but when he remembered how Joe spread out when he hit, he backed up a few feet. As the pitcher went into his motion, Joe let Betsy dip slightly down toward his back. The first pitch was high and outside. The catcher lunged for it but the ball never got to him. Joe's long arms uncoiled across his twisting body in one fluid motion, unleashing Black Betsy into a flashing black swing. The ball shot off Betsy's barrel in a flat trajectory right over the pitcher's head. Only when it cleared the second baseman, who was playing deep and on a line behind the bag, did the crowd hear the ringing *thwack!* The sound of the impact rang like a bell across the ballgrounds, a pure and fading musical note that seemed to race with the ball on its straight flight over the center fielder's head. *Thwack!*

The ball landed on the dump beyond center field. By the time the center fielder reached it, Joe was nearing third base, so the fielder didn't bother to make a throw. As Joe coasted across the plate with a stand-up home run, another cheer rose up: "Hoorah for Joey! Hoorah!"

Before the next batter stepped in, there was a pause in the game. Hats and caps in their hands, a couple of Joe's younger brothers quickly made their way through the grandstand and the crowds along the foul lines. The little Jacksons were known as the best hat-passers around, probably because they had the most practice. Their big brother hit more home runs than anyone else.

In those days the tactics of the game were different. The ball was softer and home runs were rare. Good hitters had high averages, sluggers hit a lot of doubles and triples. Long hits usually went between outfielders, not over their heads. And the classic long hit was not the towering home run that sailed over the fence — it was the level line drive, the frozen rope, the rifle shot or, as they called Joe's hits, the blue darter. So Joe's home runs were famous, particularly since he always seemed to hit them on Saturdays when the village turned out to see him play. Mill baseball was at its best on Saturdays and Joe was too. He hit so many home runs on Saturdays that they called them his "Saturday Specials."

When Joe's brothers passed their hats to take up a collection for his latest homer, many fans gladly tossed in a coin or two. They tossed in more change for a Joe Jackson home run than for a homer by any other player. Sometimes Joe's little brothers collected twenty-five dollars or more for one of Joe's Saturday Specials. Joe was then earning thirty-five dollars a month in the mill, more or less the average income of the mill hands who were watching the game. Their appreciation for Joe's homers was more than token and it was expressed with good humor and a sense of satisfaction. Joe gave them their money's worth. He showed them something they'd never seen before. And he gave them the pleasure of being proud of one of their own.

Joe's homer gave Brandon a comfortable lead. When Monoghan went to bat for their last ups, the crowd cheered Joe again as he trotted to his position in the outfield. The fans crowded along the right field foul line were closest to him, and when he got out there one of them shouted: "Hope you make a show-out, Joey! Let's have a good long one!"

Joe got set in right field. Feet close together, he crouched staring in at the batter and waited. The first two Monoghan batters went down easily. The third sent a fly ball to deep right center field. Joe raced across right field, intercepted the flight of the ball just at the edge of the dump, and allowed his stride to carry him onto the dump and farther from home plate. It was the last out; Brandon had won the game. The fans let out a happy roar that began as Joe glided toward the spot where the ball would fall to earth and increased in volume as he made the catch. Some of the fans shouted "Hoorah for Brandon!" but they were drowned out by the expectant cries of "Show-out! Show-out!"

After a few strides onto the dump Joe took one last step, wheeled around to face the plate, and fired the ball. Through the suddenly hushed April afternoon it flew toward the plate on a rising path. Every eye was on the flying baseball. As it sailed over the grandstand the crowd inhaled a collective "Ooooh!" and let loose the loudest, most satisfied cheer of the day.

Joe's show-out traveled four hundred feet or more: from the dump beyond the outfield all the way over the grandstand. The crowd loved it. Joe trotted in, a smile on his face.

Fans and players mingled on the diamond and along the sidelines. Joe's father came up and slapped him on the shoulder. When his younger brothers told him how much money they'd collected for his home run, Joe laughed. He turned toward a group of girls. "Look here, Katie," he called, "that sure was one long blow." Katie Wynn smiled back from beneath her weekend wide-brimmed bonnet.

The Monoghan players sat on the ground to take off their baseball shoes. Most put on street shoes, a few of the younger ones went barefoot. Still in their uniforms, the Monoghan players gathered up their gear and began to walk to the trolley stop. The Brandon fans and a few of the players jibed at them good naturedly. One of them called, "Next time we play I expect you'll be obliged to send your first team." The Monoghan crowd laughed and called back, "You wouldn't be struttin' now if it wasn't for Joey!"

In a few minutes one of the electric-powered trolley cars pulled up and ground to a stop. It was an open-air car, bright buff with dark brown trim. Neatly painted letters on the side spelled out GREENVILLE TRACTION COMPANY. Some of the Monoghan crowd trooped aboard, players in uniform and their fans. They reversed the backs of the oak seats so they could sit facing each other. When the conductor and the fare-taker heard the outcome of the game, they began to tease and joke with their passengers as the trolley clanked out of Brandon and headed up the Belt Line to Monoghan, about a mile away.

The Brandon fans walked home talking about Joe's Saturday Special and his show-out. They couldn't decide which had been more pleasing, but most seemed to favor the long throw. It was hard to believe, even though they had seen it.

In 1917, when he was one of the stars of the American League, Joe played in an all-star benefit game at Fenway Park in Boston. Before the game he competed in a throwing contest with Babe Ruth, Ty Cobb, Tris Speaker, and Duffy Lewis among others. Joe won. His throw traveled over 396 feet on the fly. When his fans down in Brandon read about the contest they allowed as it might have been a fine long throw, but lamented the fact that ten years had taken some of the snap out of Joe's arm. Back then, when he played for the mill, he could stand out on the dump beyond center field and heave them right over the grandstand behind home plate. That was throwing.

3

SMOKE FROM KITCHEN woodstoves rose in the air over the village as the Brandon players and their fans walked home. A small group followed Joe and they stopped in front of his house for a few last words. It was almost dinnertime. The aroma of cooking drifted out to them and they could tell that Joe's mother, Martha, was at work in her kitchen. Martha was known for her biscuits and apple jelly, but on Saturdays she was too busy to make jelly. She had to cook the evening meal and prepare the Sunday meals as well, for her husband, George, though not a churchgoing man, observed the Sabbath in his private way and did not approve of cooking on

Sundays. So Saturdays were the busiest days in the Jackson kitchen as Martha, a big woman who wore her long, dark hair pulled back and tied in a knot, calmly went about her work.

When Martha heard Joe's voice outside she called him in to tell her how he had done in the game. She'd already heard about it from others, but she always liked to have Joe tell her himself. In the kitchen Joe lifted the cover off one of the pots on the stove, took a taste, then sat down with his bottle of sweet oil and rubbed some of it into Black Betsy as he told his mother about the game. When he was done he wrapped Betsy in a cotton cloth and put her away. Many players oiled their best bats, but Joe treated Betsy with special care. She was no ordinary piece of equipment.

By the time he was fifteen or sixteen Joe was the idol of Brandon Village and the best-known player in the cotton mill circuit. To show their appreciation, the fans gave him many gifts. The best gift he ever got was from Charlie Ferguson, the local batmaker. After watching Joe play for a couple of years and hearing him talk about the kind of bat he'd like to have, Charlie decided to make him one. First he selected his best billet of seasoned lumber, one he'd been saving for something special. It was a long four-by-four, which had been cut out of the north side of a hickory tree a year or two before. Then he clamped it in his lathe and carved out a bat. When it emerged from the timber it was pale white, but Charlie changed that. He rubbed in a coat or two of tobacco juice because he knew Joe favored black bats.

Joe received Betsy in the winter and even before baseball weather came to stay that year, he tried her out. They were a perfect match. The local fans thought it was love at first sight. "Joe's got hisself a new bat," they remarked to each other at sessions of the local Hot Stove League, "and it's especially to his liking."

It was not unusual that news of Black Betsy had spread so fast. There were few secrets in a mill village, particularly about someone like Joe who was both the local baseball hero and a member of one of Brandon's oldest families.

In the sudden newness of the cotton mill villages old families were reckoned in years, not decades or generations, and in actuality the Jacksons hadn't lived in Brandon for very long. George and Martha Jackson were living in Pickens County, about fifteen miles west of Greenville, when Joe, their first child, was born in the spring of 1888, give or take a year. (Because birth certificates were not required in South Carolina at that time and because the Jackson family Bible, in which births and deaths were recorded, was destroyed in a fire long ago, the exact date is not known.)

George Jackson's occupation is also uncertain. In the "Joe Jackson Number" of *Baseball Magazine* he is described as a tenant farmer who worked a piece of land with "some twenty acres of cotton, some corn, and the customary lean cattle and razor back hogs of the poorer sections of the South." But in the memory of the late Lula Jackson Ellis, the older of Joe's two sisters, the Pickens County place was more a country house than a working farm. They kept a cow, a few pigs, some chickens, and a horse or two. They had a vegetable garden, but Mrs. Ellis couldn't recall a cotton crop. In her recollection her father and his three brothers, who lived nearby with their families, all worked in a sawmill. When work got scarce in the sawmill George and his brothers, all of whom had heard about the work available in the new cotton mills, left the countryside. Thinking he might be able to better provide for his family, George moved to Pelzer, south of Greenville, where he took a job in the engine room of a new cotton mill. A few years later he moved his family again and took a job in the engine room at Brandon.

Joe was three or four at the time his family left Pickens County. When they arrived in Brandon he was already six or seven and old enough to go to work in the Brandon cotton mill. There were many children in the mill villages and most of them worked in the mills. Usually their work was light but the hours were long. They were expected to work a full work week, which meant seventy hours and sometimes more. For five and a half long days each week they breathed the foul, lint-filled air. Respiratory infections were common among them. And when the long hours and the deafening roar of the mill had exhausted them there was always the danger of injury.

The typical cotton mill of the period was powered by one central steam engine. Power was transmitted throughout the mill by a system of overhead drive shafts mounted near the ceiling. Long belts looped down between the drive shafts and each of the individual machines on the floor. There were no safety devices; the high-speed power belts were completely exposed. Injuries to mill hands were common.

There is no record of physical injuries suffered by Joe, but his brother Davey suffered several accidents — on one occasion he was caught by a belt, carried up to the ceiling, and then slammed down to the floor.

The conditions in the southern cotton mills drew the attention of social reformers, many of whom thought that small children ought to be in school learning to read and write. They felt that children should not be working in the mills at all, but since they knew they could not yet stop the widespread practice of using child labor, they lobbied for improved conditions. The reformers urged the enactment of laws that would limit the number of hours children legally could work.

In response to these calls for reform, most mill owners took the position that business was business and the government had no right to interfere in the relationship between employer and employee, even if the employee was only six years old. In one of the annual drives against legislative reform, one owner proudly cited a gentlemen's agreement among southern mill owners, which limited any child under ten years of age from working more than sixty-six hours a week.

Among the children themselves attitudes varied greatly. Some viewed the work as a challenge and tried to learn as much as they could about the different machines and processes. Some felt proud because they were earning some money to help their families. Many of these children remained on the job until their working days were over, fifty or sixty years later. But some children didn't like the work at all. It was too dirty and noisy and the hours were so long that it took away all their time for play. Joe never said much about his early years in the mill, but while he worked there he sneaked out to play ball whenever he got the chance.

Joe worked in cotton mills off and on for a dozen years, until he was nineteen or twenty and began his professional baseball career. But he didn't work all the time and he never seems to have taken mill work too seriously. Years later some of his former co-workers criticized him for a lack of responsibility. If this criticism bothered him, he never let it show.

His longest break from mill work happened when he was ten or eleven. He had a streak of childhood illnesses, one after the other, which ended with the measles. But there were complications. For reasons the doctor was unable to explain, the measles left Joe's legs paralyzed. For several months he lay in bed with his knees drawn tightly up against his chest and locked in place.

His mother nursed Joe continually during those months when it was uncertain if he would ever walk again. She baked breads and biscuits for him and boiled apple jelly on her big black stove. She also kept a pot of water on the stove in which she soaked towels to lay on Joe's legs. The doctor gave no guarantee that Martha's nursing would bring about a cure, but after a few months Joe's legs loosened up and he was able to walk again. His strength returned rapidly and soon all traces of his temporary paralysis disappeared. It was only a year or two later that the men came to ask Martha if Joe could join them on the Brandon Mill team.

The Brandon team was typical of all the local cotton mill teams. There were twelve men on the roster and each of them had a special status in the village. They were showered with admiration and encouragement by the fans. And the owners, afraid their players might quit to join another team, paid each player $2.50 for the Saturday afternoon game and were often lenient about a little practice on company time. They made certain that their better players had choice jobs in the mill. All of these extra benefits were very significant to the ballplaying mill hands, so there was much competition for places on a mill team. The invitation to play for Brandon when he was only thirteen was a genuine compliment to Joe's ability.

The players and the men who managed the mill team had had their eyes on Joe for a few years before they invited him to join them. They had watched him from the windows of the mill when he would slip away from work to play ball for a few minutes, and they had seen him in the pick-up games he played in whenever he got the chance. Even in the beginning, when he was still a gangly boy, all the knowledgeable observers around Brandon agreed that he was a wonderful natural hitter, but when the men invited him to join the mill team they were more interested in his long right arm.

Even as a kid Joe had abnormally long arms. The mill official who managed the team once recalled that Joe had the longest arms of any man he'd ever seen. He thought Joe inherited his long arms from his father. Wherever they came from, Joe knew how to use them. Before he discovered how best to use them in swinging a bat, he already knew how to get all the strength in his long right arm into a throw.

In those days base-running was a major factor in the game and base-stealing was always a tactical highlight, so the men, confident that young Joey could throw out any base-runner with his long whip of a throwing arm, made him a catcher. He lived up to their expectations in the few games that he caught; his arm was powerful and accurate and he was not shy about using it. But his catching career was brief. A few years later his mother summed it up in an interview: "Joe has a scar on his forehead that he got in those early days. He was catching behind the plate and a great burly mill hand was pitching to him. He threw one so swift and strong that Joe didn't have strength enough to stop it. So it forced his hands back, drove into his mask and dented the mask into his forehead, leaving a deep cut. That was how he got that scar."

After this injury his mother said he couldn't play catcher anymore, so the men tried him at two other positions that required a strong arm — third base and pitcher. He played only a few games at third base, but during his first couple of years on the mill team he did a lot of pitching. At first there was nothing fancy about his delivery, he just reared back and fired one overhand fastball after another. Three surviving box scores credit him with 10, 5, and 11 strikeouts.

As he gained experience on the mound he developed a curveball and a change-up and improved his control, which had always been good. Even so, he hit an occasional batter. One afternoon a fastball got away, hit a batter on the arm, and broke his bone. After that the fun went out of pitching.

His mill team manager thought "with that whip of his he ought to be a great pitcher," but after Joe broke the batter's arm his manager regretfully reported that Joe decided that "if he were that dangerous on the mound he had better play some other position." From then on, except for a few scattered innings on the mound, Joe was an outfielder.

4

As a baseball player Joe was a natural phenomenon, and like all natural phenomena no one could claim credit for him. All that others could do was to claim that they had discovered him. He was discovered several times. All it really meant was that more people from higher and wider circles were seeing him play.

His reputation among the fans in the mill villages was already firmly established when he was first noticed by Greenville people. Although the villages were only a mile or two from Greenville in most cases, the social distance was immense, light-years away in social attitudes. The city dwellers felt free to think of themselves as merchants, clerks, doctors, blacksmiths; they distinguished themselves from each other with personal identities. But they lumped into one group all the people who worked in the mills and who lived in the villages and called them operatives. They looked down on the mill hands and did not mix with them socially. These were the prevailing social attitudes through which the city folk viewed the mill hands or behind which they ignored them. It is no wonder that the young sports of Greenville felt they had discovered Joe when they finally went out to see him play.

The first outsider to "discover" Joe was a proper citizen of Greenville. Lawrence Lollie Gray was the former star of the Clemson football team, the best-known athlete in Greenville, and the son of General J. W. Gray, a Greenville County official. Like many of his contemporaries, Lollie Gray never seemed to have enough time on a diamond to suit him. Before his college career was over he had played baseball for Clemson, Furman, Wofford, and VPI. When college was finally behind him he organized a semiprofessional baseball team in Greenville in 1906. Since he had no formal arrangement with any organized league, Gray called his team the Near Leaguers and went looking for players.

Gray recruited most of his players from among the collegians with whom he'd played, and the remainder came from other local teams. While he was forming his team he heard some stories about a mill hand named Jackson, but he assumed they were local exaggerations and didn't bother to go out to the mills to see Jackson play. But the stories persisted and Gray's curiosity finally sent him in search of Joe. He caught up with him on an afternoon when Joe was playing center field for Victor Mills in Greer, a few miles south of Greenville. Competition among the mill teams had grown so hot that the mills actively recruited players and raided the competition. Victor Mills made a better offer than Brandon and Joe had accepted it.

When Gray saw Joe play he was so impressed he didn't wait for the end of the game to ask Joe to join his team. He introduced himself between innings and Joe agreed to become a Near Leaguer. Many years later Lollie Gray recalled the first time he saw Joe play. He marveled at Joe's hitting, running, and throwing, but the thing he remembered best was Black Betsy and the sound she made when she met the baseball.

Joe returned to catching with the Near Leaguers, and played some third base and outfield too. He also continued to play for the Victor Mills, but that was not unusual. Each team played only one or two games a week, and many of the better players were on several teams.

Joe played for the Victor team but he didn't work full time in the mill. When he wasn't playing ball he helped his father, who had quit his job in the Brandon Mill to operate a small portable sawmill. Joe's busy schedule didn't seem to affect his play. The college men in Lollie Gray's crowd and the Greenville people who came to watch the Near Leaguers were as impressed by Joe's ability as the mill hands had been. His reputation kept on growing.

The Near Leaguers were only semiprofessional and their schedule was informal, but the general hunger for baseball guaranteed their success. Baseball was more than a private fever in the blood of many young men; it was in the air of the new century. Any town or city worth its own sense of pride wanted to have a team, had to have a uniformed team that could represent the aspirations of its people and make a fair showing in competition against other towns and cities. Charged with boosterism and civic pride, the acquisition of a baseball team ranked with the acquisition of electric street-lights and horseless streetcars.

The epitome, of course, was a major-league team, the purest example of the new professionalism that had entered American life. But since 1901 there had been only sixteen major-league teams, an arbitrarily monopolistic number that was to remain fixed for sixty years. So towns and cities everywhere, except in the northeast quarter of the country, had to swallow their major-league dreams and settle for less. The less they settled for ranged all the way from high-ranking professional minor-league teams to amateur teams sponsored and supported out of civic pride.

Greenville had been alive to the possibilities of professional baseball for many years, but it had had to settle for the occasional appearance of touring professional teams. Any kind of game, even a pick-up game that was announced shortly beforehand, drew a large crowd. In addition to its symbolic value as a sign of civic arrival, baseball had taken on the aura of a national mania. Everyone was invited.

As did its counterparts everywhere, the *Greenville News* frequently boosted professional ball. As early as 1900 it editorialized, "The Greenville people are again to be favored with two games of professional baseball. . . . The games will doubtless prove to be the best played here for some time. Both teams are professional and are worthy of a liberal patronage and support." A week or two later it announced, "A hot and spirited game of professional baseball will be played in the park here this afternoon. . . . A large crowd is expected. . . . Ladies will be admitted free."

The *News* also commented favorably on the fact that "goodly sums of money" were being bet on the outcomes of these professional games. The boosters saw gambling as an undeniable proof of the game's rising popularity.

Toward the end of 1907 the mounting pressure to bring a real professional team to Greenville finally had an outlet in opportunity. Several Greenville businessmen decided to field a team in the newly organized Carolina Association. Their first step was to select a manager. They chose Tommie Stouch, one of the best-known college baseball coaches in the South.

Tommie Stouch, the most important of Joe's discoverers, had a lifetime major-league batting average of .313, which he amassed by getting five hits in the four games he played as second baseman for the Louisville Grays in 1898, when they were in the National League. If he was not an all-star player, Stouch was a keen judge of baseball talent and he was an unofficial scout for Connie Mack's Athletics, the baseball kings of Stouch's hometown, Philadelphia. His first task as manager of the new Greenville Spinners was to recruit a team. That was how he met Joe. It was an occasion he always remembered.

"I had been appointed manager of the Greenville club," Stouch once recalled. "Naturally, while scouring around the country, I was on the lookout for new talent. I was playing second base on this particular occasion, when a tall, thin fellow stepped to the plate. He didn't appear to have it in him, but he drove the ball on a line toward the very spot where I was standing, like a bullet out of a gun. Now I have had much baseball experience and though getting a little old for active service, I still prided myself that I knew how a ball ought to be fielded. But that pellet caromed off my shins before I had time to make an effort to field it, and it hurt my shins, too, depend upon that. I thought to myself, 'If this Rube hits them like that every time, he must be some whale. I guess he will bear watching.' He did. That game, if I remember, he made three hits, two of them for extra bases, and they were all ringing smashes that left a trail of blue flame behind them when they shot through the air."

After the game, which was the first of a five-game series in Greer, Stouch asked his pitcher to keep an eye on Joe and see if he could discover his weakness. It didn't make any difference. Joe continued to hit the ball as hard as he'd done in the first game.

Late in the last game Joe hit a line drive right at the pitcher's head. Stouch said his pitcher looked at it "for about a thousandth of a second, and then ducked as if he were dodging a shell from a Krupp mortar." Stouch rushed over and asked, "Did you discover his weakness?"

"No," the pitcher answered, "but he discovered mine all right. I don't want to buck my head against any of his wallops."

When the final game was over Stouch was convinced beyond any doubt and he finally approached Joe. "I'm going to manage Greenville next near and I would like to have you play with me, if we can agree upon terms."

"All right," said Joe. "I'd like to play with Greenville."

"How much are you getting now?"

"Thirty-five dollars a month in the mill," replied Joe.

"Very well, how much do you want to play for me?"

"Well, you see, I am getting along pretty well. I get thirty-five a month from the mill, but I get two-fifty a game on Saturdays for playing ball, so that gives me forty-five a month in all. I wouldn't want to give up my job unless I could see something in sight. I think I ought to be worth sixty a month to you."

"Joe, if you will promise to let corn whiskey alone and stick to your business, I will pay you seventy-five a month."

"Sho'," Joe said, "I'll work my head off for seventy-five and make that much more hitting home runs."

Stouch was pleased to have signed Joe, but he wasn't exactly sure what he meant about the home runs. (He found out when Joe hit his first homer for the Spinners. A bunch of kids ran through the grandstand and bleachers carrying boxes and caps, then one of them came over to the players' bench along the sidelines and gave Joe a box filled with coins. When they added it up Stouch saw that the fans had given Joe $29.75 for his home run. He dug into the pocket of his uniform, pulled out a quarter, tossed it into the box, smiled, and said, "Here Joe, make it an even thirty.")

Shortly after the Spinners' spring training session began, Stouch announced that Joe was the first man on the squad to clinch a starting position on the team: center field. The local baseball writer, more familiar with the ex-collegiate players, didn't know where Joe came from and identified him as a native of Greer. Joe's hometown fans complained and the *News* corrected itself: "The hard hitting boy is from the Brandon Mills and is a popular idol."

By the end of spring training the Spinners were down to their twelve-man squad. Three of the men, including Joe, were from the Greenville area and a fourth lived a few miles from Greenville. The rest of the men came from such places as Illinois, Pennsylvania, West Virginia, North Carolina, Georgia, and Alabama. Several of them were college men and most were from middle-class families. Joe was the only former mill hand on the team.

The Spinners opened their season at home against the Electricians from neighboring Anderson, South Carolina. It was a cold and windy day, but a record-breaking crowd of two thousand turned out to cheer for the new team. The grandstand, which cost forty cents, was full; the bleachers, which cost only a quarter, were packed; and a row of buggies, carriages, and automobiles was parked all along the left field foul line. For this privilege the driver paid fifty cents. Those who came to the game by public transportation were the first to use the new spur line which the Greenville Traction Company had installed to service the new professional team at the ballgrounds.

The stands were filled with a cross section of the people who lived in and around Greenville: men and women; boys and girls; schoolchildren playing hooky and office boys and clerks who'd made excuses to leave work early; and black fans who had to sit in the "colored stands."

Umpire McLaughlin, a former major-league pitcher, started the game promptly at 4:30. The Spinners, in their new white uniforms, raced out to their positions and were greeted with loud cheers, which burst out of self-satisfaction, civic pride, and old-fashioned expectation. It was Opening Day.

His Honor G. Heywood Mahon, mayor of Greenville, was called upon to toss out the first ball of the season and the new league. He walked out to the pitcher's mound, peered at catcher Kelley, and heaved the ball with all his might. It sailed over the catcher's head and crashed against the wooden backstop. The crowd whooped and laughed, the mayor retired to his seat, the Anderson leadoff batter stepped to the plate, and out in center field Joe crouched, feet close together so he could get a quick jump in any direction, and stared in at the batter.

The Spinners won their first game 14 to 1. They got twelve hits and Joe, batting in the third position, got three of them, two doubles and a triple. He also made a one-handed leaping catch racing at full speed, and when the ball slipped out of his glove he grabbed it with his bare hand to save the out. The fans loved it so much they held up the game with their cheers.

Joe was a success in his first pro game. Now the Brandon fans who idolized him were joined by Greenville fans. He was an instant star and friends and strangers went out of their way to congratulate him. In the eyes of the local fans, Joe epitomized the skill and excitement of the professional game.

The arrival of a truly professional hometown team in Greenville was a major event. It not only fed the local baseball mania, it served to increase the appetite. The *News,* which had boosted professional baseball for years, announced that in response to public demand it would increase its baseball coverage. Since the start of spring training, baseball news had been prominently featured in the prime space on page two, taking at least half the page and frequently more.

A bulletin board was mounted on the *News* building so the inning-by-inning results of all Spinner games, home and away, could be posted. The paper received its rapid information by telephone reports and even invited the public to phone in for the latest scores.

The baseball fever that swept over the South Carolina uplands in the summer of 1908 matched the national mood. The game seemed to be in the air itself, part of the climate of the times, and fans were everywhere. Their attitude toward baseball was a reminder that *fan* derives from *fanatic*.

Baseball was not approached as a mere game. Even from the beginning it carried the aura of a national institution, a symbolic acting out of democratic principles and religious beliefs. Clergymen around the country based their sermons on metaphors drawn from baseball, ending with such exhortations as "Baseball shall be taught in Heaven!" Umpire Bill Klem, the "Great Arbiter" of baseball's most mythic period, spoke for many when he said, "Baseball is more than a game with me, it's a religion."

Spinner fans were typical; baseball was their obsession. Some boasted that they watched games in their dreams. Many times during the season large groups of fans who lived in outlying towns took the train to Greenville to see the Spinners play, usually on Saturdays. Once Stouch got a letter from a fan who lived fifty miles from Greenville. The man guaranteed he would bring a party of at least one hundred people to the next Saturday game if his favorite pitcher was on the mound.

Fans in Greenville took to the trains also, and when the Spinners played in relatively nearby cities — Spartanburg or Anderson — many of them made the trip just to see the game.

If the bulletin board out in front of the *News* building wasn't satisfying enough, the fans who stayed at home in Greenville could get a firsthand account of road games by going over to the Grand Opera House. For the price of fifteen cents they could hear an account of the game as it came in over a telegraph wire and was called by the operator. The telegraphic re-creations were a big hit, and crowds gathered at the Grand for the baseball matinees.

The telegraph operators who called those early games in music halls and vaudeville houses all over the country were the first sports announcers. Some of them drew followings from among the fans: D. F. Cason, the operator at the Grand, became a local celebrity.

The fans at the Grand only heard the verbal descriptions Cason improvised and fleshed out from the bare details that came clicking in over the wire in Morse code, but they cheered and booed as if they'd been out at the ballgrounds watching the Spinners in the flesh. At a matinee that featured a game in Charlotte, North Carolina, against the Hornets, emotions were particularly high. It was early in the season but the Spinners were fighting for first place and had a seven-game winning streak on the line. The fans arrived at the matinee ready to shout and cheer for the whole game, but the Hornets scored first and led three to nothing after three innings. The Grand was silent. In the top of the fourth it came to life when the Spinners put two men on base and Joe stepped to the plate. The crowd began to whoop and holler. Cason announced one strike on Joe. A fan shouted back, "Strike one! You's got two more taps at der ball Joe!" On the next pitch Joe slammed a whistling blue darter into left field. Two runs scored, Joe was on third with a triple, and the fans at the Grand jumped up and down. When the next batter drove Joe home with the tying run, they jumped higher.

Then they sat on their hands. Except for a double by Joe, Cason described nothing that was pleasing until the top of the eighth when a man walked and Joe came to bat with the tie-breaking run on first base. Another double would bring it across, and the fans at the Greenville end of the telegraph line encouraged Joe as hard as they could. Joe responded with a line drive home run over the fence in right center field, and the matinee crowd went wild. The fans cheered for Joe and cheered for operator Cason too. But their jubilation was cut short when Cason announced that the umpire had called Joe out for not touching first base. Then the crowd groaned and cursed the umpire. Cason was cursed too, as if he were responsible for the events he was merely reporting, and he let the crowd know that he would change the umpire's call if he could. After a pause the telegraph key clicked again, Cason announced again, and the crowd's emotions were swung the other way: the umpire up in Charlotte, North Carolina, had ruled that Joe was out, but that the runner on first base could score. The groans and insults changed back to cheers. The Spinners won the game, four to three, and took possession of first place.

The fans left the Grand in high spirits, though somewhat drained by the emotional experience they had had at the receiving end of a telegraph wire. If it was true that baseball had only to be seen to be loved, it was equally true that electronic media, even in their earliest forms, had only to be experienced to be deeply felt.

By mid-May Joe reached his natural level; he was hitting .350 and was generally regarded as the hardest hitter in the league. Just as he had done with the mill teams, he seemed to play his best games on Saturdays when the crowds were largest. Sunday ballgames were not allowed, and since many jobs ended early on Saturdays it was the only chance that many people had to see their new team. For the first Saturday home game a large contingent from Brandon had ridden the Belt Line into town to see Joe, and they cheered him warmly even before the game began. He got a couple of hits but his Brandon fans were disappointed; they had expected him to continue his Saturday habit by hitting a home run. He made it up to them before the season was over.

The Spinners played eleven Saturday home games that year and Joe hit home runs in five of them. It was a remarkable display. Home runs were still rare and would be until Babe Ruth and the live ball came along ten or so years later. In 1908, by comparison, the American League leader hit seven home runs and the National League leader hit twelve. Joe's five Saturday Specials gave the Spinner fans a lot to talk about.

Like other towns and cities all over America, there were special places in Greenville where fans gathered to talk. In warm weather they met on certain street corners or arrived at the ballgrounds early enough to have an hour or two of baseball talk before the game began. Unlike the players, the fans' season was not limited to the summertime. If a local gathering place had a wood-burning potbellied stove, and if the proprietor was a fan or at least tolerated them, it became a cold-weather meeting place for the endless baseball talk the fans seemed to need to get them through the winter until spring training started. The winter dialogues occurred in saloons and poolrooms, or more frequently in general stores, barbershops, and drugstores. The indispensable potbelly loaned its name to these endless discussions and in the aggregate they were called the Hot Stove League.

Harrison's Drugstore, which advertised on the sports page, was a year-round place in Greenville where the fans gathered at the soda fountain to hold their fanning bees. During the season players sat in also, offering their views and anecdotes. Joe was a regular at Harrison's and he'd drop in after games for a few glasses of his favorite drink, "dope and lime," the contemporary slang for Coca-Cola with a dash of lime juice.

Joe was always the kind of player the fans liked to talk about. Usually their stories were about his feats on the diamond, but from the very beginning of his career there was a constant thread of derision and ridicule. It began with the handful of jealous villagers who resented Joe's career and said he was a lazy, irresponsible, overgrown boy who had never matured. It continued with a few of the Greenville fans and some of the writers around the Carolina Association who jumped to the conclusion that Joe was stupid when they learned that he was illiterate.

One such story was set in Harrison's Drugstore early in the 1908 season, when Joe was batting in the .350 range. The soda fountain was crowded and the fanning bee in full swing when Joe walked in. He was so nervous and fidgety that he didn't even order his usual dope and lime. When someone in the crowd asked him what was wrong, he alarmed everyone by saying he'd heard that Manager Stouch was thinking of firing him. Several men began shouting at once, wanting to know the reason why. "Well," Joe explained, "Mr. Stouch says I've been getting only two or three hits a day and he claims that's not enough for me to hold my job."

The anecdote has someone in the crowd jeer, "What you goin' to do about it?" and concludes with Joe's humble but dumb answer, "I don't know, but I'm going to try my durndest to do better, for I like Mr. Stouch and the rest of the players and I don't want to go back to Brandon and let my pals know I couldn't make good."

It was around this time that Joe acquired the nickname Shoeless Joe. One afternoon he began to break in a new pair of spikes. By the next morning he had such painful blisters that he couldn't get his old spikes on his feet. The Spinners were in Anderson for a game against the Electricians and Stouch wouldn't hear of benching him. So Joe played in his stocking feet and nobody seemed to notice until late in the game when he hit a long home run over the right fielder's head. As he rounded third base an Anderson fan stood up and shouted "Oh you shoeless sonofabitch!" Scoop Latimer, baseball writer for the *News,* used the name in print and it stuck.

But even the stories that made fun of Joe did not hide his talent. Before he played in twenty games with the Spinners, the major-league clubs were on his trail. Connie Mack, in response to a tip from Tommie Stouch, sent his injured outfielder Socks Seybold down South to take a look at Joe and one of his Spinner teammates, Hyder Barr. It is not clear how the Boston Red Sox, in need of help after their seventh-place finish in 1907, heard about Joe, but they sent scout Fred Lake to make an appraisal of him. The scouts caught up with Joe in North Carolina where the Spinners were playing the Charlotte Hornets.

Joe went to bat four times in the game. He hit one double, one triple, and a line drive home run. It was the one called back when Joe failed to tag first base, but the scouts had seen enough. Joe was discovered by the big leagues and his reputation moved up another notch. As soon as Connie Mack got Seybold's report he made arrangements with the Spinners to buy Joe and Hyder Barr, for delivery at the end of the Spinners' season. No official word was given at the time, but from then on the *News* and several Philadelphia papers repeatedly made allusions to Joe's imminent trip north.

Everyone had an opinion about Joe's abilities. The outfielders in the Carolina Association gave theirs by playing him with their backs against the fences. This was an unusual defensive move and some fans found it amusing. A baseball doggerel of the day went:

> When Jackson steps up to the plate
> To hit the horsehide ball
> The Fielders get so far away
> They really look quite small.

Others complained that this unheard-of and faintly unsportsmanlike tactic was robbing Joe of many home runs. Nevertheless, they all expected him to hit them. When preparations for the July 4th double-header included a public guessing contest on how many home runs Joe would hit, the published guesses ranged from three to eight.

Both of the holiday games were rained out, but they still signified that baseball had become part of the fabric of Greenville life. The double-header had been planned as a morning game at home and an afternoon game in nearby Spartanburg. It was clearly the principal event of the day. In the evolution of public celebrations baseball had replaced older events. Only one year earlier the main event of the

Greenville July 4th celebration had been a horse show and some mule races.

Led by Joe's hitting, the Spinners moved into first place at the start of the season. They remained there until early July when they lost eleven of thirteen games and fell into second place. The fans and writers called for a shake-up to strengthen the team, but nobody criticized Joe, even though his average had fallen close to .300.

There were no physical causes for Joe's slump. He simply had other things on his mind: he was going to get married. He was nineteen and Katie Wynn was only fifteen, but they'd been in love with each other for so long that everyone assumed they would marry when the time was right.

When Joe played for the mills he told Katie that his aim was to be a professional and to earn his living playing baseball. She encouraged him, knowing that he wouldn't get married until he had a try at professional ball. After he signed with the Spinners, they began to plan and set a date. Joe thought it was the right time, but he wanted to be sure he could make good.

By mid-July any doubts he may have had about his ability to earn a living by playing baseball must have been answered, for he was clearly the star of the Carolina Association. And he knew that he was signed over to Connie Mack for delivery to the American League at the end of the Spinners' season. So on Sunday, July 19, Joseph Jefferson Wofford Jackson married Katherine Wynn.

The *News* reported the event on the sports page: "Joe Jackson made the greatest home-run of his career on Sunday. The home-run was made on Cupid's diamond and the victory was a fair young lady." The marriage lasted until Joe died forty-three years later.

The next afternoon the Spinners finally won a game. Joe

spent his honeymoon playing center field. The first time he came to bat the crowd gave him a rousing cheer of congratulations. With loyal fans shouting their reassurance after the Spinners' sad road trip, and with his bride of less than twenty-four hours sitting in the grandstand, Joe got two hits, made four put-outs, including one of the prettiest catches of the season, threw out a runner who was foolish enough to challenge his arm on a day like that, and led the Spinners to a victory.

Starting that afternoon Joe took off on a hitting tear and got eleven hits in the next four games including several doubles and triples and at least one more home run, another Saturday Special he whacked against the Greensboro Patriots.

On one of the hottest, steamiest days of the summer over a thousand fans came out to that Saturday game against Greensboro, which, as it turned out, was the team to beat that year in the Carolina Association. A home run against them was extra special. When Joe hit his — a blue darter over the center fielder's head — the crowd took up a healthy collection. By now Joe's brothers were not alone. Fifteen or twenty boys worked their way through the crowd passing their caps and hollering enthusiasm for Joe. All the boys in Greenville, it seemed, had chosen Joe as their favorite. Even in other cities around the league kids flocked to him. His relationship with kids was so unusual that the *News* remarked on its special quality several times.

Joe kept on hitting until his average was back up in the .350s. But the pitching staff fell apart and the Spinners struggled through the last half of the schedule. They were in second place, within striking distance, when their season was reduced to the last series of games, to be played against the first-place Patriots in Greensboro. Three single games were scheduled originally, and whichever team won two of them would win the pennant. But the teams had been rained out of a game earlier in the season and it was decided to play four games. Greenville would have to win three of them to finish in first place.

The Greensboro Patriots won the first game, 1 to 0. The next day, with the pennant still on the line, three thousand people crowded into the Patriots ballgrounds to see the double-header. Greenville won the first game, 5 to 2. In the nightcap Greensboro took an early lead. By the time the Spinners came to bat in the top of the ninth they were trailing 6 to 0. The umpire, Fred Westervelt, wrote an article a few years later, when he was umpiring for the American League, about the hardest call he'd ever had to make. It happened in the ninth inning of that third game (which was the make-up game). With their whole season narrowed down to three outs, the Spinners staged a storybook rally. Before Greensboro knew what was happening, the Spinners scored five runs and had the bases loaded with only one out. "The fleet Joe Jackson was on third," wrote Westervelt, "ready to score the run that would tie the game." But the next batter hit a sharp grounder to the second baseman who fielded the ball cleanly and made a perfect throw to the plate for a force-out. It was clear to Joe that he had no chance to beat the ball, that a slide would not help. So he took the only chance he had and crashed into the catcher.

"The catcher dropped the ball," Westervelt recalled, "and the force of the collision caused Jackson to turn a complete somersault. The catcher had the plate so blocked, however, that Jackson failed to touch it. Both went sprawling to the ground, partly stunned. The catcher recovered the ball and touched Jackson before Joe could scramble back to the plate. It was a hairline decision at that." The next batter struck out, the game was over, and Greensboro had won the Carolina Association pennant.

The teams played the fourth game, the last one of the

season, and the Spinners won it. The Spinners' owners then initiated a protest that challenged the legality of the make-up game and the accuracy of Westervelt's call on Joe's play at the plate. They claimed the catcher had dropped the ball and that the Association rules gave them the option of playing the make-up game or not, since it had not been made up within the prescribed time limit.

The season was over, but pending the outcome of the protest nobody knew with certainty who had won the pennant. If the make-up game was voided, the Spinners would have won two of the three legal games and the pennant. If the game was upheld, the Patriots would win. The dispute broke onto page one of the *News*. The Greenville fans were disappointed at the outcome of the games and many of them hotly argued the case for the protest. But their attention was divided when the emotions of one lost cause were pushed aside by those of another.

Greenville was having a hectic week. While the Spinners were up in Greensboro fighting for the pennant, the veterans of the Confederate Army of South Carolina gathered in Greenville to hold their annual reunion. "Confederate Veterans Moving On Greenville," the headline read. So the emotions focused on baseball, at their highest pitch of the year now that the pennant was at stake, were suddenly diverted by an event that evoked an even stronger emotion.

The Confederate colors were displayed all over the city. Everyone wanted to make the reunion memorable because many of the "Lost Cause" veterans were in their seventies and it was assumed that there wouldn't be many more such reunions. The Daughters of the Confederacy entertained. Main Street and the Confederate Monument were illuminated at night by the power company. The major address of the week was delivered by Colonel Robert E. Lee, Jr., grandson of General Robert E. Lee, who praised the "old boys," veterans of the battles of Chickahominy, the Wilderness, Fredericksburg, Gettysburg, and finally the surrender at Harper's Ferry.

The old boys were both the honored guests and the main attraction of the reunion. They gathered in front of the court-house for their annual sing: "When the Roll Is Called Up Yonder," "The Star-Spangled Banner," "America." Then they cheered as the fire department gave an exhibition and the chief raced through town in a big automobile at fifty-eight miles an hour.

"Thin Gray Line To Form Again," the *News* announced. Then the veterans staged their annual march down Main Street in the broiling sun all the way to the Confederate Monument. Thousands of people lined the sidewalks to watch them pass. It was the closing event of the reunion.

A day or two later, at the directors' meeting of the Caro-lina Association, the Spinners voluntarily withdrew their pro-test. No explanation was given. The directors announced that their first year of operation had been a great success. Attendance had been good, there was a surplus in the As-sociation treasury, and the public had shown great faith and interest. It probably seemed wiser to withdraw the protest than to force a challenge that might undermine the credibil-ity of the league.

Greenville fans were mixed in their reactions. Some argued that the protest should have been carried to its con-clusion, others felt it was more dignified and honorable to accept the original decision, whether it was just or not. But the Confederate reunion had taken some of the wind out of the pennant race and the protest. Besides, the big news was Joe Jackson's trip to Philadelphia to play for Connie Mack's Athletics.

5

ON THE FIRST SUNDAY after the season ended, the master of the Greenville post office informed Albert James, president of the Spinners, that the letter he'd been expecting from the Philadelphia Athletics had arrived. James went right over to the post office to get it. By the time he arrived, word had spread and there was a crowd waiting for him. The people had come to watch him open the letter and see the check inside. Nothing like this had ever happened in Greenville. Everyone was amazed at the amount of money paid for a couple of first-year minor-league ballplayers. The check was for $1,500: $600 for Joe's teammate Hyder Barr and $900 for Joe.

Hyder Barr, the former star of the Davidson College team, got on the train and went to Philadelphia as soon as he was free to go. But Joe, who was also free, played in an exhibition game instead — the Spinners against Joe's old Victor Mill team. That afternoon, while the Athletics' fans were calling for him out at Columbia Stadium in Philadelphia, Joe hit the longest home run ever seen on the Greer diamond, a whistling line drive far over the center field fence.

Connie Mack was pleased to see Barr, but he would have been more pleased to have seen Joe. The Athletics were going nowhere during the last part of that season and Mack had the opportunity to try out his rookies. He'd heard so much about Joe that he particularly wanted to see him in some American League action. After waiting a few days, Mack wired Stouch in Greenville and asked him to accompany Joe north to make sure he got there. Stouch agreed.

Tommie Stouch had heard rumors that Joe would not go north at all, but he'd not heard anything directly from Joe, so he went out to Brandon to talk with him. He assumed that Joe just needed a little extra time to get ready. He could not believe that Joe would not go; he naturally assumed that no man would refuse an invitation to join a major-league club. But when he talked with Joe he was surprised by his lack of enthusiasm. When he asked what was wrong, Joe confided, "I hardly know how I'd like it in those big northern cities."

"Oh, you'll like it fine," Stouch replied. "There's nothing to worry about, and I'll be going with you."

Joe thought it over and agreed to go. The next morning he and Stouch boarded the northbound train, but along the way Joe changed his mind again. In Charlotte, North Carolina, one hundred and fifty miles away, Joe got off the train and caught a southbound back to Greenville.

Stouch, unaware at first that Joe had left the train, continued on and arrived in Philadelphia alone. "Joe Jackson disappointed the fans yesterday, but he is expected to be here tomorrow," the *Philadelphia Evening Times* wrote. "All you have to do to raise a smile from Connie Mack is to mention Jackson's name." Mack smiled because he was used to the erratic ways of some ballplayers, but he wanted Joe badly enough to send Socks Seybold, his injured outfielder who had scouted Joe earlier in the season, down to Greenville to bring Joe back with him personally.

Joe's game of hide and seek with Connie Mack, as some of the writers called his indecision, was so unusual that it was reported on sports pages all around the country. Tommie Stouch's belief that any man would leap at the chance to play in the major leagues was shared by writers and fans everywhere. It was widely believed that making the majors was the highest aspiration of every American male. Nobody could remember another rookie who had failed to report, so Joe's hesitation surprised everyone, particularly since his reputation as a gifted player had spread so far and so quickly.

As early as June, when he had had only thirty Spinner games to his credit, Joe was featured in *Sporting Life,* a national publication, which labeled him "a ballplayer of the first magnitude" and said he was better than Ty Cobb had been at the same point in his career. A short time later *Sporting News*, the longtime "Bible of Baseball," identified Joe as "the Southern whirlwind who is to be Ty Cobb's rival of the future." In light of his talent and the praise he'd been receiving, Joe's actions were perplexing.

In Greenville the headlines on the sports page of the *News* reflected the confusion. "JOE JACKSON LEAVES TOMORROW FOR PHILADELPHIA" was the announcement when the Athletics' check arrived. A week later it was "JOE JACKSON LEAVES TO JOIN PHILADELPHIA: LEFT YESTERDAY." After he got off the train in Charlotte and came back, the *News* retracted: "JOE JACKSON DID NOT GO TO PHILADELPHIA: WILL STAY HERE."

Joe gave no reason for his behavior, which seems to have been based on his misgivings about large and unknown northern cities. The *News* said he was making a great mistake by not reporting to Connie Mack: "If he persists in staying here it means that he will be blacklisted and can never play in organized ball." The *News* was correct in its warning to Joe. Blacklisting was real. It had been a part of organized baseball since the nineteenth century, when the club owners made the reserve clause a standard part of every players' contract. This clause, which remained in players' contracts until the mid-1970s, gave the owner an exclusive and perpetual option on the player's professional services.

When the owners adopted the reserve clause they also agreed not to employ or tamper with any player reserved by another club. They further tightened their control of the players by agreeing not to play against any team that employed a player reserved by another club or to let such a club use their ball parks. If Joe did not report to Mack and if Mack refused to sell Joe's contract to another club, Joe's career in organized baseball would be over.

In Philadelphia, Joe's delayed arrival was the baseball topic of the day. Expectation was so intense that many Athletics' fans cheered him even when they knew he was still in Greenville. Though there were many rookies with the team, and players' uniforms in those days had neither names nor numbers on them, the mistake was unusual. One afternoon, with the game tied in the ninth inning, Connie Mack sent in a left-handed batter to pinch-hit. A fan who was at that game recalled that when the pinch hitter stepped to the plate, "The fans in the grandstand commenced hollering 'Jackson!' and I sat straight up. I shouted at the top of my voice along with the other crazy fools, and afterward found out that it wasn't Jackson at all."

The *Philadelphia Evening Press* acknowledged the general disappointment over Joe's failure to arrive and hoped Socks Seybold's mission would succeed: "If Manager Mack's scheme works the followers of the White Elephants will see the fence-breaker in action this week."

On arriving in Greenville, Seybold immediately rode out to Brandon and talked with Joe. The next morning the *News* announced, "JOE JACKSON HAS CHANGED HIS MIND — Heavy Hitting Center Fielder Packed His Trunk and Left for Philadelphia Yesterday to Play Ball." This time they were right.

Philadelphia, one of the five cities in the country with two major-league teams, had a long baseball history, but 1908 was not a banner year for baseball in the City of Brotherly Love. The National League Phillies finished fourth, sixteen games behind the pennant-winning Chicago Cubs. Outfielder Sherwood Magee had been the Phillies' best hitter the year before when he had been second in the National League in batting and first in runs batted in. Magee had a poor year in 1908, but his exploits off the diamond kept the fans entertained. Magee was a veteran sleepwalker. One night when he and his wife were asleep in their third-floor hotel room, he got out of bed, walked across the room and right out the window. He woke up with a crash when he landed on the roof of a stable ten or twelve feet below. Only his pride was injured, but he had a good excuse. He blamed it all on green grapes and ham. "Green grapes and ham sandwiches always did have a bad effect on me, but I thought I would take a chance."

Across town the Athletics were having a rebuilding year. They finished a dull sixth, winning only sixty-eight games.

But Mack was in the process of putting together one of his greatest teams and that summer the Athletics' fans got their very first look at Jack Barry and Frank ("Homerun") Baker, and their first long look at Eddie Collins.

The Athletics and the Phillies were the centers of baseball interest in Philadelphia, but they weren't the only interest by far. Amateur and schoolboy baseball flourished at a level of activity that lived up to the title "National Pastime." The Amateur Baseball Association sponsored by the *Philadelphia Inquirer* had 254 teams and 4,000 players in a dozen cities throughout Pennsylvania, and it was only one of many amateur leagues. Pennsylvania was one of the hottest centers of baseball activity, but it was not unique. The whole of the Northeast was packed with amateur teams, and the rest of the country was not far behind. Baseball, on the amateur level, was the country's most popular participant sport just as on the professional level it was the biggest spectator sport.

This was the baseball atmosphere Joe stepped into when he finally got off the train in Philadelphia. His delayed arrival had only heightened interest. The papers wrote about him every day. They even interviewed Hyder Barr, who said, "The fences around Columbia Park will have some dents in them when Joe Jackson gets into action." In all, it was the biggest press buildup a rookie had ever gotten in Philadelphia, perhaps anywhere.

And when it was announced that Joe had actually arrived and would play against Cleveland the next day, three thousand fans came to Columbia Park in a cold rain to see him.

In his first major-league game Joe played center field and batted fourth. It was an honor for a rookie to bat in the cleanup position, even more so when it was his very first game. As he approached home plate for his first at bat, the crowd gave him an ovation. He responded with a slight smile, stepped into the batter's box, and got Black Betsy ready on his left shoulder. The Athletics had a man on second and there were two outs.

Heinie Berger, the Cleveland pitcher, was known for his fast spitball (then legal). It was particularly hard to follow and hit on a dark, drizzly day, so he threw it almost every pitch. He looked in at Joe, went into his big windup, and threw a fast spitter. Joe stepped smoothly up to meet it, unleashed Black Betsy, and sliced a foul down the right field line. The fans cheered. They liked a man who swung his bat. On the next pitch, another fast spitter, Joe stepped up again, but this time he moved his front foot a little less and timed his swing a little differently. He hit a clean blue darter into left field for his first major-league hit. The man on second base scored and Joe had his first run batted in. The crowd gave him another long cheer.

He didn't get any more hits in the game, but he did drive two more blue darters at the third baseman, who caught them in self-defense, and late in the game, with the Athletics trailing by one run, he tried to hit one out of the park. By now the ball was wet and heavy and Betsy was wet and slippery, but Joe stepped into a pitch and uncoiled a flashing black swing. He drove the ball all the way to the right field fence where the fielder caught it. The ball was hit so hard the crowd cheered him again.

The crowd had come just to see him play. Everyone in the ball park knew it, including Joe. He gave them something to watch. When they weren't cheering him at bat they cheered him in the field. In the second inning, with pitcher Berger at bat, Joe positioned himself in shallow center field. But Berger caught hold of one and sent a line drive over Joe's head. At the swing of the bat Joe spun around and raced toward center field. He looked back over his left shoulder and raced the trajectory of the ball until he was almost out to the flagpole next to the fence. Running at full speed, his back to the plate, he caught the ball just as it sailed over his shoulder.

Joe also demonstrated his throwing arm. Early in the game he made a throw from the left center field fence to third base. The ball bounced once, about ten feet out, and skipped into the third baseman's glove. It was estimated that the throw traveled nearly four hundred feet.

Later in the game, with a runner on second base, he fielded a one-hop, line drive in right center field and let loose a throw to home plate. The ball came in like an arrow, level and low to the ground. But the pitcher, judging there was no play on the runner racing home, cut off Joe's throw and fired the ball to first base in time to get the batter, who had rounded the first-base bag.

Joe also showed good baseball instincts and base-running ability when he raced from first to second on an outfielder's throw to third.

When the game was over his team had lost and he'd had only one hit in four attempts, but Joe's debut was a grand success. One writer summed it up briefly: "Thus in all respects Jackson looked extremely good in his first game and as if he didn't possess a single weakness: good at bat, good on fly balls, good on the bases and fast on his feet."

The papers were full of long reviews of Joe's performance. One of the men who covered the game for the *Evening Times* was most amazed by Joe's arm: "Such strong arm throwing was a reminder of Treadway, the old Baltimore star." The writer for the *Philadelphia Telegraph* was most impressed by the over-the-shoulder catch: "He went after and judged the ball and timed himself much like Curt Welch used to do in making those great catches that electrified baseball crowds twenty years ago." In search of comparisons the writers looked back to the 1880s and 1890s to find players who could throw with such power and accuracy and make such electrifying catches. It seemed they had already sensed Joe's baseball immortality and were casting about for names with which to establish his link to baseball's legendary past.

Connie Mack, whose judgment as owner and manager was the most important one, was most impressed. He smiled broadly when a reporter asked him what he thought of Joe. "If nothing happens to him," Mack replied, "he should develop rapidly into one of the greatest players the game has yet produced." Then, mindful of the great pressure under which Joe was breaking into the majors, Mack added, "But give the boy time to learn and develop and don't expect too much of him from the start. Remember, he is only a boy and this is his first year out."

After Joe's debut game, the Detroit Tigers arrived in Philadelphia for four games. The Tigers, in the second of three straight pennant years, were in first place by four games over second-place St. Louis. They were the Tigers of Wahoo Sam Crawford and Germany Schaefer; of pitchers Wabash George Mullin, Wild Bill Donovan and Kickapoo Ed Summers; of manager Ee-Yah Hughie Jennings. But most of all they were the Tigers of Ty Cobb, the Georgia Peach, star batsman of the American League.

In 1908 Cobb was in his fourth major-league season. He had already posted batting averages of .240, .313, and .350, and was on his way to a .324 mark in 1908. In 1907 he'd won the first of his twelve American League batting titles with his .350 average and had also led the league in runs batted in, hits, slugging average, total bases, and stolen bases. He had also been among the leaders in home runs, runs scored, and triples, and he was involved in more double plays than any right fielder in the league. His average dropped to .324 in 1908, but he still won the batting title and his statistics were again among the best in the league in most departments. Cobb was the first man seriously to challenge the mighty Honus Wagner for the title of greatest baseball player in the world, and many already felt Cobb was the better of the two. There was little disagreement that he was the best in the American League. This was the player against whom Joe was compared.

With the Tigers in town, the chief topic of baseball conversation was the coming confrontation between Joe and Ty Cobb. But the foul weather that had threatened Joe's debut game turned worse and the first two games against Detroit were rained out. With time on their hands and little else to talk about during the rain delays, the fans and the writers inflated Joe's first head-to-head meeting with Cobb into an epic showdown, which matched the reigning king against the heir-apparent.

Following the customs and interests of the times, the rain-idled players hung around their hotel lobby and talked baseball. Joe could not help hearing the many anecdotes his Athletics teammates told about Cobb's greatness and fierce determination. The fact that these anecdotes served to increase the pressure on Joe was not lost to his teammates. In part, at least, they wanted to see Joe put in his place by Cobb.

When rookie players joined a club they were usually subjected to harassments of one kind or another because the veteran players regarded them as competitors, younger men who might take away their jobs. Rookies were frequently forced away from the plate during batting practice. If they suffered silently they never got the chance to show what they could do. If they spoke up for their rights or fought their way into the batter's box for hitting practice, they increased the enmity of the veterans, who then regarded them as fresh bushers who didn't understand the ways of a big-league club or their own inferior position on it.

Joe's case was different. He had been preceded by such an extensive press coverage that he was not forced to fight for his rights like other rookies. But the veterans resented the publicity, the most ever given to an untried and unproved minor leaguer, and many of the Athletics were contemptuous of his background. For one reason or another, many of the Athletics were bitter toward Joe and tried to drive him from the team with taunts and insults. When they saw it would not pay to ridicule his physical abilities, they chose other targets. They quickly zeroed in on his illiteracy and naïveté and made him the butt of all their yokel tricks. One night in the hotel dining room they tricked him into drinking the water in the finger bowl and then laughed him out of the room. Early the next morning, without a word to anyone, he got on a southbound and went back to Greenville.

Joe never gave a public explanation for his return home, but forty years later he told a Greenville friend, a playing colleague from his mill team days, that his Athletics teammates had made him feel as bad as he had ever felt in his entire life.

As soon as Joe's departure was discovered, stories circulated in Philadelphia saying he had run away because he was afraid of the big city, the American League, and, most of all, Ty Cobb. As if in answer to this charge, the next day Connie Mack received a telegram that informed him that Joe had returned home because there was illness in the family. Joe's mother, who probably sent the telegram, defended him in a public statement. She said it would be a mistake to believe he ran away or lacked courage. "Joe is game," she stated, "and he has always been game. He left Philadelphia because I sent for him. His wife was very sick and his uncle was not expected to live."

There was some illness in the family, it was even reported in the *News,* but Joe's mother just used it as a convenience.

She knew the real reason why Joe had left Philadelphia, but she thought it best to give the public a simple explanation. But once again Joe himself said nothing to explain or excuse his actions. And the *News* warned again of the blacklist: if Joe refused to return to Philadelphia, his major-league career would end after one game.

When the weather cleared in Philadelphia, the Athletics and the Tigers played two consecutive double-headers to make up the two rained-out games. Not knowing yet that Joe had left town, over twelve thousand fans turned out for the first double-header, to see him play against Ty Cobb. As we know, the much-heralded first confrontation never took place because Joe was back in South Carolina. We are left to speculate about what would have happened. In all the anecdotal versions about Joe's flight from Philadelphia and his fear of facing Cobb, no mention is made of the effect the challenge had on Cobb. Perhaps he had welcomed the test and suffered a letdown when Joe disappeared. In the two double-headers, Cobb went to bat a total of fourteen times and got only one hit.

Tommie Stouch was already back in Greenville when Joe returned, and Mack wired him to bring Joe back to Philadelphia. He also wired Joe: "Report at once." The *News* kept the Greenville fans informed of Mack's efforts to recapture Joe, and in the same editions that carried the warnings about the blacklist, the *News* reprinted from the Philadelphia papers the rave reviews Joe had received for his debut game a few days earlier. The fans must have been almost as confused as Joe, who maintained his public silence but listened to his mother, who advised him to go back. Ten days after he fled the Athletics he got on a train and returned.

Joe had left Philadelphia on August 28 and did not return until Monday, September 7; he was gone ten days. But when he got back nothing had changed. His teammates continued to torment him. On Tuesday he played against New York and on Wednesday against the Red Sox in Boston. On Friday the Athletics played a double-header in Washington. In the first game Joe went 0 for 4 against Walter Johnson. He was 0 for 5 in the second game. Then he left again. He quietly got on another train and went back to Greenville. This time he stayed.

It had been an eventful year for Joe. He had turned professional and had led his league with a .354 batting average. He had married Katie. He had made it to the major leagues and had gained a national reputation. He was unanimously considered the next great star of the American League. But he ended the year back in Brandon Village, his future uncertain.

When Joe ran from the Athletics the second time, Connie Mack tried to get him to come back, but Joe was stubborn and Mack lost his patience. The *News,* which had opened the baseball season with headlines about Joe's exploits with the Spinners, closed it with headlines about Joe's adventures with the Athletics: "JOE JACKSON HAS BEEN SUSPENDED BY MACK . . . The Brandon Boy Can Never Play Organized Ball Again."

6

JOE AND KATIE spent the winter in the Jackson household in Brandon. Joe was now the family's biggest money earner. Earlier in the year he had helped his father start a butcher shop, and during that winter he worked in the shop with him. Joe's father, George, was a quiet man, but his venturesomeness set him off from most of his village neighbors. Unlike many mill hands who were disappointed with mill work and moved from one mill to another in search of work that would satisfy them, Joe's father chose an independent course and went out on his own. His quiet independence made a great impression on Joe, but it was his mother, Martha, who was the center of the family.

Martha Jackson was a big woman and family tradition has it that Joe inherited his size from her. When the family first moved into the cotton mill area from Pickens County, Martha already had three children, but she went to work in a mill all the same. By 1908 she was a full-time housewife and mother to seven children.

Her life was busy but she always found time for Joe, her oldest child and the one to whom she was closest. She always liked to hear about the places he'd been and the things he'd seen, and he liked telling her. Usually they talked in the kitchen. If she was baking apple pies, Joe sat at the kitchen table and peeled the apples. He saved the peels and cores for making jelly.

Joe also discussed his plans with his mother; he valued her advice. During the winter they discussed Joe's baseball career several times. We don't know what Martha said but by springtime Joe was ready. He packed his gear and, carrying Black Betsy wrapped in a cotton cloth, he got on the train to report to the Athletics spring training camp in Atlanta.

Connie Mack divided the Athletics into two teams for the 1909 spring training, the Regulars and the Yannigans. The Regulars had big-league experience on their side, but they were no match for the young Yannigans, who won most of the practice games that spring. The Yannigans included Eddie Collins, Frank Baker, Stuffy McInnis, Amos Strunk, and, of course, Joe.

Joe had a great spring training and when Connie Mack broke camp and headed north, Joe was still with the team. Following big-league tradition, the Athletics played their way north in a series of exhibition games, which helped the players round into shape and helped the club to defray training expenses. Clubs frequently split their rosters into two teams so they could play twice as many exhibition games, and Mack was set with his Regulars and his Yannigans.

Mack took his youngsters into Eclipse Park in Louisville for a game against the Louisville Colonels. When the Colonels' general manager learned that Mack had brought his rookie team, he complained loudly: "That isn't fair. Why, we'll murder those kids." Mack told his young players what the Louisville general manager thought of them and they got sore. As one observer reported, "With young Jackson battering down the fences, the Athletics kids won by a score of 21 to 2." Among Joe's cluster of extra base hits was the longest home run ever hit at Eclipse Park, a screaming blue darter over the right-field wall.

Joe made it all the way to Pennsylvania with the Athletics that spring and then he changed his mind. There is a much-repeated story of how he informed Mack that he did not want to play in Philadelphia. One version of this story was told by baseball writer Frederick Lieb: "After an exhibition game in Reading, the players were on the station platform, awaiting a train for Philadelphia. There was a row of milk cans, with red labels attached to them on the platform. 'I wish I had one of those labels on me, and that I would be sent away somewhere,' said Joe. Mack overheard the remark and asked: 'Do you mean that Joe?' 'Yes I do,' he replied. 'All right,' said Connie, 'we'll see whether we can oblige you.' "

The next day Mack sent Joe down to play for the Savannah Indians in the South Atlantic League.

Savannah, Georgia, had been the second city in the South to adopt the "New York Game," the direct forerunner of modern baseball. Savannah's conversion took place in 1866 when the local gentlemen's amateur team adopted the rules and format of baseball which had been designed by Alexander Cartwright in 1845. Before they adopted the "New York Game," the gentlemen's clubs in the South had played by the rules of the "Massachusetts Game," which they'd learned from Union soldiers in southern prison camps during the Civil War. In 1867 Savannah played Charleston, South Carolina, for the baseball championship of the South. Thus the modern game had had over forty years of local history when the first *hurrah* for the 1909 season unfurled in a banner headline across the top of the sports page of the *Savannah Press* in early April: BASEBALL IN ELEVEN DAYS!

To set the stage for the new season, the *Press* reprinted an article from the *New York Evening Telegram,* which boasted that two million dollars had been spent in less than a year to improve professional ball parks around the nation, mostly in the major leagues. Everything pointed to a great season, which was the way it was supposed to be, for, according to the *Evening Telegram,* "Baseball is a national game, our national game, for all good Americans are proud of it, and its great prosperity is the most conclusive testimony to its purity, its honesty, its attractiveness and the hold which it has on the national heart."

In support of its by now obvious contention that the game held a unique place in our national life, the article cited a statistician who speculated that on one single afternoon, probably a Saturday, over one million fans watched baseball games in New York State alone. By including all the baseball states, the total number of fans attending baseball games on a single afternoon was estimated at twenty million.

In 1909 there were ninety million Americans, so this estimate would have us believe that over twenty percent of the population was at a baseball game at the same time. We do not know if these estimates were grossly inflated or not, but their appearance in print demonstrated the way the game was viewed by its writers and how it was promoted to the public. The success of professional baseball was treated as a national cause and it was inserted into the American Way of Life at every opportunity.

Free newspaper promotions and organized civic support for ball teams was a great advantage for the club owners in all leagues. It was not their only source of support. The owners' desire to promote their product was matched everywhere by the self-promotional needs of politicians. In Greenville, the mayor had been one of the Spinners' most ardent fans and supporters. As he advanced through his political career he had recognized the value of baseball and had exploited it. When he first ran for office he campaigned at country fairs. A year or two later he campaigned at every baseball game he could find. Politicians everywhere wanted to be associated with baseball because it had the ideal image: wholesome and all-American. Also, a lot of fans were voters.

The owners were only too pleased to accept the attention of the politicians. Politicians got news coverage and that meant extra publicity. In their roles as public officials or statesmen, politicians also lent prestige to the game.

While local politicians and club owners helped each other, the owners of the Washington Americans had higher aims. In 1909 they went after the President of the United States, and they got him. President Taft and Vice-President Sherman showed up in the second inning of the Washington home opener and stayed for the rest of the game.

Taft's decision to attend a much-publicized Opening Day game was not impulsive. It was based on his understanding of public image making. The gesture was a great success and Taft's appearance at the ballgame was widely reported. Down in Savannah the *Press* ran an editorial entitled "Big Bill at the Game":

"Bill Taft is all right. He may not indulge in athletics himself except to enjoy a game of golf but — and he will win his way into the hearts of his countrymen because of it — he loves baseball."

The Savannah Indians played their first game in Jacksonville, where opening day had been proclaimed a legal holiday. Led by the mayor of Jacksonville and a marching band, the teams paraded through town out to the local ballgrounds where the band played "The Star-Spangled Banner," and four thousand fans cheered for some action. The Indians lost their opening game and the team didn't look very good, but the Savannah fans had something to anticipate when word got out that Joe Jackson was coming to town.

The *Press* responded to the news with exuberance: "Everybody in South Carolina knows Joe Jackson," the paper announced, and assured the fans that Joe would be one of the best players ever to appear in the South Atlantic League.

When Joe arrived a week later, he lived up to the advance notices. In his first eighty times at bat he got thirty-six hits for a .450 average. The fans liked him immediately and he felt comfortable. Savannah was much easier for Joe than Philadelphia. It was smaller, it was southern, and its baseball writers did not treat him as if he were a rare specimen captured at the edge of civilization. His teammates played no humiliating tricks on him and Bobby Gilks, his manager, understood him.

Gilks was a big-city man from Cincinnati, but he seems to have understood Joe at first sight. In the late 1890s Gilks played the outfield and pitched for Cleveland when it was in the American Association and later when it joined the National League, so he had the experience to recognize immediately how marvelously talented Joe was. He also seems to have intuitively understood Joe's temperament, and he gave him the emotional support he needed.

The fact that professional baseball players needed emotional support would have been a surprising thought to most fans in those years — they were hardly used to thinking of them as mere mortals or even as human beings at all. When they went to a game they could see how well or how poorly a player performed, but the image they had of what a player was like as a human being came almost completely from the writers who, with few exceptions, were only interested in presenting flat, two-dimensional characters.

The subject of the players' real lives could have easily come to mind, for just at this time the national sports headlines were focused on the suicide of Harry Pulliam, president of the National League. The *Press* was one of the papers that carried a syndicated piece called "Baseball Suicides." This short piece pointed out that Pulliam was the only non-player among the "surprisingly long list of prominent baseball men who have taken their own lives." Of the dozen certified cases of baseball players who had committed suicide — or "suicided," as the papers used to put it — up until 1909, most drank poison. Of the two who used guns, one first murdered his wife and three children. His act was so horrifying that his former colleagues disowned him. Connie Mack was the only baseball man who attended his funeral.

As the season wore on Joe enjoyed Savannah more and more. The pace of the city itself was pleasing and the fans had singled him out as their special favorite; everyone was pleased with Joe, but nobody was pleased with the team. The Indians lost eighteen of their first twenty-two games and were in last place. The fans cried for new infielders and pitchers. The *Press* warned of a shake-up and added bluntly: "We have paid good money for that club, and they are going to start in to win!" When the shake-up came, it was superficial. Manager Gilks was fired and the team continued to lose.

The biggest change probably happened to Joe. In the

month he had played under Gilks, Joe had quickly learned to trust and respect him. Joe had been aware of the shake-up rumors, but he'd assumed the changes would take place among the players — the infielders who made too many errors and the pitchers who gave up too many hits. He was surprised and confused when Gilks was suddenly fired with hardly a word of explanation; his hitting slowed down until his average fell to .350. It was a drop of one hundred points, but he still had the highest average in the league.

Joe's hitting and all-around play were the one bright spot in an otherwise dull season, so the Savannah baseball writers wrote as much copy as they could about his exploits. When they tired of that, they complained. They complained about their own Indians, but mostly they complained about the Chattanooga Lookouts, who won so often that they ran away from the rest of the Sally League.

When the Lookouts seemed to have clinched the pennant before the season was half over, writers in Savannah and in other cities around the league accused the Lookouts of "lying down" because they'd already won the pennant. Accusations of gambling surfaced with such insistency that the president of the Sally League was forced to acknowledge the problem: "The Gambling Must Stop!" This stern warning must have been undermined when the *Press* ran a photograph a few days later of a group of men sitting in some bleachers, wearing white shirts with round collars, black ties, and straw skimmers. The whole caption read, "Betting at American League Games."

The complaints against the Chattanooga team included the accusation that the team owners had broken the league's salary limit rule and were paying their players too much money. The concept of a salary limit for players was not new. It had first appeared in the major leagues in the 1880s, when the owners defended it as an attempt to equalize player hiring power between the wealthy and the poor clubs. The players saw the salary limit from another point of view. To them it was a self-serving rule by which the owners could keep salaries perpetually depressed, no matter how well a player performed or how much profit an owner made. The players protested, and when the owners refused to repeal the salary limit, a group of major leaguers organized the short-lived Brotherhood of Professional Ballplayers.

The Brotherhood gave rise to the Players League, an independent, player-controlled organization that competed with the major leagues for one season before it collapsed. The Brotherhood was eventually successful in its fight against the salary limit, which was dropped by the major leagues. It continued in the minors, however, where the owners had some justification in their claim that high salaries might bankrupt many clubs.

The loudest complaint against Chattanooga that year was directed at the club's home grounds, a shabby, run-down ball park that the other clubs felt was a disgrace. The issues behind all the complaining were not merely civic rivalries and frustrations. Chattanooga's lead was so great that all excitement faded from the pennant race. Fans around the league lost interest and attendance fell below the danger line. The owners of the Macon team were forced to sell. The Charleston team was moved to Knoxville with the hope of drawing larger crowds. All the teams in the league were in financial trouble. Facing serious losses and even bankruptcy, the owners took action. They declared that the season would be divided into two parts, the First Season (the first half of the original schedule) and the Second Season (the remainder of the original schedule). Chattanooga was hastily awarded the First Season pennant and the Second Season got under way.

Mostly on the strength of Joe's hitting, the Savannah Indians got off to a good start in the Second Season. The fans were annoyed by the happenings of the strange season, but Joe seemed not to have been bothered at all. He came out of the slump which followed the departure of Bobby Gilks and batted over .375 in the last fifty games he played for Savannah. His fielding improved as the season wore on and he was considered the best base-stealer in the league. He even pitched a few times. One afternoon he went three innings against the Macon Peaches, giving up one hit and striking out two. The cartoon of the game showed a pitcher in his windup saying, "Dis ball will beat itself to the plate." The caption reads, "And Jackson was right, for he certainly had ten brands of speed."

When the writers around the Sally League chose their all-star team, Joe was the unanimous choice for center field. "Jackson is a sensation in all departments of the great American game," wrote one, "and that's saying a whole lot."

Joe's hitting and fielding were not enough to carry the whole team and the Indians settled back into fourth place. When they were mathematically out of the pennant race, a message from Philadelphia called Joe back to the Athletics for the last month of the American League season.

There were still a few games on the schedule when Joe left Savannah. He had played in 118 games and his .358 batting average was the best in the Sally League. In his first two professional seasons he had won two batting championships.

Joe stopped over in Brandon for a few days to visit with his family, then went on to Philadelphia. This time Katie went with him. He did not hang back, or play hide and seek, but his heart was not in it.

The Athletics fans had followed his progress on the sports pages and they were delighted to have him back. His return was noted by the press: "Jackson, the youngster who is known as Stonewall, Home Run Joe and other aliases, reached town Monday night." But Joe was not the center of attraction he had been the year before. This time he came up to an Athletics club that was in the middle of a pennant race. Connie Mack's rebuilding had progressed much faster than he had expected. By early September the Athletics were in second place, a few games behind the Detroit Tigers.

When Joe arrived, Mack put him in center field in a game against New York. In a repeat of his major-league debut in Philadelphia the year before, he got a hit his first time at bat and drove in the first run of the game. But his play in the outfield was spotty. He looked listless and uncomfortable. In the fifth inning he misplayed a long drive to left center by Hal Chase. It should have been a double, but by the time Joe got the ball back into the infield, Chase had a home run.

After the game, Connie Mack may have realized what was really troubling Joe, for Joe made no attempt to pretend. The problem was personal: Joe did not want to play baseball in Philadelphia. Talking about Joe years later, Mack recalled, "We brought him and his Mrs. up in the latter part of the 1909 season. We tried to teach them our way of doing things, but it still was difficult for them to get adjusted. Our players played pranks on Joe, and he regarded them with suspicion. My players didn't seem to like him, though I told them at the time he was going to make one of the greatest hitters of baseball."

Following the one game against New York, Joe sat on the Athletics' bench for the next three weeks while the battle with Detroit reached its climax. The year before the fans would have howled for Joe to appear in the lineup, but now all attention was focused on the pennant race. In mid-September the Athletics won three out of four against Detroit and pulled to within one and a half games, but they never got any closer.

Since Joe was still a rookie, Mack's decision not to play him in the middle of a high-pressure pennant fight could easily be accounted for by Joe's lack of major-league experience. But several of Joe's fellow Athletics, who'd resumed the needling they had begun the year before, attributed Mack's decision to Joe's cowardice. Joe had a yellow streak, they told some reporters, and that was why Mack wouldn't let him play when the pennant was on the line.

Joe got into a few more games after the pennant race was decided, but his American League totals for 1909 were lackluster: he appeared in five games and got five hits in seventeen times at bat. Seen in light of his minor-league record, his performance for the Athletics was ordinary and disappointing. By the end of the season, Mack, who understood the reason for Joe's lack of enthusiasm, must have wondered if Joe would ever become a full-fledged member of the team. He had no doubts about how good a player Joe was, but Joe just didn't seem to fit in.

Mack knew he had a good young team, one that would be in contention for the pennant for the next few years, with or without Joe.

This team, which in fact did win pennants without Joe in 1910, 1911, 1913, and 1914, was built around such players as Chief Bender, Eddie Plank, Jack Coombs, Lou Krause, Jack Barry, and Eddie Collins, all of whom were college men. Amos Strunk and Stuffy McInnis, among other Athletics, were high-school graduates, a mark of educational distinction in 1909. Most of the men on the club were from middle-class backgrounds or from families with middle-class aspirations. Joe was the only illiterate man on the team and, with the exception of Connie Mack himself, who had worked in a cotton mill in Massachusetts for several summers, the only ex–mill hand. The attitudes of the men on the Athletics toward Joe were about the same as those held by the people of Greenville toward the mill hands out in the villages.

The situation posed a dilemma for Connie Mack. He

doubted that Joe would ever want to play in Philadelphia, but he was hesitant to sell him to an American League rival for fear that Joe would live up to his potential and return to haunt the Athletics. Selling a potential star to the National League, still a hated rival, was out of the question. Mack thought about it over the winter and when Joe gave no sign of increased enthusiasm over playing for Philadelphia, Mack chose a temporary solution. He sent Joe back to the minor leagues.

7

JOE WAS PLEASED, even relieved, when he learned that Mack was sending him down to play for the New Orleans Pelicans of the Southern League and he was in high spirits when he reported for spring training in March of 1910. He was ready to begin training the day he got to New Orleans but he was held out of action until the business arrangement between the Athletics and the Pelicans was settled.

While waiting to see him play in practice games, the New Orleans writers welcomed Joe: "Jackson is a star of the first magnitude," said the *New Orleans Times Picayune*. A few days later, when reporting the rumor that Mack wanted to call Joe back to Philadelphia, the paper warned, "If Joe got away it would crimp enthusiasm, for he is destined to lead Southern League batsmen this season and is needed here."

As soon as an agreement was reached — Mack retained complete ownership of Joe's contract and Charlie Franks, owner-manager of the Pelicans, received a guarantee that Joe would play for New Orleans at least until the Southern League pennant race was decided — Joe began to play. The Pelicans had a close working relationship with the Cleveland Naps and that spring the two teams trained together in Pelican Park. Most of their training consisted of games played against each other. Joe got into a dozen of those games and got twenty hits off the Cleveland pitchers, half of them for extra bases. Charles Somers, owner of the Naps, immediately began the negotiations that eventually brought Joe to Cleveland.

Joe batted .340 in the practice games, highest of any player on both teams except for Larry Lajoie, who hit .465. In addition to Joe, the rest of the Pelicans looked promising too, and the fans and writers began talking about winning the championship of the Southern League. When pennant fever breaks out in a city, the perceptions of the fans and the actions of the players suddenly gain new dimensions. The meaning of events are heightened, small occurrences grow portentous and almost everyone becomes a fan. The excitement generated through New Orleans by the Pelicans that spring grew as Opening Day approached. The excitement mounted when the Pelicans announced that their all-electric scoreboard, installed the year before and then damaged by a storm, was repaired and ready for the season.

The Pelicans were scheduled to open their season at home against the Mobile Sea Gulls on April 14, but the game was advanced one day to accommodate the schedule of the Mystic Order of the Shriners, which was holding its national convention in New Orleans. The front-page headline of the

Times Picayune blared: "Magnificent Metropolis Is the Mecca for Mystic Shriners!" Over 30,000 Shriners gathered in New Orleans, which had a population of under 350,000. The Shriners took over the city and on Opening Day they joined in the general festivities.

An early concert by Boehler's Marching Band started things off: "Hail to the Chief," "Pelican March," "Take Me Out to the Ballgame," "America," and "Jungletown." At two o'clock the big parade started out from City Hall, headed by a guard of mounted police. The parade included over forty carriages and stretched out for blocks as it wound its way through the packed streets of the city and out to Pelican Park. Boehler's Marching Band was joined by a band from Mobile and they blared their way through town. The lead carriages carried the mayors of New Orleans and Mobile and such notables as the New Orleans inspector of police, the postmaster, judges, and other city and state officials. Newspaper reporters got two carriages, the Mobile team and some of their fans got three, and the Pelicans got three. Joe, in uniform like the rest of the players, rode in the middle of the parade. He was singled out for cheers by the crowds along the route. The parade wound through newspaper row, making a stop in front of each newspaper office to tender a musical salute; then, cheered on by the crowds along the sidewalks, made its way to Pelican Park.

The park was decorated with flags and bunting, and the Mobile Sea Gulls were led to their bench by a brightly costumed honor guard from the Mobile Temple of the Shriners. The bands played, the crowd of over five thousand cheered and whistled, and the season finally began. The Pelicans built up a 6-to-1 lead by the eighth inning, but the Sea Gulls scored seven runs in the ninth to win the game. The fans were disappointed at the loss, but everyone was pleased with the parade, the biggest ever held for a New Orleans baseball team.

The next day, in the nation's capital, the Washington Americans improved on their public relations success of the year before. This time President Taft arrived at the Washington ball park before the Opening Day game of the American League began, accompanied by his wife, Vice-President Sherman, and other notables. Newspapers around the country announced, "FIRST CHIEF EXEC. TOSSES FIRST BALL IN OPENER!" The *Times Picayune*, congratulating Taft for his good Americanism, added, "What was more, he sat through the entire nine innings and seemed greatly to enjoy the contest." Any fan would have. Washington opened against the Athletics, who were on their way to a pennant. Connie Mack's ace left-hander, Eddie Plank, allowed one run, but he was no match for Walter Johnson, who pitched a one-hit shutout.

Taft's appearance at the game and his symbolic gesture of throwing out the first ball gave the Opening Day of major-league baseball everything short of formal recognition as a national holiday and established a presidential custom that continued as long as Washington, D.C., had a major-league team.

In the territory of the Southern League (Alabama, Arkansas, Georgia, Louisiana, and Tennessee), the spring of 1910 was one of the coldest on record. Sea lions swam in the ship canal at Galveston, Texas, where they had never been seen before. And for the first time in its history, the Southern League had had to cancel all its games one day because of the cold spell. Many of the players in the league were bothered by the cold weather, but not the Pelicans. They won ten of their first fifteen games and moved into first place.

The pitching staff, which would post over thirty shutouts before the season was over, looked very strong. And in those first fifteen games Joe went to bat fifty-two times and got twenty-seven hits, including six doubles and six triples, for a .519 batting average. He became the immediate hero and idol of New Orleans baseball fans.

Joe had liked New Orleans at first sight, and as the season progressed he liked it better and better. The fans were more cosmopolitan and varied in their backgrounds than any he'd known before, and they were warm and full of praise. His heroics on the diamond drew people to him. His open, easygoing manner made friends of many of them. He developed friendships with other players as well.

One afternoon before a game against the Mobile Sea Gulls, Joe fell into a conversation with Sea Gull outfielder Joe Phillips. They struck up a friendship and later palled around together when they got the chance in Mobile or New Orleans. During the off season Phillips operated a vaudeville house in his hometown in West Virginia, and he introduced Joe to the world of show business. Phillips told him how easy it was for a person with a famous name, particularly for a star baseball player, to earn extra money in vaudeville, then the most popular form of show business. Joe was interested. He accompanied Phillips on the rounds of New Orleans vaudeville houses, observing and learning whatever he could.

While the fans in New Orleans were enjoying Joe, the fans around the rest of the league, after watching him break up game after game against their home teams, jealously agreed he was the best hitter they'd ever seen. The other players, always the best judges of a man's ability because they confronted it on the playing field, paid Joe the compliment of their respect. The outfielders played him deeper than any other hitter in the league, and the pitchers were afraid of him. They felt good when they held him to a single.

An occasional pitcher, his judgment clouded by pride or stubbornness, insisted on pitching to Joe as if he were an ordinary hitter. One afternoon in a game against the Sea Gulls, Joe came to bat in the ninth inning against such a pitcher. The Pelicans were one run behind and they had two men on base. The Sea Gulls' first baseman, who was also the team captain, huddled with the pitcher and told him to give Joe an intentional base on balls. "Walk?" shouted the pitcher. "He looks just like the rest of them to me!" On the first pitch, Joe hit a blue darter against the right field fence, driving in two runs and winning the game. The Sea Gull captain scolded his pitcher, heated words led to a fight, and in addition to losing the game the pitcher took a drubbing behind the clubhouse.

The Pelicans were in first place for most of the season and there were other exciting players on the club, so the New Orleans writers did not have to concentrate on Joe. But they did anyway. Almost every day he did something on the diamond that drove them in search of new superlatives and new stylistic twists. For the most part they wrote about his hitting. In a June game, while "cracking out two three-baggers and a single, Joe Jackson starred with his ebony stick." A few days later, "The young Ty Cobb of the Southern League threw himself into the game with added zest with the big crowd looking on. His triple was a pippin and his two-bagger was a peach." By July one writer answered his own rhetorical question: "Did Joe hit? Well, the Candy Kid from Carolina copped it to left like a bullet. . . ." In an away game the next week, a writer with the home team recorded the mood of the home-team fans: "The bases were bulging, none down, and the terrible Joe Jackson was at bat. A shiver of apprehension swept over the stands, and it seemed that nothing short of three or four runs would inevitably ensue."

The writers were fascinated with Joe's hitting. His average

passed .400 a few times during the season and at no time was the second-place batter in the league any closer to Joe's average than thirty or forty points. Sometimes the second-place man was almost a hundred points away. By season's end, Joe's average leveled off at .354. In the whole Southern League that season, only two or three other players batted over .300. And if Joe's high average weren't enough to make the writers marvel, the kind of hits he got made it certain. He hit his blue darters to all fields and against all pitchers. He hit the ball harder, farther, and more frequently than any hitter they'd ever seen.

Then there was his fielding. One afternoon when an opposing batter "laced a long, lurid drive to right centre field, Joe made the most sensational one-handed catch ever seen at Pelican Park. The batter smashed the spheroid on the nose with such savageness that it seemed sure the hit would be good for two or three bases. Jackson ran hard to get in the comet's path, pulling it down out of the ether by a marvelous leap and stab with his left (gloved) hand. Such a fielding stunt thrilled the record Monday crowd with wildest enthusiasm. It was really far more wonderful than the three-base hits so common to the Candy Kid from Carolina's repertoire."

At the end of August the writers around the Southern League chose their personal all-star teams. Joe was on all of them, including the one selected by Grantland Rice, who was already one of the best-known "sporting writers" in the South. Rice said he had had a few close decisions to make, but "there wasn't any argument about Jackson's status. He is lengths out in front and still breezing."

After the naming of the traditional all-star teams, the only thing left for the Pelicans was the clinching of the pennant. They had held first place for almost the entire season, but the second-place Birmingham Barons had won just enough games to remain in mathematical contention. There was little doubt that the Pelicans would ultimately win the championship, so the fans were unworried as the season entered September. Until the pennant was clinched they would keep Joe Jackson.

But the Cleveland team had expressed interest in obtaining Joe during spring training, and their interest was heightened when they learned from Mack that Joe was, in fact, available. Mack's asking price for Joe was Cleveland first-string outfielder Briscoe Lord, whom Mack had traded to Cleveland only the year before. He wanted Lord back so he could add another experienced veteran to his outfield.

Mack's asking price was low. Briscoe Lord never became more than a good journeyman outfielder with an exceptional arm. But at the time Lord was a proven commodity and Cleveland might have questioned Joe's motivation. After all, hadn't he run away from the Athletics and asked to be sent back to the minor leagues? Perhaps he would refuse to play in Cleveland.

Cleveland was interested in the deal but they wanted to get the opinion of their best scout, so they sent him to New Orleans at the end of June to take a long look at Joe and talk with him. The scout loved what he saw his very first afternoon in Pelican Park, which isn't surprising, for he was none other than Bobby Gilks, Joe's first manager in Savannah. Gilks had admired Joe from the first moment he saw him step into the batter's box the year before, and now he saw that Joe was even better.

Joe welcomed Gilks warmly, happy to see him again. The two spent much time together. After several long conversations, Gilks was convinced that Joe would go to Cleveland and play for the team if the deal was completed. After Gilks filed his report, Cleveland quickly agreed to Connie Mack's terms. At the end of July the trade was announced: Joe would report to Cleveland as soon as the Southern League pennant race was decided.

News of the trade met with surprise. Whatever else the fans around the country believed about Joe, they knew about his marvelous talents. They couldn't understand why such a respected judge of baseball talent as Connie Mack would make such a move; it seemed to call for an explanation. In the fifty years that Mack managed the Athletics, Joe Jackson was the best hitter who ever got away from him. Some observers insisted it was the biggest mistake he ever made. Years later Mack still felt the need to explain his action.

"I knew exactly what I was doing when I let Jackson go to Cleveland," Mack once said. "Lord, of course, helped me at the time. I knew our players didn't like Jackson, but that isn't why I traded him. I also knew Joe had great possibilities as a hitter. But at the time things were going none too well for Charlie Somers in Cleveland, and I was anxious to do him a good turn in appreciation for the way he had helped us out in Philadelphia in the early days of the League. So I let him have Jackson."

On another occasion, though, shortly after Ted Williams hit .406 in 1941, when the Athletics were in one of their prolonged weak periods, Mack confided during an interview, "I wish I had a Williams. I had one once and I lost him. Joe Jackson, one of the greatest hitters of all time."

Joe's fame had spread since his first appearance in the national press in 1908 and he had fans all over the country. Now his Cleveland fans rooted for the Pelicans to clinch their pennant so Joe could head north and join the Naps. His New Orleans fans found the trade dismal, but they hadn't expected Joe to remain in the Southern League for more than one season anyway.

At the end of August all of Joe's fans got a scare when he got hit on the head by a fastball. He was out of action for a few days, but when he returned he relieved his fans' worries. The *Times Picayune* prefaced its report of Joe's return game with a few lines of doggerel:

> Jackson, Joe, was a dashing young beau, and a slashing
>   young beau was he:
> He larruped to left, and he hammered to right, both of
>   them good for three.

"When in the course of human events," the report continued, "a noble ballplayer is badly biffed on the bean and has to lay off for a couple of days, then comes back and bats 1.000, drawing a pass, hitting two triples and one double and scoring three times, said kingpin pellet-puncher deserves commendation. That's what the Carolina Confection received, and in such copious quantities that other hard-working Pelicans were almost forgotten. The bugs do love a batter, and Jackson jolted the most staid and settled fan into a fury of excited approbation."

In that return game Joe also stole a base and made four put-outs, one of them a wonderful running catch. He more than met the expectations of the large crowd and played as if the beaning had been a mere irritation. But he was having headaches and his vision was a little blurry for a few days.

The Pelicans finally won the pennant in a double-header against Chattanooga, which had joined the Southern League at the start of the season. A version of Joe's role in the pennant clincher was presented to major-league fans the following spring in an article in a Boston paper: "Joe clinched the pennant for New Orleans in 1910 by breaking up both games of a doubleheader at Memphis three weeks before the season closed. He made four hits in four times up in the first game and three hits in three times up in the second game. His batting average was .394. He took things easy after the pennant was won and his average dropped to .354."

This account of Joe's heroics was complimentary but extreme. Going into that double-header, played only one week before the end of the season, Joe was hitting .361. He did not get seven hits that day; he went to bat four times and got none. His average dropped during the last week of the season because he was still suffering the after-effects of the beaning. He was also worried about Cleveland.

His life seemed to be repeating itself. For the third year in a row he had played his first season in a new league with the same result: he had been the batting champion of the league and its star attraction. Now, again for the third time, he was called north to the big leagues for the tail-end of the season.

As his departure day approached, he was quoted as saying he really preferred to stay in New Orleans. In Greenville the *News* eagerly sensed the possibility of another game of hide and seek. They interviewed Tommie Stouch who said Joe was a "real Southerner" who wanted to play in the South. When rumors were reported that Joe would return to Greenville rather than go to Cleveland, the *News* responded with its own speculation that Joe would play with a Mill League all-star team. But Joe did not return to Greenville. He got on a train in New Orleans with Katie and Bobby Gilks and started north. When the train reached Memphis, Tennessee, Joe's reluctance made him hesitate one last time. He said he didn't want to go to Cleveland.

When Bobby Gilks asked him why he'd changed his mind, Joe shrugged and answered, "There's not enough elbow room in the big city." Joe hesitated but he did not threaten to return to Greenville. By chance the Pelicans were also in town for a series of games against the Memphis team and Gilks, who guessed that Joe only needed one small shove, brought Charlie Franks over to talk to him. Joe listened. Then he got back on the northbound with Katie and Gilks. All he'd needed was a final bit of reassurance. He remembered how painful Philadelphia had been. He hoped Cleveland would be better.

While the train carried Joe and Katie across Tennessee and Kentucky on the way to Ohio, a feature article about his career appeared in several papers around the country. It was an interesting article because it set a pattern for most of the features written about him from then on. It was a blend of fact and fancy, all presented under a laudatory headline which proclaimed Joe the "Rival of Cobb" and a wonder. The facts detailed Joe's unmatched minor-league record, and the writer flatly called Joe one of the finest batters the game had ever seen. Then he retold several of the growing store of barefoot yokel yarns and finally concentrated on Joe's illiteracy. "Jackson is not an apt student of anything," he declared, "but his inaptitude in other matters has developed an apparent abnormal baseball acumen and he is one of the coolest players in the business, knowing always what to do and when."

The abnormality, of course, was not in Joe. It was in the manner of judgment applied to him by some of the writers. Other players had their private lives judged by their performance on the diamond; but Joe's performance was judged against the image of him that these writers had created. It was a winless situation, for if he succeeded these writers could explain away his success by labeling it an abnormal achievement, an accident, a lucky fluke. If he faltered they could declare he fell because he was stupid. Since they viewed the game and its players through their own preconceptions, these writers never saw Joe clearly. But he was too talented and exciting to ignore, too good a source of copy to pass up. They couldn't let him alone, but they didn't know what to do with him. Joe must have wondered what Cleveland would do to him as the train rattled across Ohio and headed for the shores of Lake Erie.

Cleveland, Ohio, was flushed with civic pride in the early fall of 1910. The newly released national census figures revealed that the city had grown by fifty percent since 1900 and could now boast a population of 560,000. It had moved up a notch or two in the ranking of American cities by size. The news stories of the day were about robberies, graft, murders, corruption, and labor strikes. But these were seen as perfectable flaws in a system that could only improve with time. A headline in the *Cleveland Plain Dealer* reflected the pride and optimism of the moment: "CLEVELAND — METROPOLIS OF THE MIDDLE WEST — CELEBRATES AS RIVAL CITIES FALL BEHIND."

Most of the growth occurred during the four terms of Mayor Tom Johnson, inventor, businessman, and disciple of Henry George's economics. Johnson's eight years in office were marked by his attempt to create a system of public ownership of all public utilities. The vested interests defeated public ownership, but Johnson gained a temporary victory by maintaining the three-cent trolley fare. This was an important issue in a city whose underpaid laborers relied on public transportation to get to their jobs, and for this and other reasons Johnson was one of the most popular mayors Cleveland ever had. The public love affair he carried on with the Cleveland baseball team did not hurt his popularity.

Cleveland first fielded a team in the National League in 1879. Over the next two decades, except for a few years in the late 1880s, Cleveland was a major-league city. The star player of the Cleveland Nationals over their last decade was Hall of Fame pitcher Cy Young, who won nine games in his rookie season of 1890. Over the next eight years he won 232 more, winning as many as thirty-four, thirty-five, or thirty-six games in single seasons. Outfielder Jesse Burkett, another eventual Hall of Famer, was on that team too. For a few seasons the club was joined by the colorful and popular outfielder Louis Sockalexis, a Penobscot Indian who had one of the strongest throwing arms ever seen. Despite these players, the team never won a pennant and, more importantly, it did not draw large crowds.

In 1898 the Cleveland Nationals won over eighty games and finished a respectable fifth in the twelve-team National League, but their attendance was very poor. Eighteen ninety-eight was a poor year for all professional baseball clubs. The Spanish-American War was the center of public interest, and the country was also suffering from an industrial depression. While club owners everywhere moaned about their losses, the owners of the Cleveland team took action.

Frank and Stanley Robison were "Streetcar Tycoons" in the Cleveland area. When they bought the Cleveland team they were intent on making a profit (civic pride was not one of their main interests). Unlike other owners, they said so publicly. When attendance fell off, their profits suffered, as did their vanity. They took the low attendance personally, as if the Cleveland fans were trying to insult them. Out of their peevishness, they criticized the fans and said they did not deserve to watch a baseball team. The fans replied that the Robisons did not deserve to own one.

For spite and for what they thought was good business, the Robisons did not sell the Cleveland team. Instead, when the National League franchise in St. Louis was forced into bankruptcy by lawsuits resulting from a fire that destroyed the club's wooden grandstand during a game, they bought that team too. Now they owned two teams in the National League, an uncommon but not unknown practice, which was called syndicalism.

The next season, 1899, the Robisons concentrated the best players from both teams in St. Louis. They thought St. Louis was the better baseball market and they were still angry at the Cleveland fans. Those who took the trip south to play in and for St. Louis included Cy Young, Jesse Burkett, five other first-string players, and two more starting pitchers. The players who remained in Cleveland and the cast-offs who joined them compiled the worst season record of any major-league club in history — 20 wins and 134 losses.

Soon after the season began, the Cleveland team acquired two new nicknames: the "Misfits" and the "Leftovers." The fans made fun of the team, but it wasn't too bad for the players because hecklers were scarce. Attendance averaged less than two hundred per game. It was so low that visiting clubs lost money in Cleveland; their travel expenses were far greater than their share of the puny gate receipts. When the other National League owners complained bitterly enough, the Robisons fired the Cleveland manager and changed the schedule. For the rest of the season the Cleveland team played all its games on the road. The fans and writers responded by immediately renaming the team the "Exiles" or the "Wanderers," and they laughed at the Robisons, whose St. Louis team finished fifth and didn't make any money either.

The fans and writers may have laughed, but they were bitter. The Robisons had insulted Cleveland by their outrageous behavior, had damaged the city's pride and its public image. All of Cleveland was offended by this shabby treatment. The Robisons' message, gleefully reported in newspapers all over the country, was clear. Cleveland was not a major-league city.

After that season the National League owners met and decided to drop the four weakest clubs from the league. Losses had to be trimmed and the public had rejected the practice of syndicalism. Cleveland, the weakest franchise in the league after the fiasco of 1899, was the first to go. Now it was official. The city of Cleveland was second rate. But not for long.

In 1900 the old Western Association reorganized itself under the leadership of its ambitious young president, Ban Johnson. It changed its name to the American League and challenged the National League's twenty-five-year-old self-proclaimed status as the one and only major league. By 1901 the American League was on its way. One of its charter franchises was placed in Cleveland.

When the new Cleveland club played the first American League season in 1901, Tom Johnson (no relation to Ban) was beginning his first term as mayor. He had progressive plans for the city, which included the success of its new team. He did all he could to help, for the success of the team was psychologically important to the city. An early financial success was almost guaranteed because the fans were out to erase the humiliation of 1898 and demonstrate that Cleveland was indeed a major-league city.

In his political role, Johnson had been critical of the Robison brothers' lack of civic concern. Later, in his struggle to take the ownership of public transportation out of private hands, he tangled with them directly. It is impossible to say if Johnson hated them more for their economics or for their shabby treatment of Cleveland baseball fans. As a fan himself, Johnson never forgave them for the wound they had inflicted on the city's baseball tradition.

Johnson was one of those lucky politicians who could gain high public visibility, receive favorable press coverage, and win the goodwill of the voters by doing one of the things he loved best — going to ball games. He was a true fan, and starting in that first season he developed friendships with several of the Cleveland players.

Ten years later, in the springtime when the Cleveland club was training in the South, the entire city performed a public deathwatch for its ex-mayor. Tom Johnson lay on his death-bed in a coma, attended by family and aides. Suddenly he roused out of his coma and asked for a secretary — he wanted to dictate a letter. His attendants assumed he was delirious and humored him with pretense. He dictated a let-ter to his good friend Larry Lajoie and fell back into his coma. The deathwatch continued. Several hours later he sat up again and asked for the letter so he could sign it. An aide hastily wrote the letter as best it could be recalled; Johnson signed it and sank back into his coma.

After he had signed the letter, Johnson regained con-sciousness one more time. "I hope the boys win the pennant this year," he said, and then he died.

Since their first long look at him during spring training in New Orleans, the Cleveland writers had kept an eye on Joe and from time to time the Cleveland fans read reports of Joe's progress in the Southern League. Then, when the deal which would bring Joe north was publicly announced, the papers began to publish daily accounts of his exploits, so Cleveland was ready for Joe when he got off the train in the middle of September and reported to the club.

He got into town on a Thursday evening, they gave him a uniform, and on Friday he played center field against the Washington Nationals and batted third. The uniform was white with a blue *C* on the left side of the blouse. The pants were baggy, reaching only to his knees, and were drawn in at his waist by a thick black leather belt. The knee-length woolen socks were blue, as was the small cap, which had a small *c* and a narrow peak. It looked as if it would never stay on his head. His fielder's glove was not much bigger than his hand.

"SOUTHERN STAR IS TO PLAY TODAY," declared the morning headline. The fans were primed for Joe and a large crowd turned out to see him. The early arrivals cheered when he stepped in for batting practice, then sat in near silence as Black Betsy's ringing notes sounded through the stadium and blue darters flew to all parts of the field. Katie, alone in a seat in the last row of the grandstand behind home plate, had been anxious, but after the game she said Black Betsy's song had calmed her nerves.

There was a man on first and one out when Joe stepped to the plate in the first inning. He was greeted with a mighty cheer. A slight smile was his only response. He set himself in the batter's box in his cool, relaxed way, Black Betsy resting on his left shoulder. He seemed perfectly at ease. On the first pitch thrown to him he unleashed Betsy and sent a screaming blue darter toward right field. It was the kind Tommie Stouch said left a trail of blue flame behind. But the second baseman got in the way. "After being turned around and almost knocked off his feet by the drive," he picked it up and threw to second base to force the runner. His glove had been torn right off his hand. Joe felt good. He knew he was in the big leagues to stay. He'd announced to the baseball world that when he didn't hit the ball by the fielders or past them, he could turn them around or knock them down. The crowd gasped at the impact of the blue darter. A moment later they were on their feet again as Joe put on a gliding burst of speed and stole second base.

Joe got one single in four times at bat that afternoon and hit the ball so hard that the fans believed everything they had ever heard about him. And once again, though he was billed as the "Champion Batter of Dixie," he stood them on their heads with his fielding. The first man up in the seventh inning caught one just right on the end of his bat and sent it like a rifle shot toward right center. Joe raced over and made a tumbling shoestring catch. The fans got what they had come for. When they poured out of the stadium at the end of the game, all they talked about was their new center fielder.

The next day in its long account of Joe's first game with the Naps, the *Cleveland Plain Dealer* made an observation about Joe's character. It was unusual because it was not the standard practice to comment on a player's character at all, particularly after seeing him play in only one game: "Jackson showed that he was not a dirty ball player," declared the paper, "when he refrained from sliding into second base on an attempted steal. Had he done so he would have spiked [shortstop] McBride, who overran the bag."

Perhaps the writer commented on Joe's sportsmanlike behavior because it was so different from Ty Cobb's, with whom Joe was still being compared. Cobb too was a Southerner and a great left-handed hitter, but the resemblance ended there. In character and background the two men were opposites. Joe was easygoing and Cobb was a fiery competitor. Known for his basestealing, Cobb spiked more infielders than any player of his day, perhaps of all time. To a game that was never known for brutality, Cobb brought a steely kind of violence that was unique. Years later, toward the end of his life, Cobb was asked what had driven him. "I did it for my father, who was an exalted man," he answered. "They killed him when he was still young. But I knew he was watching me and I never let him down."

Ty's father, Herschel, had been both a Georgia state senator and a school superintendent. He disapproved of his son's desire to become a professional baseball player; he wanted him to attend West Point. When Ty left to join a minor-league team, Herschel Cobb told him not to come back unless he was a success.

While Ty was away playing baseball Herschel Cobb developed the suspicion that his wife was unfaithful. One night after leaving the house he sneaked back and peered into her bedroom window. His wife, who later explained she thought it was a burglar, took up her shotgun and blew her husband's head off. Three weeks later, not yet nineteen years old, Ty Cobb joined the Detroit Tigers and began his career as the most aggressive man ever to play the game.

While Joe and his new fans in Cleveland were being introduced to each other, his old fans were kept informed. In New Orleans the *Times Picayune* ran a front-page story under the headline "JOE JACKSON'S DEBUT AT CLEVELAND SETS NAP SUPPORTERS FAIRLY WILD."

The next day the *Greenville News* featured his second game for the Naps. Half-inch type announced: "JACKSON DRIVES BALL TO THE TALL AND UNCUT — Longest Hit Ever Recorded in Cleveland — Greenville Boy Making Good in Rush."

In its eagerness to publicize and share in Joe's success, the *News* exaggerated. There is, of course, no firm standard by which to evaluate the various claims put forth for the longest hits in the different ball parks, but it seems that Joe's drive was only the longest hit at League Park that season. The ball was hit so far into the deep outer reaches of center field that the center fielder didn't bother to make a throw. The fans gave Joe a long ovation after he returned to the players' bench. "He cemented his place in the estimation of the fans," one writer observed, and a day later another flatly said Joe was the "favorite of the bleacherites." Calling Joe the favorite may have been an overstatement because Larry Lajoie was still on the team.

Larry Lajoie was thirty-five years old in 1910 and in his fifteenth major-league season. On the field he carried two reputations: the first as one of the hardest and best hitters in baseball, and the second as the most graceful of all infielders.

He was also one of the most respected and best-liked players in the major leagues. In Cleveland he was an all-time favorite, though he got there by a fluke.

Lajoie began his career in 1896 with Philadelphia in the National League. In 1901, along with several of his teammates, he jumped to Connie Mack's new Philadelphia Americans. It was a matter of money. Mack offered him $4,000 a season, almost twice the National League's salary limit of $2,400. In that first American League season Lajoie batted .426, still the record batting average for the major leagues in this century.

Lajoie and Mack, fellow New Englanders, looked forward to a long association, but the Philadelphia Nationals got in the way. They wanted their players back, particularly Lajoie, so they went to court and they won. The Pennsylvania Supreme Court enjoined Lajoie from playing with the Athletics. In an emergency meeting called by Ban Johnson, founder and president of the American League, the problem was solved by sending Lajoie to play for Cleveland, where he could avoid Pennsylvania's jurisdiction and still play in the American League. In his first few years with Cleveland Lajoie was left behind when the team traveled into Pennsylvania to play the Athletics.

His career in Cleveland was a great success. He was the best player on the team and also managed it for five years. It was during his managerial years that the team's nickname was changed to the Naps, after his Christian name Napoleon. He won many friends in Cleveland, including Mayor Tom Johnson. He also won three consecutive American League batting titles, but the last had been in 1904 and he was tapering off.

Going into the 1910 season, Lajoie was coming off the three worst seasons of his career, having posted successive batting averages of .299, .289, and .324. His career batting average slid to .345 and his fans feared that Larry's best days were behind him.

In 1910 the Chalmers Motor Company inaugurated the Chalmers Award by offering one of their automobiles to the batting champion of each of the two major leagues. Philadelphia outfielder Sherwood Magee laid off green grapes and ham and won the Chalmers in the National League by hitting .331.

The pre-season favorites in the American League were Lajoie and Cobb. Though Lajoie got off to a strong start, most observers felt he wouldn't be able to keep up with the younger Cobb. But as the season progressed and he kept pace, fans all over the country began to root for Larry and against Ty Cobb. It might be Larry's only chance at a Chalmers and the fans wanted him to win it.

Only a few points separated the two when Cleveland arrived in Detroit in early September for a series of games. Lajoie, who had fans everywhere, was greeted with a warm ovation when he stepped to the plate for the first time. The Detroit fans cheered for Cobb too, but they didn't know what to make of him. He was the most exciting player on a team that had won three straight pennants. But in 1910, as the team went bad, Cobb publicly blamed his teammates. One of them, Sam Crawford, the barrel-chested heavy hitter of the Detroit outfield, made a public response. Crawford usually spoke only with his bat, but he could not tolerate Cobb's attack silently. Cobb was the problem, Crawford said. Among other things, he was pampered by the club, which caused hard feelings among the other players. If he missed practice, for example, he received no fine. It demoralized the other players, who were expected to follow the club's rules. "I vouch," said Crawford, "that if I did the same things I would be reprimanded right."

With two games left on the American League schedule,

the outcome of the batting duel remained uncertain; the margin between the men was small and the figures were unofficial. But most of the unofficial figures placed Cobb ahead, and many observers felt Lajoie could not catch up. Cobb also must have thought his lead was insurmountable, particularly if his own average did not drop, because he withdrew himself from the lineup for the last two games of the season.

The *Plain Dealer* ran a photomontage of Cobb, in his batting stance, standing on a cake of ice. "Tyrus Cobb, the leading batsman of the American League," the caption ran, "suffering from that peculiar disease, 'congealed condition of the pedal extremities,' known to card players as 'cold feet.' Cobb was similarly stricken a few weeks ago. His present attack is expected to pass away by Monday [when the season would be over]. In some sections of the country it is known as chrome streakitis."

Lajoie went into the last two games, a double-header in St. Louis, needing eight or nine hits to have a chance at the batting title and the Chalmers. Ten thousand fans came out to cheer for him and some members of the St. Louis club, out of hatred of Cobb and regard for Lajoie, tried to make sure he got the hits he needed. Under orders from his manager, the St. Louis third baseman played very deep every time Lajoie came to bat, as if inviting him to bunt. Lajoie was not a speedster, yet by the end of the day he had eight hits, one of them a clean single to the outfield and seven of them bunt singles to the third baseman.

On the strength of the eight hits, most newspapers declared Lajoie the winner of the Chalmers. He immediately received a telegram of congratulations from eight of Cobb's Detroit teammates (their names were not revealed) and one letter from a fan in Morgantown, West Virginia, who enclosed eighteen cents' worth of postage stamps for Larry's first gallon of gas.

The effort to help Lajoie had been so blatant that the league was forced to investigate. Everyone seemed to agree that the hits were tainted, but the St. Louis third baseman was exonerated on the grounds that he had only followed the manager's orders. The manager and another club official who had offered the official scorer a new suit to make sure the bunts were scored as hits were also exonerated. But they were both fired anyway.

While the controversy over the tainted hits held the sports pages, Cobb was not completely forgotten. Baseball writer Hugh Fullerton, once described as a worshipper of Cobb, frequently served as official scorer at American League games. Earlier in the season he'd scored a disputed play as an error for an infielder and not a hit for Cobb. Now he submitted a report to league headquarters, changing that error to a hit. When asked to explain his actions, Fullerton was reported to have said, "Fair is fair."

When the official figures were finally released, Cobb's average was .385 and Lajoie's .384. The Chalmers Motor Company, making the best of the situation, gave an automobile to each of them, thus pleasing everyone but the rulers of the major leagues, who promptly prohibited any such prizes in the future. They feared that further expressions of favoritism toward players would undermine the game's image of integrity.

The Auto Chasers, as Cobb and Lajoie were called that year, drew much news coverage toward the end of the season, but writers in all major-league cities noted Joe's return and wondered if he was up to stay. He convinced them quickly. He played in twenty games for Cleveland. In seventy-five trips to the plate he got twenty-nine hits, eight of them for extra bases. His batting average hovered around the .400 mark, but by the end of the season it settled at .387. It was the highest average in both the American and the National leagues, though he had not been at bat nearly enough times to qualify for the batting championship. But he maintained his personal streak of leading each new league the year he entered it.

Joe played with an enthusiasm that had been missing in his previous American League games. He demonstrated this in a game against the first-place Athletics. He didn't get any hits, but he prevented defeat in what became an eleven-inning scoreless tie. In the fifth inning the Athletics loaded the bases with two men out. Eddie Collins tried to slice a sinking line drive between the fielders, but Joe simply outraced the ball, made a diving catch, and retired the side.

In the top of the tenth, with a man on third and one out, Collins came to bat again. This time he sent a drive to deep center. As Joe glided back to catch it, the Naps fans groaned. The ball was hit so deep that the runner on third was sure to score. As Joe caught the ball the baserunner tagged up and began his dash for the plate. He ran hard, for though the ball was hit very deep he had seen Joe throw before.

Out in deep center Joe caught the ball, braced his feet, and in one fluid motion brought back his right arm and whipped his throw to home plate. Time seemed almost to stop as the ball flew in a straight line across the field and into the catcher's mitt. The runner was out by ten feet and Joe had his double play. The crowd roared its amazement.

Even the Athletics were impressed. "Jackson doesn't look like the same player he was with us," one of his former Athletic teammates remarked. "He has improved one thousand percent." Joe's former teammate was correct, but most of the improvement was emotional. In Cleveland Joe was happy and he wanted to play.

8

JOE'S LYRICAL PERFORMANCE in the final twenty games of the 1910 season was more than enough to keep his name in the news. Most of the writers and fans thought he was the best player to come along since Cobb, and they spent the winter fueling the Hot Stove League with speculations on how Joe would do when he went up against Cobb over a full season. But the praise that sounded for Joe was not unanimous. Some writers said that his .387 average was a fluke, that the pitchers would soon discover his weakness and make him look foolish.

When their minority opinions about Joe did not gain wide favor, his critics introduced a new argument: Joe would fail, they said, because he was a coward. This was an unusual kind of attack, particularly on a rookie. To support their new argument, they claimed that people who'd watched Joe in the South swore he lacked nerve. They said they were reporting the opinions of the fans in Brandon, Greenville, Savannah, or New Orleans, all of whom idolized Joe and had always seen him lead his league in hitting.

The origin of the stories about Joe's lack of courage lay in his ambivalent escapades with Connie Mack and in the stories spread by his former Athletics teammates. Some of the writers never forgot Joe's game of hide and seek with Mack. Joe's cautious attitude, coupled with his unequaled natural talents, puzzled some of the writers at first, then caused them to respond aggressively, as if they viewed Joe's indecisiveness as an intentional insult to baseball and to them. These writers were receptive to stories about his flaws.

Most of the fans and some of the writers defended Joe, or at least adopted a wait-and-see attitude. After all, he had yet to play his first full season. But the players around the league were quick to believe that Joe was yellow, for it was to their advantage. Any weakness or foible that could be discovered or invented about an opponent was used against him. Taunts and insults were a constant part of the game and some men were more renowned as bench jockeys than as players. Verbal attacks were an accepted strategy, and if a player was bothered by them the word was sure to spread through the league. Some players, out of their own sensitivity or because of the viciousness of the attacks, were actually hounded from the game.

Back in 1908, after his debut game with the Athletics, the writers had compared Joe to George Treadway, one of the big-league stars of the 1890s. They recalled Treadway's great skill as an outfielder, but they did not mention that Treadway had been driven out of baseball by opposing players and fans who bombarded him with taunts and slurs about his alleged or real Negro blood. Everywhere he played they screamed "Nigger" at him until he couldn't stand it any longer and he quit.

When it came to throwing they had compared Joe to another brilliant player of the 1890s, Lou Sockalexis, one of Joe's predecessors in the Cleveland outfield. Sockalexis, whom many felt had the strongest throwing arm ever seen in the game, was a Penobscot Indian from Maine. He was an educated and gentle man, but everywhere he played he was greeted with derisive Indian war cries and hooted at as "Chief." The writers always remembered his powerful arm, but they forgot to recall that the unending racial taunts had so pained and unnerved him that he had begun to drink. When alcohol had ended his career before he had played three seasons, a few writers casually accepted his downfall as further proof of the old adage that Indians and firewater don't mix, and years later, when the Cleveland club was in search of a new name, the war cries that had greeted "Chief Sockalexis" were recalled and the club was named the Indians.

With the help of a few writers the word spread rapidly through the ranks of the American League: Joe Jackson was a coward and he could be had. By the time the 1911 season started the other seven clubs in the league were primed to go after Joe and ride him as hard as they could. They knew they couldn't take away his natural talent, but they thought they could destroy his confidence and perhaps even drive him back to South Carolina.

After his triumphant 1910 season — the highest batting average in each of the two leagues he played in — Joe spent a satisfying winter at home in Brandon. His neighbors in the mill village welcomed him back, a bigger hero than he had been before. They shared a communal pride in his great success, for now every baseball fan in the country agreed with their assessment that Joe Jackson was, indeed, a wonder.

He was the center of endless fanning sessions with his neighbors and with members of the Greenville sporting crowd who came out to see him. When they told him with alarm and anger that some of the writers were saying he was a coward, Joe shrugged it off and quietly confided that he felt he could beat Cobb and Lajoie for the next batting title.

Before the Naps opened their spring training camp in Alexandria, Louisiana, Joe took the train to New Orleans and got an early start by training with the Pelicans. The city received him well; the writers named him the most popular ballplayer in the city's history, and on a rainy, muddy day, over twenty-five hundred fans came out to see him play in an exhibition game against the Chicago Cubs. Joe got three hits in the game. When it was over he reported to the Cleveland training camp.

The Cleveland writers who covered spring training filed a story about Joe almost every day. The very first one, which announced his arrival in camp, called him the "Beau Brummel of the Squad" and featured a photograph of Joe standing on the wooden veranda of the Bentley Hotel in Alexandria. He wore a fashionable double-breasted gray suit and a pork-pie-style felt hat. "Nap's Beau Brummel Jackson, barefooted when he started, is now a fashion plate," the caption read.

Joe was more relaxed and feeling loose enough to be himself. He joined the general conversations with his teammates and clowned with some of the other young players. Many of the Naps had formed opinions of Joe based on the Shoeless Joe yokel stories and they were surprised to find an easygoing fellow who could hold his own in the players' exchange of banter and tell a good tale in his pleasing South Carolina drawl. While Joe was enjoying spring training another prediction was made of his inevitable downfall.

During an exhibition game a group of writers was sitting in the grandstand discussing the players of the day. Joe's name came up frequently and the writers speculated on his future. Several of them seemed certain he would be a great major-league star and they told each other of the marvelous hits, catches, and throws they had already seen him make. They sang praises for Joe until Hugh Fullerton spoke.

Fullerton, the same man who had changed an error to a base hit for Ty Cobb the year before, was one of the best-known baseball writers of his time. He spoke with great authority and the younger writers listened with respect. One of them, Joe Williams, listened with extra care, for Joe Jackson was his own idol. He never forgot Fullerton's words about Joe. "A man who can't read or write," Fullerton insisted, "simply can't expect to meet the requirements of big league baseball as it is played today." As Williams recalled it, "There was a sickening, shattering finality to his words." Nine years later Fullerton had the opportunity to help his prophesy come true.

Before the 1911 season even began, Joe's teammates warned him of what was coming, then sort of held their breaths to see how he would stand the gaff. It began on opening day and never let up. The cruder bench jockeys simply cursed at Joe whenever they had the chance, and the subtler ones said such things as, "I understand you have a keeper, Joe, so no one will kidnap you," or "Honestly, Joe, what made you quit Connie by the light of the moon?"

By the time the season was two or three weeks old, a story out of Chicago flatly stated, "Joe Jackson is having the hardest time of any young player to break into the American

League for years. The sharp tongued players on every team are after Joe. They are urged to get Joe's nerve by the managers and club owners. . . . Joe was kidded in St. Louis, abused in Detroit, and insulted in Chicago, but they didn't get his nerve." The players who rode Joe, and the managers and owners who had given the orders, had misunderstood their man. They took Joe's soft-spoken manner and his usually gentle way as signs of weakness.

Nixey Callahan, a veteran outfielder in his eleventh year, was one of the more accomplished bench jockeys on the White Sox. He was described as a witty Irishman whose aim was not to insult, but simply to exasperate. After Callahan gave Joe his treatment, Joe laughed at him and said, "You're another of those fellas after my nerve. Well, keep on after it. I like to have you fellows chase me. I know I'm a good player when the whole pack of you are after me. I didn't know if I would make good before the season started, but I'm certain now."

In addition to the attacks on Joe's character, some players and writers made the mistake of criticizing his batting style. Wabash George Mullin, the ace of the Detroit pitching staff who won one hundred thirty games in the six seasons from 1905 through 1910, was the most outspoken of these. "A player who pulls away from the plate as Jackson does is not a real hitter. Jackson is bat shy. The pitchers know it now and will throw a ball at his head, then three over the outside corner and he will go to the bench. The pitchers know it now." Mullin predicted that Joe would be lucky to hit .250 in 1911.

In the first three games that Mullin pitched against Cleveland, Joe faced him fourteen times and got six hits, most of them for extra bases, for an average of .428. By the end of the season he raised his average against Mullin to .435.

Long Tom Hughes was a right-handed journeyman

pitcher with the Washington Nationals (Senators) in the days when they were proving the truth of the popular adage: "Washington — first in peace, first in war, and last in the American League." He was another pitcher who learned the truth about Joe's ability the hard way. One afternoon he shared a taxi out to the Cleveland ball park with his team-mate Herman ("Germany") Schaeffer.

"How do you feel, Tom?" asked Germany Schaeffer.

"Great," replied Sir Thomas. "I'm fit, Herman, I'm fit. I'm going to show up this fellow Jackson."

"Going to show up Jackson?" from Schaeffer with a broad grin. "Tom, my boy, you're a wonder. You're a great pitcher, but stay away from that stuff, it'll prove the death of you, don't mix up with it at all."

"Is that so? Well now, look here, Jackson is a left-handed hitter, isn't he?"

"He is."

"Well, I never saw a left-handed hitter in my life touch one that breaks sharp down on the inside. They all look foolish when you give it to them. I've made Ty himself look like a sucker with it. You watch this Jackson person today. I'll lay a little ante of two bits that he won't even scratch a bingle today. The only way to stop a left-hander is to keep feeding him this one breaking low on the inside. When he crowds the plate, bean him one. That'll drive him back and then let him have the low one. He'll break his back going down for it."

"It listens good, it listens good," replied Schaeffer.

When Joe came to bat in the first inning, Hughes's first pitch was a fastball aimed right at his head. Joe ducked out of the way. On the next two pitches, both low-breaking balls on the inside of the plate, Joe swung and missed. Then Hughes came back with the same wicked, low, quick-breaking ball near the shoes, but this time Joe caught it and sent a blue darter into right field. The ball was hit so hard and rebounded off the wall so fast that Joe was held to a single. While standing on first base Joe laughed at Hughes until the whole crowd took it up. Later in the game Joe got another hit.

That evening, on the boat ride across Lake Erie to Detroit, Germany Schaeffer asked Hughes, "What do you think of Jackson now?"

"What do I think of him? There I was beaning him and shooting 'em in that low, and there he was stepping back and clouting to the fence. That guy ain't human, that's all!"

A few days later Hughes was on the mound again. This time Joe hit two of his inside pitches for doubles against the right field wall. In between the two doubles Hughes sent Joe to the ground with another beanball thrown at his head, and finally, out of sheer frustration and rage, he hit Joe in the ribs with one of his fastballs. The sound was so loud that the writers could hear it two tiers up, in the press box. In the first two games he pitched against Joe, Hughes held him to a .375 average.

In a game played in Washington a few weeks later, Hughes was on the mound again. The first pitch he threw to Joe was a fastball aimed right at his head and Joe hit the dirt. Then he came in with his low "sweeping drop." Joe was ready. He unleashed Betsy into her flashing black swing and hit a blue darter toward right field. The right fielder didn't move his feet at all, he just turned his head quickly to watch the ball fly over him in a rising streak. It was still rising when it flew over the right field wall. It was only the second time that anyone had hit a ball over that wall. Tris Speaker had done it the year before, but Joe's drive was harder and traveled farther. It was still rising when it crashed against a brick building across the street. The Washington fans cheered him wildly. Many of them had come out to the weekday game just to get a look at Joe and he gave them something to remember — the longest home run hit in the Washington park.

The next time Joe stepped into the batter's box Hughes took drastic action. He fired a fastball behind Joe, the sure sign of a pitcher's intention to hit the batter. The ball hit Joe squarely on the spine and knocked him flat. After a stunned moment he jumped up and took a step or two toward the pitcher's mound, then changed his mind and trotted down to first base. "You deserve something for that," Joe hollered at him, "but I respect your gray hairs." Joe remained in the game, and even got another hit.

Later that night Doc White, the Cleveland trainer, found Joe wiggling and twisting in a hotel lobby chair. When he asked what was wrong, Joe answered, "Some way that smash in the spine today has all upset me. It feels as if there was something dripping back there." The trainer quickly took Joe to his room and worked over him for two or three hours. Later he said the blow had been a terrific one and that Jackson had been kept awake all night by the pain. Even so, Joe was in the lineup the next day and got one hit in four tries against Walter Johnson.

The writers who believed that Joe's inability to read or write was his most important characteristic never tired of writing about it or asking him about it during interviews. Once, when he was asked directly if he thought his lack of education would hurt his professional career, he was quoted as answering, "I ain't afraid to tell the world that it don't take school stuff to help a fellow play ball."

A few fans, more influenced by what they read than by what they saw, joined in the attacks on Joe. A much repeated anecdote of the day describes Joe pulling into third base with a long triple. A home team fan sitting in the grandstand cupped his hands to his mouth and shouted, "Hey Jackson! Can you spell CAT?" The fans nearby tittered. Joe peered over and hollered back, "Hey mister! Can *you* spell SHIT?" The crowd roared with laughter.

Unlike Shoeless Joe, who was drawn as a thoughtless, carefree, natural wonder, a big kid who was oblivious to pressure and immune to ill will, the real Joe Jackson played his entire rookie season under the most intense kind of pressure. After the season was over Umpire Billy Evans, a frequent contributor to the sports pages, summed it up in the title of one of his articles: "Joe Jackson Made Good against Fearful Odds. Ballplayers Thought He Had a Yellow Streak and Did Everything on Earth to Make It Crop Out, But the South Carolina Kid Stood Fast and Fairly Set the American League Ablaze."

The Victor Mill baseball team, 1907. Joe Jackson is standing, second from left.

The Greenville Spinners of the Carolina Association, 1908. Joe is fifth from the left.

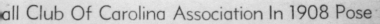

all Club Of Carolina Association In 1908 Pose

Joe in an unidentified uniform. This was probably taken in 1908 or a little later. Note the size of his forearms.

The New Orleans Pelicans of the Southern League, 1910. Joe is seated, second from right.

Joe in his Cleveland uniform, probably in 1912.

Katherine "Katie" Wynn Jackson, circa 1913.

A posed photograph of Joe in his batting stance, 1912.

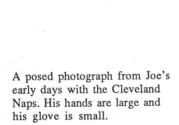

A posed photograph from Joe's early days with the Cleveland Naps. His hands are large and his glove is small.

Posed "action" photo of Joe sliding into second base. The other player is pitcher Jim Baskette. Probably in 1912.

The Cleveland Americans, 1913. Joe is standing, second from left.

Getting some tape from the trainer's bag, probably in 1914, perhaps in spring training.

George Jackson, Joe's father. Date unknown.

The Jackson family in one of Joe's first cars. Katie is driving, Joe is in the front passenger seat, his little sister Gertrude is standing behind Katie, and at the extreme right in the back seat is Joe's mother, Martha. Probably 1915.

Joe with his sister Gertrude on the front porch of the house he bought for his parents in West Greenville, 1915.

The Famous Joe Jackson Deal

Why Jackson Was Traded by Cleveland to Chicago as Explained by Owners Somers, Comiskey, Huston, and Ban Johnson

Joe Jackson and his bandaged right arm. Joe pays little attention to injuries so long as he is not entirely disabled. The above picture was posed specially for the "Baseball Magazine" on the day before Jackson made the longest home run on record at the Polo Grounds

The famous Jackson trade was easily the sensation of 1915. How he left the club where he had made so brilliant a record and joined the White Sox is graphically explained in the following brief statements by the principal actors in that historic deal.

"The Famous Joe Jackson Deal," an article about Joe's sale to the Chicago White Sox, 1915.

Title page of the feature article in the "Joe Jackson Number" of *Baseball Magazine*, March 1916.

Joe Jackson and the Brandon Cotton Mill where he toiled for six years and where he began his baseball career

The Man Who Might Have Been the Greatest Player in the Game

Joe Jackson and His Extraordinary Career—A Humble Beginning—His Sensational Rise—His Strong Points and Weaknesses as a Popular Star

9

From the very first game of the 1911 season, Joe's average never fell below .360. It moved up all year, rising a few points, then dropping one or two, then rising again. By the end of July he neared the limit of his ability. That was when he went on his great thirty-seven-game hitting streak. He hit in all but one of those games, and got a total of sixty-eight hits for an average of .462. Within the streak was a smaller superstreak: twelve games, twenty-six hits, .509 batting average.

By this time most of the writers had forgotten about their coward stories and outdid each other in hyperbolizing Joe's feats. The truth was, the game had never seen a hitter like him. Cobb and most of the other high-average hitters were scientific in their approach. They took advantage of the situation on the field and tried to place their hits. They swung more carefully and usually choked up on the bat handle. Cobb gripped his bat with his hands placed several inches apart. As he began his swing he could move his bottom hand up or his top hand down and adjust to a pitch or a change in the defense.

Joe's approach was different. He always held Black Betsy the same way, the way Charlie Ferguson had shaped her to be held, at the very bottom with the small finger of his right hand curled around the knob. He never choked up on the bat and he rarely adjusted his swing. Only against Walter Johnson, perhaps the fastest of all fastball pitchers, Joe shortened his swing and slapped at the ball. His career average against Johnson was almost .500, which prompted Johnson to remark, "Jackson didn't seem to have a weakness. I was always glad when [he] had been disposed of without having him break up the game."

All the other pitchers looked pretty much the same to Joe. With the taunting insults of the bench jockeys buzzing around him, he sliced the air with the full beauty of his flashing black swing. As one writer viewed him, "Joe stood silent and alone at the plate and banged out the best the pitchers could offer him to the tune of .408. Surely his like as a natural batter has never been seen."

As the season progressed, thousands of fans came out to watch and cheer for Joe all around the league. In Detroit he was cheered more loudly than Cobb. In New York the fans booed when their own pitcher gave Joe a walk — they had come to see him hit. In Washington, they fell silent with dread when he was hit on the spine, cheered him mightily when he got up and trotted to first base, and joined him in laughing at their own pitcher. And in Boston the Red Sox fans greeted him with his favorite encouragement — "Give 'em Black Betsy Joe! Give 'em Black Betsy!"

Other opposing players were sometimes cheered also, but usually after they had made an excellent play. Joe was cheered everywhere and always, out of the fans' expectation that he would do something to amaze and please them. As measured by their response to Joe, it seems as if they held him above hometown pride or the outcome of the game. It often didn't seem to matter if their home team won or not . . . they wanted to see Joe slash his blue darters and rifle his throws to home plate. When Joe was on the diamond, competition narrowed down to Black Betsy against the pitch, or Joe's arm against the speeding runner. Their attitude toward him seemed to rise above mere victory or defeat to focus on the beauty of his game.

One afternoon in New York, when Joe stepped to the plate for the first time, the game was interrupted for a moment as a few fans walked onto the field and presented him with an immense bunch of roses. When the flowers were safely on the Cleveland bench, Joe stepped in and returned the compliment. He drove a flaming blue darter to center field for two bases. The crowd cheered with gratitude, then buzzed with astonishment at the power of the line drive. Joe hit them harder than anyone and his blue darters were still the standard against which all other line drives could be measured. He hit them hard and often, but the fans never ceased to be amazed.

Some writers felt Joe hit the ball too hard for his own good, pointing out that he was robbed of many hits when infielders got in the way of his line drives and were charged with errors by the official scorers, even when their gloves had been literally knocked off their hands, or they had been spun around and even knocked to the ground by the impact of the ball. Joe himself was aware of this phenomenon, and though he rarely complained, he was quoted after one game as remarking, "I got only one hit out of four times at bat according to the scorer. I don't know how he figured it out. I knocked a pitcher down with one and tore the glove off the second-sacker with another. Both of them were called errors." Other infielders took a wiser course: they ducked. One cartoon about Joe's line drives showed an infielder ducking down as a smoke-ringed artillery shell whizzed past him. "No wooden overcoat for me!" the infielder says.

Infielders were not the only ones endangered when Joe unleashed Black Betsy. In one game he hit a screaming line drive over second base that drilled the center fielder right in the stomach and ricocheted so far that Joe got an easy double. The next time up he hit an even harder drive to right field. The right fielder tried to get his glove up, but the ball hit him on the wrist. The trainer came out and applied arnica and iodine, but the right fielder had to retire for the day.

In yet another game he hit a blue darter in the direction of Tris Speaker, regarded by many as the greatest center fielder ever to play the game. Speaker stood his ground as the ball whistled at him, but even his glove was not quick enough and the ball hit him in the neck. Speaker got no error, and Joe was credited with an inside-the-park home run.

A few years later, after watching Joe hit a double and a home run, Ring Lardner wrote, "I walked out with Mr. Jackson's hitting on my mind and I was thinking to myself how dangerous it must be to play the outfield or the infield against him as you are always liable to get murdered." At the end of an adventurous cab ride back to his hotel, Lardner wondered "which was more dangerous — to ride in a St. Louis taxi cab or play the outfield or infield against Mr. Jackson because you are bound to get killed sooner or later either way."

Joe's hits were almost always level line drives. Frequently they reached and rebounded off the outfield walls so quickly that fielders were able to hold him to singles. The levelness of his drives also cost him many home runs. In an article about a game in Philadelphia, a writer commented that Joe's line drives against the fences were hit harder than most home runs that sailed over them: "Yesterday he missed having two home runs because the fence was just about one yard too high." He did get three doubles in the game, though, denting the walls in left center, right center, and right field. Rising again to the challenge of playing in Philadelphia against his former Athletics teammates, most of whom were the same men who had tormented him a few years earlier, Joe hit three singles and six doubles in the three-game series.

In a two-game series in Boston he burned the air with blue darters, getting six hits in nine at-bats, including three doubles and a triple. His performance prompted a sports-page headline: "YOU CAN'T MAKE THE BOSTON PITCHERS THINK FOR A SINGLE MINUTE THAT A PLAYER LIVES WHO CAN HIT THE BALL AS HARD AS GENERAL JOSEPH JACKSON."

Not all of Joe's line drives were stopped by outfield walls. A few had the altitude to go right over them. In April he hit such a mighty home run in Cleveland that the feat was carried by the wire services. In the first inning he swung at the first pitch and hit a rising line drive that flew over the exit gate in right center field, about 340 feet from home plate. The ball carried across Lexington Avenue and landed between two houses on the other side of the street. Several men measured the distance and said the ball traveled approximately 418 feet. It was only the second time anyone had hit a ball out of League Park. Just the year before Sam Crawford had hit one over the wall at the right field foul line, 290 feet away. But Joe's drive, according to those who saw both, traveled at least 90 feet farther than Crawford's. It was the longest home run hit at League Park. The only long hit they could compare it to was the triple Joe had hit the year before, which flew over the center fielder's head and rolled to the center field wall 460 feet away.

Joe performed many amazing feats on the diamonds of the American League in 1911. He got 233 hits and batted .408. It was probably the best performance ever turned in by a rookie. But the thing best remembered about Joe's 1911 season was the way in which he lost the batting title to Ty Cobb.

10

TY COBB'S VICTORY in the 1911 batting race is part of base-ball lore. It is often cited as the perfect example of Cobb's cunning, the clearest demonstration of how he put his keen intelligence to work in the service of his career. The story has appeared in print frequently. The details vary in the telling but the basic tale remains the same. Of all the many versions perhaps the most interesting is the one told by Cobb himself in his autobiography.

My Life in Baseball — The True Record appeared in 1961 with a foreword by General Douglas MacArthur, in which the Old Soldier wrote, "As baseball's greatest competi-tor . . . this great athlete seems to have understood early in his professional career that in the competition of baseball, just as in war, defensive strategy never has produced ultimate victory and, as a consequence, he maintained an offensive posture to the end of his baseball days. . . . His aggressive exploits . . . vitalized the competitive spirit among the youth of the land."

MacArthur's remarks were in line with Cobb's perceptions, for a central chapter of his autobiography is called "The Ultimate Secret: Make Them Beat Themselves or Waging War on the Basepaths." The chapter is devoted to Cobb's playing philosophy ("The Great American Game should be a war of nerves") and ends with Cobb's version of his 1911 showdown with Joe.

In the battle of wits I was lucky enough to join in [Cobb wrote], you sat up nights plotting ways to win . . . and it was on such a night that I won a league batting championship that it seemed I was about to lose. [With more modesty than his biographers, some of whom set the lead at thirty-five points, Cobb puts Joe's lead at only nine points.]

Jackson was a Southerner, like myself, a friendly, simple, and gullible sort of fellow. On the field, he never failed to greet me with a "Hiyuh, Brother Ty." . . . So now we were in Cleveland for a season-closing six-game series, and before the first game I waited in the clubhouse until Jackson had taken his batting practice. I had one of the clubhouse boys tip me off when he was finished, so I couldn't miss him.

Ambling over, Joe gave me a grin and said, "How's it going, Brother Ty? How you been?"

I stared coldly at a point six inches over his head. Joe waited for an answer. The grin slowly faded from his face to be replaced by puzzlement.

"Gosh, Ty, what's the matter with you?"

I turned and walked away. Jackson followed, still trying to learn why I'd ignored him.

"Get away from me!" I snarled.

Every inning afterward I arranged to pass close by him, each time giving him the deep freeze. For a while, Joe kept asking, "What's wrong, Ty?" I never answered him. Finally, he quit speaking and just looked at me with hurt in his eyes.

According to Cobb, Joe's perplexity and loss of concentration quickly led to his complete collapse at the plate. And when Joe stopped hitting, Cobb rallied in the six games until he caught Joe and finally passed him to win the batting title. Cobb ended his account of the episode with a word of advice: "It helps if you help them beat themselves." On another occasion he said of all his competitors, "I had to fight all my life to survive. They were all against me and tried every dirty trick to cut me down. But I beat the bastards and left them in the ditch."

In the public story of Cobb's life, the episode is taken as further proof of his desire and shrewdness. Since batting championships were becoming commonplace to Cobb — the 1911 title was his fourth in a row — the point of the episode rests on his come-from-behind victory and his cunning tactics, as if beating Joe Jackson was not achievement enough for the insatiable Cobb.

Within the traditional version of Joe's life, the episode has a different meaning. This other meaning was explored by Joe Williams, longtime sports columnist for the *New York World Telegram*. Williams, who readily identified Joe as his boyhood idol, wrote several columns about him. In one of these, entitled "Shoeless Joe Was Weak As Cobb Proved," Williams began by repeating some fictions about Joe playing barefoot when Connie Mack discovered him. Then he offered a standard version of the 1911 episode and an interpretation of its meaning. Joe Jackson, he wrote, "revealed a significant weakness of character, for when Ty Cobb began to crowd him and then openly taunt him, Shoeless Joe faded. . . . Here was proof, stunning proof, that he wasn't a competitor, wasn't capable of meeting a crisis head on."

Among the baseball writers, Williams was one of Joe's staunchest defenders. But the proof Williams offered to demonstrate the defective character of his old boyhood idol, the "stunning proof," was all false. The episode, so carefully detailed and elaborated by Cobb and numerous writers, never happened.

Cobb, of course, did win the 1911 American League batting title by hitting .420 and Joe did finish second with .408. Cobb probably did try to upset and confuse Joe, and he may have used the silent treatment or he may have repeatedly cursed him for no apparent reason. But there was no showdown in the last six games of the season and there was no come-from-behind victory by Cobb. There was also no failure of Joe's nerve or his will. The facts are less dramatic. Joe simply had the bad luck of running into Cobb at his peak. Of all his marvelous seasons, 1911 was Cobb's best; he was never below .400 all year and he reached his career seasonal highs in batting average, runs scored, hits, doubles, triples, runs batted in, and slugging average. Cobb got off to such an incredible start — after eighty games he had over one hundred forty hits and an average of .450 — that he publicly announced his goal for the season was three hundred hits.

While Cobb was batting .450 after eighty games, Joe was seventy points behind, at .380. After a hundred games Cobb had dropped to .417 and Joe had climbed to .398. The gap between them fluctuated from day to day, and over time it seemed to be narrowing. Yet after one hundred thirty games Cobb was at .416 and Joe was still at .398. In the final averages, the twelve points that separated them was about as close as Joe ever got. There was no day in the 1911 season on which Joe led Cobb in batting.

The final six-game series during which the showdown supposedly occurred was also an invention. The Tigers came to Cleveland for a three-game series that began on Monday, October 2. The Tuesday game was rained out, so they played a double-header on Wednesday. Before the series began, the last meetings between the two teams for the season, Cobb held a lead over Joe of some sixteen or seventeen points. In the three games Cobb was 3 for 10 and Joe was 3 for 8. Joe had closed the gap a little, but time was running out.

After the games in Cleveland the Tigers headed to St. Louis for their last three games of the year. Cobb, still thirteen or fourteen points ahead of Joe, was not with them. Just as he had done the year before in his race with Larry Lajoie, Cobb withdrew from his team's final games. When pressed to explain his behavior, Cobb said that the St. Louis Browns had such a poor pitching staff that he would have been certain to fatten his average at their expense. What some of the writers had called cold feet the year before was now palmed off by Cobb as a kind of sporting gesture.

The Naps, still in a battle with the White Sox for third place, got on a train for Chicago to play the last two games of their season. Chicago had to win both games to finish third, so they went with their money pitcher, Big Ed Walsh, who loaded up his spitball and went after his twenty-seventh win of the season. Walsh was a pitcher in the iron-man tradition — in 1911 he led the American League in strikeouts, innings pitched, games pitched, and games saved. He was a hard, determined man from the coal fields of Pennsylvania, who once said his main incentive on the pitching mound was the shadow of the mines which hung over him. But his determination and the maddening flutter of his spitball were not enough to stop Joe, who got three hits off Walsh that day, including a clutch blue darter single in the eighth inning, which brought in the tying run. The Naps won the game, 4 to 3. Now that third place was clinched, Joe gave in to the various injuries which he had sustained during the season and he sat out the meaningless last game.

In all likelihood, Cobb himself created the story of his dramatic come-from-behind victory over Joe. This kind of self-promotion was not new to him. When he had been an eighteen-year-old minor leaguer, he had bombarded a young sportswriter named Grantland Rice with anonymous telegrams and letters: "Tyrus Raymond Cobb, the dashing young star from Royston . . . is a terrific hitter and faster than a deer. At the age of eighteen he is undoubtedly a phenom." Rice followed up the lead and "discovered" Cobb, who eventually confessed his trick over forty years later.

It is easy to understand Cobb's motivation for inventing the story, but we are left to wonder why the writers accepted and promoted it, particularly men like Rice, who covered baseball in 1911 and surely knew better.

In *The Tumult and the Shouting,* Rice's autobiography, he introduced Cobb as "perhaps the shrewdest man I ever knew," before he told of Cobb's self-promotional letters. Then he presented a stock version of Cobb's great "last minute victory" over Joe in 1911. He made several errors of fact in his brief account and seems to have gone out of his way to portray Joe as the shoeless yokel. For no intrinsic purpose, since he tells us nothing else about Joe except to remark on the "rhythmed beauty of Jackson's black bat," Rice retold one of the classic Shoeless Joe yarns:

One day, while in the minor leagues, Joe was playing the outfield. As usual, he was playing barefoot. But the diamond was "cluttered with sharp stones and broken glass." After several innings, Joe "came in shaking his head, slammed down his glove and blurted, 'I quit!' When his manager asked if the outfield was too tough on his feet, Joe complained, 'It ain't the feet, it's just that all that busted glass is fuzzin' up the ball so's I can't peg it good.' "

In the early 1940s, by which time Cobb's version of the showdown had become a part of baseball lore, Joe tried to set the record straight. "A story you now hear from time to time that Ty bulldozed me by getting my goat in a conceived plan to ignore me in Cleveland in that important final series is just a lot of hooey. Ty was able to beat me out because he got more hits than I did." Joe told the truth but few people believed him. Cobb's fictional version continues to be told to this day.

11

IN CLEVELAND JOE and Katie took an apartment on Lexington Avenue, not far from the right field wall of League Park. Joe walked over for morning practice and sometimes even came home for lunch. When he did, he walked back to the ball park with Katie, who attended almost every Cleveland home game. It was always her custom to sit alone, even after she became as well known around League Park as Joe, and she always sat in her favorite seat in the last row of the grandstand, directly behind home plate. She cheered when he got a hit and sighed when he didn't, then marked it all down on her scorecard.

"Joe Jackson's Wife a Strict Judge of Husband's Bingles,"

the title of one article read. "She won't even give me a hit unless I poke the ball a mile away from a player," Joe was reported as complaining. "I've almost got to get a home run to get credited with a hit by *my* official scorer. She's a pretty good judge, but we can't always agree on my hits."

When Joe disagreed with the ordinary official scorers, he never let them know it. He never argued about hits and always spoke about them quietly. After overhearing Joe at the end of a game in New York, one writer wrote, "Joe Jackson does not call the things for which he is famous hits, they are 'blows,' and Joe speaks the word very softly. After a defeat he says very little, but after a victory he is very likely to tiptoe up to the official scorers and whisper 'How many blows did little Joey get this evening?' "

Joe couldn't ask Katie how many hits he got in home games because she never kept score beyond the seventh inning. No matter what was happening in the game, when the seventh was over she got up and left. When a curious reporter asked her why she never stayed to the end of a game, she told him she was on her way home to cook dinner. Reminded that most ballplayers ate in restaurants, Katie replied that it was healthier for Joe to eat at home.

But their life in Cleveland was not only baseball and home cooking. They went to the movies and the theater, amusement parks and summer band concerts. When Joe bought a car, they took rides out into the countryside. Despite Katie's rule about home cooking, they also ate in some of the better restaurants. The Lajoies were their closest friends on the team, and the Jacksons' friendly manner made them attractive to many people. Sometimes when they were taking a stroll, strangers would invite them home for a pitcher of iced tea, or insist they come along to the nearest soda fountain or ice-cream parlor.

If Joe was the Beau Brummel of the squad, Katie was the

belle of the wives. She had a sparkling smile, pale blue eyes, and a trim figure. When the *Plain Dealer* ran a photographic spread on the front page of the Sunday rotogravure section that featured "The Wives of the Mighty Naps," Katie's photo dominated the page and the other women were shown in insets the size of postage stamps. Katie's hair was upswept and she was fashionably dressed in a soft silk blouse and a tight-waisted ankle-length skirt. She was smiling.

Katie became such a fixture at League Park, sitting in her usual seat and dressed in one of her lovely ballgame outfits, that the papers commented if she missed a game. When someone else took her seat, it would be noted: "Mrs. Jackson Loses Usual Seat — Joe Makes One Hit in Two Days." She was the unofficial mascot of the Naps and Joe's lucky presence.

They shared the "hunch," as they called it, that Katie's presence in her usual seat was the only way for her luck to work. Joe also had another superstition: he collected hairpins. He would quickly stoop and pick up any hairpin he happened to see on the floor or on the street. If he was hitting well, he would keep the collection and add to it whenever he got the chance. If his hitting fell off, he would toss out that collection and start a new one. His superstition was a mild one compared to those of many other players. Columbia Eddie Collins, for example, always stuck his chewing gum on his cap when he entered the batting box. And when Ty Cobb was hitting well he'd try to repeat the same actions from day to day. He'd eat the same food at the same restaurant, wear the same clothes, say the same things to his fellow players (when he was talking to them) and try to perform every action, however minute, in the identical manner as on the day before.

At first Kate stayed behind in Cleveland when the Naps went on the road. The club knew Joe would miss her, so they assigned a player to be his roommate and companion. One story claimed that the roommate helped Joe to order his meals in hotel restaurants because Joe couldn't read the menu himself. Another described how he read Katie's letters to Joe and then wrote out his replies.

The club was being considerate. It's true they wanted to protect a valuable property, but they also wanted to make things easier and more comfortable for Joe. As Connie Mack had done a few years earlier, they offered to hire a tutor who could teach Joe to read and write. Joe refused again and he never explained why. When he said he didn't have to know how to read or write in order to hit, he was correct, but he was avoiding the issue of his own illiteracy. It is impossible to know why Joe refused these offers and we are left to specu-late. Perhaps the ridicule heaped on him by so many of the writers made the risk too great to take . . . what if he tried to learn and couldn't? And perhaps there was an element of stubborn pride: if illiteracy was good enough for many of the folks back home in Brandon Village, it was good enough for him up in the North.

Joe may have missed Katie when the team was on the road, but he rarely missed a pitch. He continued to burn up the league. And more importantly, from the club owner's point of view, he drew large crowds wherever the Naps played. Home teams featured him in their advertisements: "GENERAL JOE JACKSON WILL LEAD THE NAPLANDERS INTO . . . ," and the fans cheered every move he made. He sud-denly passed Larry Lajoie as the team's biggest drawing card, and the papers observed that Joe was a wonderful attraction in every city.

The fans around the American League swarmed out to see him: adults, like the ones who invited him home, and kids who came to see him if they had the money for a ticket or not. In the older ballgrounds, enclosed by wooden fences, the kids could peer between the slats. In the newer steel and concrete stadiums they had to discover new ways. At League Park in Cleveland the best free view was from under one of the gates. A newsphoto shows a group of kids lying on the ground. Four or five of them are barefoot and one has a big hole in the bottom of his shoe. Most are wearing floppy caps and one holds a tattered satchel in his hand. The caption reads: "Here are some of the Naps' most ardent rooters with whom the fans in the grandstand pavilion and bleachers are not acquainted. They never miss a game. Lying prone on the ground outside the park, they peep under the right field exit gate and join in the ringing cheers."

One of the kids is facing the camera. His floppy cap is pulled down sideways on his head and there is a big tear in his knickers. His mouth is open, he is shouting: "Jackson's up fellers!" Joe hit a single and scored the only run in the game when Lajoie doubled him home.

Kids waited for him outside the gates of every park. He talked with them as they followed him along the sidewalk, and sometimes he'd join them in an empty field or lot and lob a few pitches or fire a show-out to a kid standing four hundred feet away. He laughed with them and showed them how to hold their bats or how to stand in the outfield. "The best outfielders keep their feet close together," he told one group of kids. "The men who are slow starting are the fellows who spread out. They can go to the left or right pretty well, but need time to shift their feet to start forward or backward."

Every year the Cleveland newsboys chose two Naps to umpire their annual Newsie's Picnic Game held out at Euclid Beach Park. Joe was always one of them. "Joe is the newsies' idol," a Cleveland reporter wrote, "but this will probably be forgotten in the heat of the game and for once the great Nap will get in bad with the small boy fans."

One day a couple of railroad switchmen caught a possum

in the Union depot. Since they were on their way to League Park, they took the possum along and presented it to Joe before the game as a good luck mascot. Joe laughed, then lifted the small animal by the tail to see if it was fat enough for possum pie. After several photographs were taken, Joe called Heinie Wexler, the Naps' young mascot, and Heinie took the possum to the bench. When Joe came up in the first inning, he signaled to Heinie and the possum was brought out to home plate. Joe petted its head, then stepped in and hit a single to center. When the next batter came to the plate Joe called time, ran to the Naps' bench and carried the possum to home plate so his teammate could pet it too. The crowd chuckled, and whooped it up when the next man got a hit too.

Another afternoon Heinie Wexler came up with an idea to help Joe against one of his few pitching nemeses, spitballer Russell Ford of the New York Yankees. Heinie figured that Joe had to fight fire with fire or — in this case — spit with spit. Since Joe couldn't hit Ford's spitball and admitted it, he thought he had nothing to lose. His last two times up he let Heinie spit on Black Betsy for good luck. The charm worked both times, and Heinie immediately claimed credit for Joe's two hits. Joe laughingly agreed.

In June 1913 Joe faced Russell Ford in a game played in the Polo Grounds. We don't know if Heinie Wexler spit on Black Betsy before Joe stepped into the batter's box, but a writer who was at the game left an account of what happened next. The first pitch Ford threw "was much below the knee, sweeping not very far above Joe's ankle and it was not over the plate, but pretty close to Joe's foot. He swung the bat like a golf stick, caught the ball fair on the nose and lifted it in a wide, sweeping arch clear over the roof of the [right field] grandstand, halfway up near a floating pennant on one of the flagstaffs for the most sensational home run ever made on that historic field."

It was the first time anyone had hit a ball over the roof of the Polo Grounds, and even after Babe Ruth had played there for several seasons oldtimers still insisted that Ruth never hit one there that was longer than Joe's.

Joe seemed always ready to go along with the playfulness when the opportunity arose. One of the Cleveland papers featured a running gag called the "Bug Club." A player who had "bug ideas" or "acted like a bug" was automatically added to the membership roll, which included the names of Herman ("Germany") Schaeffer, Eddie Plank, Tris Speaker, and a few of the Naps. Joe was listed as the president.

So some of the time, at least, Joe was presented as an entertaining and engaging fellow whose actions spoke for themselves. One feature article which told of Joe's desire to return to a more rural life as soon as he was able, defended his preference as a matter of personal choice, and added, "Jackson is as kind and thoughtful a fellow as you would ever meet, possessing an abundance of good nature and an ever ready lending hand, and well deserves the popularity that is coming his way. Yes, Joe is alright."

Another writer, refuting the rumors that Joe was a roughneck off the field, pointed to his behavior on the diamond. He never argued with the umpires — his most strenuous objection to an umpire's call was "a slight turn of the head." He was as much a gentleman off the diamond as on, this writer claimed. "He is a mild mannered chap, not the least affected by his success, talks in a low tone and has that soft Southern accent that makes you wish he was more talkative. I have often started a conversation with Joe just to hear him talk."

While a few of the writers were trying to present Joe as

they actually saw him, most of them were still offering invented yarns about his hick background and yokel ways. Joe still spoke to the writers, but he grew more guarded. At first he was bewildered by the stories that lied and made fun of him. At first he didn't understand. The writers seemed friendly when they spoke to him, and often they promised to write exactly what he said, but when someone read the article to Joe he could hardly recognize a word.

Joe told a writer from the *Washington Star* that he would give an interview if the writer stuck to baseball and left the yokel stuff alone. The writer promised and got his interview. But in his article he prominently featured a sampling of the yokel yarns anyway. "Jackson is . . . a bit sore and asked this writer to go light on that mill talk," the writer explained. "Silence is pledged."

If many of the writers could not be trusted, the fans could. They always said what was on their minds; deception was not their style. Pete, a well-known Nap fan who always sat in the right field bleachers armed with a cardboard megaphone, carried on a public monologue addressed to Joe. One afternoon, as Joe stepped to the plate with two men on and the Naps trailing by one run, Pete's encouragement blared across League Park. When Joe tripled in the tying and winning runs, Pete boomed out, "Guess I'll go home now, Joe! You won the game!"

The greatest affection for Joe came from his fans, young and old, but his biggest compliments came from his peers. During one game Oscar Stannage, the Detroit catcher, gave up all attempts at stopping Joe. When Joe stepped to the plate with a single and a triple already to his credit, Stannage said, "You've hit everything we've pitched you this season. What do you want this time?" "Give me one high and outside," answered Joe. The next pitch was high and outside and

Joe drove it into left field for a single. He finished with four hits for the game.

While he was warming up one day to pitch against the Naps, Chief Bender was asked by a reporter if he had any special plans for pitching to Joe. Bender, Connie Mack's choice as the brainiest pitcher he ever had, admitted he didn't. "I've watched Jackson in a half-dozen games now. He likes them high or low and over the inside or outside corner of the plate. I've concluded there's no use trying to fool him."

Aside from the bench jockeys, who were still under orders to ride him, the other players around the league accepted him as a member of their fraternity once they got a chance to play against him and meet him. Most of them were as awed by his talents as the fans were, and they particularly appreciated the fact that he was not a braggart. They took to him because he was friendly, if shy, and he didn't seem to take himself too seriously.

12

FROM 1912 TO 1914 Joe's batting averages remained high —
.395, .373, and .338 — but he never managed to beat Cobb
for the title. Some of the writers kept the rivalry alive, pointing to Cobb's titles as proof of Joe's failure. In their readiness
to prove that Joe was flawed — if he couldn't beat Cobb he
wasn't any good — they usually forgot to mention that Joe's
averages were far above everyone else's in the American
League and in the National League as well.

At first Joe accepted the challenge of the rivalry created
by the writers and said his chief goal in baseball was to beat
Cobb for the batting title. But when asked about the rivalry
for the hundredth time, Joe only replied "What a hell of a

league this is. I hit .408, .395 and .373 the last three years and I ain't won nothin' yet. Perhaps if I hit .450 Ty will bat .475. He sure is an aggravatin' cuss." His response was disappointing. It didn't seem to have enough competitive spirit and it sounded as if Joe would not accept the outcome of the rivalry with Cobb as the final measure of his worth.

Several writers compared Joe's personality to Cobb's. One saw their differences very distinctly: "Jackson's ambition is to make a lot of hits, score a lot of runs and steal a lot of bases. When his baseball career is over he wants to go to Greenville and stay there. Cobb wants to steal more bases than any other player, make more hits and score more runs. He wants to be crowned king of the ballplayers. He wants to be rich and own autos and property and he won't stop until he attains his ambition. Cobb seldom stays in one spot a minute. He hurries off the field, gets a drink, slides from one end of the bench to the other, walks around, returns to the bench, fidgets around the bats, then scurries to the field again. Between innings Jackson likes to loll on the bench or in the grass outside the foul line."

Joe's relaxed manner was his natural way of being. He was comfortable and felt free to be himself. He fit in well with the other men on the Naps and he liked Charles Somers, the Cleveland owner. Years later he described him by telling an anecdote: "We couldn't play Sunday ball in Washington then, and when we were playing the Senators over a weekend, we'd make a jump back to Cleveland for a Sunday game, then back to Washington Sunday night. There never was a time we made that jump that Charley Somers didn't come down the aisle of the train and give all the players $20 gold pieces."

Joe didn't always ride with the rest of the Naps. After he established himself as a genuine star player, he got a drawing room. Now Katie usually accompanied him on road trips, and sometimes they brought along their pet parrot. Passengers walking past the drawing room door sometimes would be startled by an odd voice, which squawked, "You're lousy O'Loughlin!" O'Loughlin was an American League umpire.

On some train rides Joe would invite a couple of his teammates and perhaps a writer or two into his compartment to share some of his South Carolina "triple distilled corn" liquor. As they sipped they swapped yarns, and Joe was known as one of the better yarn tellers. Even his teammates liked to hear him talk. After they got to know him, they couldn't understand why so many of the writers kept insisting he was stupid.

Joe played under five managers at Cleveland and they all praised him. He formed a close and lasting friendship with Deacon Jim McGuire, his first Cleveland manager. Even after they'd both left the Cleveland team, they went on some off-season hunting trips in Michigan. Manager Harry Davis, after giving the customary compliments — "Joe is the kind of ballplayer that makes a manager's heart glad; he hits the ball harder than I ever saw anyone hit it" — went on to assess Joe's mental capacities for the game. "Joe has as level a baseball head as I ever saw in the game. He pulls no bones and I find, the better I know him, that he has a head for things outside of baseball. For instance, he turned a little trick for a few hundred dollars just a few days ago. Those who advised him were good businessmen, but he saw little angles to the deal that others had overlooked. As a result it turned out better for him than the others had figured it."

Not only did Joe make few mistakes on the field, he also reacted quickly to new situations. Once, while playing right field against the Yankees, his quick thinking earned him a put-out at first base. During a confused rundown, with three Yankees on the bases, Joe quietly came in to cover first base.

The New York fans gave him a bigger hand for his quick-witted defensive move than for the two doubles and the triple he hit that day.

Before Joe was the Naps' right fielder, line drives against the right field wall were generally good for two bases or even three. After playing a few games, Joe devised a new way to play the rebounds. A reporter credited him with the discovery: "Joe Jackson is an inventive genius. . . . Now line drives against the wall are good only for singles."

Every season Joe had his share of injuries, most of them from beanballs or from running into fences. Like many of the other players, Joe played when he was hurt. Once a pitch broke his finger. He missed a game or two and came back hitting. But sometimes the pure fun of the game was missing. He had to play, even when his heart was not in it.

One morning while he was lying in bed resting his body for the afternoon game, a reporter arrived to interview him. He only asked one question and he asked it with belligerence. He demanded to know why a player of Joe's talents was not hitting better and was not stealing more bases. "You ought to be stealing as many bases as Cobb," the reporter chastised. "Yes," Joe replied, "I suppose so, but you don't know all about it. I have family troubles. My father is very low, isn't expected to live out the week. I may have to leave any time for the south. It looks bad. And about speed. How many bases would you steal with this?" Joe got out of bed and showed the reporter his knee. The whole side of it was skinned and raw. "I got that sliding bases. . . . You would not want to slide very far on that, would you? When a ballplayer isn't going just right, the chances are people don't know what they are talking about. The chances are a player isn't doing any better because he can't. There is a reason for all these things, you know."

With early retirement from the big leagues a real possibility in his own mind, Joe set out to earn as much money as he could. His salary with the Indians never exceeded $6,000 a year, but he claimed to have various bonus agreements with Somers, one of which reportedly called for a $1,000 bonus if he hit over .350. He invested some of his money in business — a poolroom in Greenville, a farm out toward Pickens County — and he speculated on business deals. He also bought a house in West Greenville. His parents, his sister Gertrude and the younger of his brothers lived in the house all year, and he and Katie joined them for most of the off season.

In the beginning Joe was content to spend the off season in Brandon, helping his father in the butcher shop, resting, visiting with his friends. He quickly learned that he could put his fame to work. People wanted to see him in person and they were willing to pay. One fall he organized his own barnstorming team and had a successful tour through the South. With an eye to gate appeal and on keeping the profits in the family, Joe built his exhibition team around his five brothers and two first cousins.

Joe's interest in vaudeville, first aroused in New Orleans, now carried him onto the stage. Vaudeville was always receptive to acts that carried guaranteed publicity, and well-known players had been presenting skits, monologues, and even song-and-dance routines for years. The fans, particularly those who lived away from major-league cities, filled the local vaudeville houses when the players appeared. Christy Mathewson was reported to have earned almost $1,000 a week for a seventeen-week stage engagement, and John McGraw was said to have received $2,500 a week on the Keith Circuit for delivering a monologue on big-league baseball. Joe's first stage appearance was a modest one. He had a small role in *The College Widow*, a vehicle featuring Ty Cobb. Joe had no lines. A year or two later he had his own show.

In the winter of 1915 Joe toured throughout the South with "Joe Jackson's Baseball Girls." One writer described it as a "tabloid musical farce comedy." The principal attraction of the show was Joe's monologue, which the same writer called a "sob rendition of his rise in the baseball world and how he rose from a minor place in the cotton mill to a major place in the baseball world."

Later on, a few writers used his "Baseball Girls" as an example of Joe's foolish investments. They said he'd lost his money, but actually the tour was profitable; one of its highlights was a two-week run in Atlanta before a capacity house every night. The show was so successful that Joe talked about retirement more seriously. He told one reporter that he could make as much or even more money on the stage, but he feared his drawing power would fade as soon as he quit baseball.

By the winter of 1915 his life had grown complicated. He spent much of the off season on the road with his show. When the contract sent out by the Naps finally caught up with him, he was not satisfied with the terms. He wanted more money and he threatened to hold out if he didn't get it.

The schedule of the show conflicted with the start of spring training, and Joe remained with the show. Joe Birmingham, the current Nap manager, ordered him to come to the training camp at once, then fined him for not reporting. "Joe has not even tried to get into condition for playing ball," Birmingham charged.

While all these things were going on, Katie remained at home with Joe's family in Brandon. She worried when Joe did not report to spring training on time; she knew how wearing the long season was on him and she wanted him to be in his best condition. She also worried about the rumors that kept coming back to her: Joe was spending a lot of time with one of the actresses in the show.

We do not know what messages passed between them, nor their feelings in the matter. Katie wanted Joe to come home or, at least, to report to spring training. When he refused and chose to stay with the show on its tour through Georgia, Katie saw a lawyer and announced that she was considering a divorce and would start the proceedings in Cuyahoga County, Ohio, their legal residence. It was her only place to bring the action. Divorces were illegal in South Carolina. But Katie did not stop with the threat of divorce; she went to the sheriff of Greenville and swore out a warrant to have Joe brought back. The newspapers said she charged him with lavishing too many attentions on one of his Baseball Girls.

The sheriff took the train to Atlanta, went to Joe's hotel, and served the warrant. Joe agreed to return and quickly packed his clothes. But on the walk to the station the sheriff said something that angered Joe. They got into an argument, which the sheriff tried to settle by putting Joe in handcuffs. Joe said he wouldn't be handcuffed. When the sheriff grabbed Joe's wrist, Joe hit him.

On the basis of his physique and strength, a few writers had speculated about Joe's potential as a boxer. They talked about his speed and the great reach of his long-muscled arms and concluded he would have been a star in the ring as well. The short, one-sided fight with the sheriff supported their view. Joe knocked him down with one or two punches and walked away. The papers said the sheriff was "badly battered."

After leaving the sheriff, Joe walked through the streets of Atlanta thinking about his problems. When his anger cooled down he walked back to the station, got on the next train and went back to Greenville alone. He reported to the sheriff, posted a bond for the charges against him, and went home to Katie.

They must have sat up all night talking out their problems, for the next morning Joe got back on the train and left for the Naps spring training camp. Katie announced that she had dropped her charges against him. As one reporter put it, "She gave him another chance. It's the old case of too much prosperity," he continued, "from a shoeless butcher's boy who didn't know his ABCs to a popular star feted by fans and fawned upon by chorus girls — it was too much for his mental makeup."

13

THERE WAS AN AIR of expectation and uncertainty in the Cleveland training camp. Like many other major leaguers, some of the Naps had received offers to quit their club and play for the rival "outlaw" organization, the Federal League. Whether they accepted or not, these offers made them think. As a group, their situation as employees was paradoxical. They had glamour and high public esteem, but when it came time to sign a contract, they had no real bargaining power at all. Since the reserve clause in their contracts gave their owners perpetual control of their careers, their only option was to sign at the salary offered by an owner or retire from their profession. Even when they signed they had no real security, for the ten-day clause in their contracts gave an owner the undisputed right to cancel the contract with ten days' notice. No explanations were required and there was no appeal. These conditions had already led many of the players to join the Baseball Players' Fraternity, an early attempt at a kind of players' union. Then the Federal League appeared and seemed to offer an alternative.

When the Federal League first appeared in 1913 it directly challenged the monopoly of major-league baseball held jointly by the entrenched owners in the National and American Leagues. The National League was already forty years old and even the upstart American League, itself a former "outlaw," had over a decade of successful business behind it. As the established power, the major leagues' first response to the Federal League was disdain — if it was ignored it would go away. But the Federal League did not go away. The owners of the Federal franchises mostly were men who had made large personal fortunes. They were accustomed to success in other businesses and they expected to succeed in baseball too. Their tactics were in the tradition of American business — they offered competition and fought for a share of baseball talent and the baseball market — but the newspapers generally viewed this challenge as un-American and hostile. They named this attempt at free enterprise the Federal League War.

The Feds placed teams in some major-league cities and recruited players wherever they could find them. Since the power of the reserve clause was limited to teams in organized baseball, the Feds took advantage of their outlaw status and enticed major leaguers to jump their contracts. The Feds knew they needed big-name players to compete, so they went after as many star players as they could. Their first big catch was Joe Tinker, star shortstop of the Chicago Cubs and a member of the famous Tinker-to-Evers-to-Chance combination. Tinker jumped the Cubs to become playing manager of the Chicago Whales, or ChiFeds as they were also known. Tinker also became the leading recruiter for the Feds and he traveled around the country visiting players at home during the off season.

The Feds offered bonuses, salaries frequently more than double a player's major-league salary, and long-term contracts. But they could not really guarantee that their league would survive. On this important issue all they could do was express their high hopes and refer to the strength of their financial backers, among whom was oil tycoon Harry Sinclair, perhaps now best remembered for his role in the Teapot Dome scandal.

The Feds' uncertain future deterred some players from jumping, and others refused out of loyalty to their team or their league. But by 1915, at the height of the Federal League War, over eighty major leaguers had jumped to the Feds. Some played a season or two, and others jumped back and forth. One winter Walter Johnson jumped, then returned before the season began when the Washington club met his salary demand of $12,500 for the season. When Johnson jumped, many of the writers accused him of being a "mercenary." *Sporting News* lumped all the jumpers together and bitterly condemned them for putting "money before honor."

When it was reported that Harry Sinclair had offered and Ty Cobb had refused $100,000 for four years, most of the press praised Cobb for his loyalty to the American League and his sound business instincts. When Joe turned down an offer, his decision was offered as further proof that he was a yokel.

Joe Tinker and other Federal League officials visited Joe in Greenville. The papers reported they had offered Joe a three-year contract for $65,000. Whatever the offer actually was, it is certain it was larger than Joe's Cleveland salary, which never exceeded $6,000. He was interested but he did not jump. Though his salary was relatively low, he liked Cleveland and he respected his owner, Charles Somers. When his decision to refuse the Federal League offer was made public, *Leslie's Weekly* published an article called "How Jackson Lost the Coin," which quoted an anonymous baseball star: "The Fed's mistake was made in not showing Joe the money in pennies." Another anonymous wag added: "If Jackson really had been shown the money in this form, he would have swum up Niagara Falls to get it."

The Federal League War was complex and it was fought on several fronts. One of them was in the courtroom. After several legal skirmishes in state courts over the legality of the reserve clause, the Feds made their most serious legal challenge. In January 1915 they brought suit against organized baseball in a federal court. Their suit claimed that the sixteen owners of the major-league teams had monopolized the interstate business of baseball. In short, they claimed that all of organized baseball was operating in violation of the federal antitrust laws. They entered their suit in the United States District Court of Northern Illinois, the bench occupied by Judge Kenesaw Mountain Landis. Commenting on the Feds' choice of federal court districts in which to bring their suit, historian Harold Seymour observed, "The Feds doubtless chose Landis' court mindful of his reputation as a trust-buster; they did not know, or chose to ignore, that Landis was also a baseball fan. He soon disabused them."

The judge had been a passionate fan of the Chicago Cubs since 1876, when he was ten years old and the National League began. His special favorites among the Cubs were Joe Tinker and pitcher Three-Fingered Mordecai Brown. During the Federal League War he could only watch help-lessly as some of his lifelong idols jumped to the Feds.

How strange it must have been for Landis when the fabled

Three-Fingered Brown entered his courtroom one morning. Brown was a witness for the Federal League and he offered testimony on the abuses suffered by players in organized baseball. When he told of a minor-league player who had been traded to another team in exchange for a dog, Landis joined in the general laughter. But he did not think the suit was a joke. He believed it endangered the structure of major-league baseball. When the testimony unfolding before him began to give support to the Federal League's case, Landis grew irate and snapped at one of the Fed's lawyers: "Do you realize that a decision in this case may tear down the very foundations of this game so loved by thousands . . . ?" Toward the close of the hearings the judge swept away any doubts there may have been about his position. "Both sides must understand," he announced from the bench, "that any blows at the thing called baseball would be regarded by this court as a blow to a national institution."

Landis took the case under advisement in April 1915. Though he was famous for acting on impulse and whim, in this case he didn't act at all. Eleven months later he had not yet reached a decision, but by then the dispute was over. Economic realities had forced the parties to settle out of court. As part of the settlement, some of the outlaw owners were admitted into organized baseball and allowed to buy major-league franchises (St. Louis Americans, Chicago Nationals): Thus reconstituted, organized baseball continued to operate as it had done before the war started or the suit was brought to court. The legal question about organized baseball's monopolistic practices was left unanswered.

Several commentators attributed Landis's inaction to his fear of harming baseball. He knew, they said, that if he based his decision on the law, he would have had to strike down the contractual pin which held their monopoly together: the reserve clause. Rather than take that action, which would have amounted in his own words to "striking a blow at a national institution," he did nothing and remained silent. Some said it was the greatest thing he ever did for baseball.

The 1915 major-league season began and progressed, but when no decision came from Landis, the air of uncertainty that had clouded spring training hung over the whole season. The competition offered by the Federal League hurt gate receipts everywhere, but the poorer teams suffered most. The Naps, who always lacked consistent pitching during Joe's years with the team, had dropped to the bottom of the American League in 1914, finishing last. Attendance dropped sharply in 1915. In August, when the club's financial position became precarious, Somers sold Joe to Chicago.

The Cleveland fans were shocked and disappointed. Their mood was not improved when the papers published a summary of Joe's career with the Naps. In 673 games he had gotten 937 hits, over 400 of them for extra bases. His cumulative batting average was .374. Asked what he thought of the team's chances now, one fan answered, "Team? What team? They sold *him* to Chicago!"

Joe was sorry to leave Cleveland. Katie and he had learned enough about the city to feel comfortable, and Joe felt the Nap management had always treated him fairly. But he was pleased to be going to a contending team and said he hoped to help the White Sox and owner Charles Comiskey get into the World Series.

When he stepped to the plate for the first time as a White Sox, the Chicago fans tried to make Joe feel right at home. "Give 'em Black Betsy!" they roared. "Come on you, Joe, give 'em Black Betsy!" Joe was sold to the White Sox on August 21. On August 23 he came up in the bottom of the eleventh inning in a 3 to 3 game against New York. There was a man on first base. Joe promptly hit a blue darter against the right field wall and won the game. A group of fans waited outside the clubhouse after the game to give him an added cheer.

He wasn't in Chicago long before he became a favorite of the fans and a hero of their anecdotes. A stranger stopped his automobile at the curb and asked a man, "What's the best drive in Chicago?" "Well, sir," replied the Chicagoan, "the best drive I've seen in many a day was made by Joe Jackson at Comiskey Park today."

Charles Comiskey also valued Joe; he boasted that he owned "the greatest straightaway hitter in baseball," and let it be known that he was paying Joe $10,000 per season. Joe does not seem to have refuted the figure publicly, though it was $4,000 higher than his actual salary. Perhaps he shared the feelings of other players who remained silent when Comiskey gave out grossly exaggerated salary figures: if they were not getting that much money, at least the appearance of it would keep them in the fans' esteem.

Charles Comiskey's biggest boast was that he was the only man who had ever risen from the ranks of the players to become the sole owner of a major-league club. He was proud of his image as a self-made man, though he never denied his father, John, who had been a Chicago alderman, clerk of the Cook County Board, Deputy Internal Revenue Service Collector, and owner of the construction company that rebuilt much of City Hall after the great Chicago Fire. The inconsistency between the father's success and the son's claim of being self-made went unremarked by the press. Early in his career Comiskey realized the value of courting newsmen. He set a lavish table for the writers who covered his club and served them fine food and drink. He presided over a private social club called the Woodland Bards, which gathered at his country place in Wisconsin for hunting, fishing, and epicurean meals. All the writers, many of them Woodland Bards, agreed the "Old Roman" was a good fellow and a generous man.

They called him the "Old Roman." Nobody knows the origin of the nickname, but it came early. It was already well known when he opened his new stadium, Comiskey Park, in 1909 and decorated his private box to resemble the emperor's box at the Roman Colosseum. The writers loved the gesture and applauded Comiskey for whom, they said, such lavish spending was merely "a merry little incident." But such gestures were never made in the direction of his ballplayers. When every other team was giving the players four dollars per day for meal money, Comiskey continued to give only three. He even skimped on the team laundry bill. And though the White Sox were one of the most profitable teams in the major leagues, the club's payroll was among the lowest.

Comiskey's financial dealings with the players caused much resentment. In face-to-face bargaining sessions he used all the advantage the reserve clause gave him, particularly when bargaining with uneducated or poorly educated players from working-class backgrounds. He would not rely on a player's performance or his value to the team when he set a salary figure. The question he always asked was what the player could earn if he left baseball and returned to his former occupation or took up the occupation of his father. What could you earn down in the mines, he asked, or back in the mills? He offered salaries that were hardly greater. The players could take them or leave the game.

He had a different relationship with at least one of his players, second baseman Eddie Collins, the only man on the team who was making more than $10,000. Collins had demanded $15,000 a year and a five-year contract when Comiskey bought him from Connie Mack after the 1914 season. Comiskey agreed. He knew he had to pay Collins enough to prevent him from jumping to the Feds. And he also knew that his standard approach to salary negotiations would not work with Collins, a college graduate who could presumably earn a good living outside baseball.

Joe began to hear the complaints the players made about Comiskey and each other as soon as he joined the club. Unlike Cleveland, where Somers had set a friendly tone and the players were easygoing, the Chicago clubhouse was a mixture of backbiting and angry silence. A couple of players gathered around Collins and catcher Ray Schalk, but most of the men went their separate ways. The resentments and bitterness, though not particularly aimed at him, made Joe uneasy. He spent most of his nonplaying time with Katie.

They took an apartment in Chicago and Katie continued her practice of going to every game. The Chicago writers were as intrigued by her as the Cleveland writers had been. "Mrs. Joe Jackson Is White Sox Mascot" was the title of one article, and "Wife of Star Slugger Travels with the Team" was another. Few wives traveled with their husbands and Katie was the most famous. They called her "The White Sox Girl" and she was known everywhere the team played.

As the team's acknowledged but unofficial cheerleader, Katie had much to cheer about, but Joe was not the magical player he'd been in those first years in Cleveland. The bad feelings on the team bothered him and now and then he'd remark that the fun of the game was fading. Even so, he could still make plays that stood everyone on his head, including the other players. The White Sox were playing a close game in Cleveland one afternoon and Joe was out in the familiar territory of right field. Cleveland had men on first and third with one out. The runner on third was Tris Speaker, the man who had been brought to Cleveland to replace Joe as the idol of the fans. The next batter hit a powerful drive toward right center. Felsch, the Chicago center fielder, started back on the ball, but it looked to be beyond his reach. The runner on first base broke for second. But Speaker, on third, watched Joe streak across right field toward the deepest reaches of League Park, where the center field fence was 460 feet from home plate. Joe reached the ball in deep right center and caught it one-handed in his glove. In midflight he whirled around and fired a strike back in to his first baseman, which got there in time to double-up the base runner and end the inning. After the game Tris Speaker admitted he'd "pulled an ivory play, a boner pure and simple." He should have tried to tag up and score after Joe made his catch, but he was so intent on watching Joe's stunning play that he forgot what to do.

Just as he always seemed to play harder against the Athletics, Joe now approached games against Cleveland with an added incentive. On one of his first trips back to Cleveland, Joe mentioned that he would like to show his old club that it had made a mistake when it sold him. That afternoon he hit a line drive home run over the right field wall, and two doubles against the wall in right center. The fans loved it and cheered for him as they had done before. After listing his feats on the field, one writer said, "He also ate three square meals at Cleveland's most expensive hotel, took in the movies with his wife, yawned and went to bed well satisfied."

Joe had some big games for the White Sox but overall his performance was disappointing. He had arrived from Cleveland with a .330 batting average, but in the forty-six games he played for the White Sox he hit only .265. His average for the entire 1915 season was .308, the lowest he had ever had. His critics were quick to say he was all washed up. *Baseball Magazine* sent a man to Greenville to collect material for the "Joe Jackson Number," the issue of the magazine published in March 1916. They called the feature article about Joe "The Man Who Might Have Been the Greatest Player in the Game."

Joe's first full season with Chicago was 1916. He batted .341, led the league in total bases and triples, and was among the leaders in hits, runs batted in, doubles, and slugging average. Powered by his hitting the team was in the pennant race all season, but finally lost to Boston by two games. During the season Joe was the subject of a long editorial in *Sporting News*, "There Is But One Joe Jackson." The editorial complained that Joe was not receiving the accolades his performance had earned and tried to correct the oversight. After pointing out his positive attitude — "There is today no ballplayer more conscientious or more loyal to his manager and his team and none who works harder" — the writer commented on the style of Joe's performance: "In Jackson the baseball fan sees the clean-up clouter of the old school without the necessity of tricks to get by. . . . When he gets hold of the ball it goes, and there is a thrill in his giant swing that every fan can feel. . . . When it comes to hitting the ball on the nose, he doesn't take his hat off to any player in baseball."

The editorial alluded to Joe's background, but stressed his growth. "Unlettered and unlearned in the ways of the world when he broke into the limelight a few years back, he is today a person in whose company one finds pleasure and profit, a gentleman of manners, at ease in any gathering, his homely wisdom a delight to those who meet him, and his sheer honesty and straightforwardness a relief in these sordid times. . . . Joey has grown into a well-rounded gentleman of parts."

After the close miss of 1916 Comiskey tried to strengthen his club. He bought first baseman Chick Gandil, a tough sure-handed veteran, and he brought up rookie shortstop Swede Risberg. During spring training Comiskey promised his players a substantial bonus if they won the pennant. No figure was mentioned.

The Chicago White Sox won one hundred games in 1917, still the highest total in the team's history. They won the American League pennant by ten games. On the train ride home after the pennant-clinching game, Comiskey made good on his promised bonus. The players could not have had very high hopes. How much could they have expected from a man who was the only owner in the majors who charged his players a laundry fee for dirty uniforms of fifty cents a garment? When some of them refused and played in dirty uniforms, Comiskey had the dirty uniforms taken from their lockers when they were away and docked the laundry fees from their salaries. But as low as their expectations had been, Comiskey disappointed and angered them. In recognition for turning in the best performance in the club's history, he gave his players a case of cheap champagne to share among them. Ring Lardner, who rode the victory train with other baseball writers, said it tasted like "stale horse piss."

Though Joe had the lowest batting average of his career in 1917, .301, his statistics did not blind the baseball world to the fact that he was the man the New York Giants would have to stop if they were to win the World Series. One article opened with the prediction that Joe would be the major threat to the Giant's pitching staff, but it concluded with a long and pointless account of his yokel background. It was an exact repeat, word for word, of a yokel article that had first appeared three and a half years earlier while Joe was still with Cleveland. Though the nickname "Shoeless Joe" had all but disappeared from use — one writer said it was "definitely passé" — some of the writers continued to revive it.

In the six games of the 1917 World Series Joe got seven

hits and batted .304. But beyond the mere numbers, and to the pleasure of the fans, he demonstrated what one writer had in mind when he'd written before the series began, "Joe is a poem at bat." The series opened in Chicago and the White Sox won the first two games. After the second game one paper featured a photograph of Joe holding Black Betsy on his shoulder. The caption read: "Chicago's Hard Hitting Outfielder Whose Great Catches Saved the First Game and Whose Hitting Helped to Win Yesterday's Battle."

The Giants evened the series by winning two games in New York, then the teams returned to Comiskey Park for the remaining games. The White Sox won the fifth game, but their victory was tainted. After building up a 5-to-2 lead, John McGraw had allowed his starting pitcher to remain in the game long enough for the White Sox to tie the score. Since McGraw was known for his usually shrewd handling of pitchers, the New York fans loudly questioned his decision to let the faltering pitcher remain in the game. Gamblers in New York and Chicago circulated rumors that the game had not been honest. McGraw deflected the criticism toward the Giants' second baseman, first by accusing him of letting ground balls go by him intentionally and then by trading him away from the team as soon as the series was over.

The sixth game was also tainted. The White Sox scored all four of their runs on errors to win the game and the series. As one of the leaders of the new World Champions, Joe received the recognition *Sporting News* had called for. After the Chicago victory celebrations, in which Joe was singled out for special praise, he and Katie returned to the South.

Ever since his season with the Savannah Indians in 1909, Joe had thought of moving to Savannah. Then his sister Lula got married and moved there. Finally, in 1916, Joe and Katie bought a house on the Savannah waterfront for ten thousand dollars. His mother and little sister Gertrude came to live with them, but Joe and Katie were there only during the off season.

Joe's off seasons were busy. He owned a new version of his "Baseball Girls," which he sent on tours of the southern vaudeville circuit. He had an investment in a poolroom and he also owned some other property. He had told a Chicago writer, "If all my business interests were not down South, I reckon I'd live up here in the North all the time." But he only said what the writer wanted to hear. He never seriously considered living in the North. As Tommie Stouch had said in the beginning, Joe was a "real southerner," and he especially liked Savannah.

Soon after returning home Joe and Katie were featured in a newspaper advertisement, sitting in an open, four-door motorcar. Joe, wearing a white wide-brimmed fedora, is behind the wheel. Katie, a dark cloche hat on her head and a ruffled white scarf at her throat, sits beside him. The white-walled tires are narrow and the spokes of the wheels are made of wood. The famous White Sox slugger says: "The Oldsmobile Eight for me every time."

Savannah honored Joe's World Series triumph with several celebrations. And the Bijou Theatre, the local house on the Keith Circuit, invited him, as guest of honor, to attend the opening night of a new vaudeville show and the first public showing of "The Retreat of the Germans at the Battle of Arras," the latest newsreel from World War I.

14

By early 1917, when America's entry into World War I seemed inevitable, public concern began to grow about raising an adequate army and changing over to a wartime way of life. The public was warned that luxuries would disappear and necessities might be scarce. Because of its high visibility and symbolic value, baseball was singled out as one of the expendable luxuries. If the nation goes to war, the *New York Times* editorialized, professional baseball should close down for the duration.

No official government policy had been announced, but the owners were worried nevertheless. Business was good — the 1916 season had been one of their best ever — and they had begun to recoup some of the losses suffered during the battle with the Federal League. Business was good and the owners did not want to lose it, so they tried to join the patriotic war effort. Some of them made their players go through the motions of military marching drills as a pre-game attraction ("PLAYERS EXCHANGE BATS FOR RIFLES"). They even offered a prize for the best-drilled team. Ban Johnson, President of the American League, invented "Wake Up America Day." On that day appeals were broadcast over the public-address systems in American League parks, urging spectators to enlist in the military, immediately, before the game began, in special enlistment booths that had been set up for their convenience.

A few players were called up for conscription in 1917, and a few enlisted, but the major-league rosters were not truly affected until the government's *work or fight* order was issued in May 1918. All able-bodied men between the ages of twenty-one and thirty had until July to get jobs in "essential work" or face military conscription. The owners tried to get special consideration for their players, but they could not get them exempted from the *work or fight* order. Now that the message was clear, the players began to leave. By the end of the war, over two hundred of them had entered the military. Many others chose to take jobs in essential work. Joe was one of them.

During spring training, before the *work or fight* order had been issued, Joe talked about enlisting so he could join his three brothers who had already volunteered. But Katie was against it. She did not want him to go and she thought he would be exempt from the draft anyway because he was the sole support of four dependents — his mother, a brother, a sister, and Katie. At first it seemed that Katie was correct, and Joe traveled north with the White Sox and began the season. He started to hit on opening day and was batting over .350 when the Greenville draft board, after some question and hesitation, classified him 1-A. Joe then accepted a position with the Harlan and Hollingsworth Shipbuilding Company, a subsidiary of Bethlehem Steel, located at Wilmington, Delaware. As "essential work," the job qualified Joe for draft exemption. It also made him eligible to play in the Bethlehem Steel Baseball League, one of the strongest leagues outside of organized baseball in the country. Its players included many former major and minor leaguers, some of whom reportedly were paid as much as five hundred dollars a week to play baseball.

Many of the players who entered the military were assigned to special services and spent their time playing exhibition games for the troops. By performing what were essentially entertainment duties, these players happily escaped the horrors of trench warfare. Nothing was said against them. Some of the players who went into essential work also continued to play ball for industrial teams, often playing in exhibition games that raised money for the war effort. Nothing was said against them either, at least not by name. They were criticized as a group and condemned as "slackers."

Many players chose essential work. Joe's teammates on the Harlan ballclub, for example, included two or three of his White Sox mates. But in all the newspaper attacks, only Joe was singled out. The *Chicago Tribune* published an editorial, called "The Case of Joe Jackson," which set the tone for these attacks. With heavy-handed sarcasm the editorial pointed out that Joe was "a man of unusual physical development, and presumably would make an excellent fighting man, but it appears that Mr. Jackson would prefer not to fight." Because he neither enlisted nor allowed himself to be drafted, the editorial concluded, "Good Americans will not be very enthusiastic over seeing him play baseball after the war is over." Though the editorial concedes that Joe is not the only major leaguer in essential work, he is the only one mentioned by name.

In an article entitled "Retreats to a Shipyard," a sportswriter put the case more bluntly. "The fighting blood of the Jacksons is not as red as it used to be in the days of Old Stonewall and Old Hickory, for General Joe of the White Sox has fled to the refuge of a shipyard." The writers never forgot the inside dope about a player, even if they had invented it themselves. They recalled the gossip early in Joe's career that marked him as a coward and felt free to call him a coward again.

The newspapers weren't alone in their attacks on Joe. Charles Comiskey, his owner, blasted him too: "There is no room on my club for players who wish to evade the army draft by entering the employ of shipbuilders." He followed with threats about not taking the "jumpers" back into organized baseball.

Some of these attacks were answered. One or two writers argued that Joe should not have been classified 1-A in the first place. Another, first pointing out the perfect legality of Joe's choice, declared he was not a slacker at all. And several wondered why Joe was picked on and singled out for criticism.

Among Joe's defenders was Alfred von Kolnitz, a utility player with the White Sox who left the team in 1916 to enlist in the army. He was one of the first major leaguers to enlist, perhaps because he felt he had to answer for his obviously Germanic name. He became a major, the highest rank attained by any player, and when the war was over he remained in the army as a career officer.

When the attacks on his former teammate and fellow South Carolinian were at their loudest, von Kolnitz published an answer. First he talked about Joe's climb from the cotton mill to stardom, then he stressed the fact that Joe should have been exempted anyway. "There are thousands of men walking the streets in civilian clothes and with exemptions in their pockets with far less claims than Joe." Von Kolnitz concluded his defense by offering an answer to the question of why Joe had been singled out from all the others. He said the small-mindedness of some writers made them delight in criticizing a famous man, particularly a public man who responded to character attacks by saying nothing.

Von Kolnitz's explanation had some truth to it, but there were other reasons as well. The attacks on Joe were not only supported but often were led by Comiskey. By threatening Joe and the other "jumpers" with expulsion, he was preparing for future contract negotiations. How could a player, with the threat of expulsion hanging over his head, refuse any "reasonable" offer? If Comiskey threatened often and loudly enough, perhaps Joe and the others would feel they were lucky to return to the White Sox at all.

The official record for Joe's 1918 season lists seventeen games with the White Sox and a batting average of .354, but he played more ball than that, although at a lower level. His .393 batting average made him the undisputed star of the Bethlehem Steel League. He carried the Harlan team into the championship series, the last game of which he won with two home runs. When he hit the second one, the fans were so pleased they showered him with coins. The game was interrupted to sweep up the money.

While denunciations flew around him, Joe said little and went along doing the thing he did best. He played in the Harlan games, often when he was hurt, and he played in exhibition games that raised money for the war effort. In one of these games, played in the Polo Grounds, Joe was the main attraction and six thousand dollars was raised for the Red Cross. And sometimes Harlan loaned him out to other teams.

On Sundays he traveled to Reading, Pennsylvania, apparently at his own expense, to play for the Reading Steel Casting team in a series of Red Cross benefit games. For the last scheduled Sunday game he drew a record crowd of fourteen thousand and broke up the game with a home run. Two days later he received a copy of a letter sent by the vice-president of Reading Steel Casting to Harlan and Hollingsworth Shipbuilding. The vice-president thanked Harlan for allowing Joe to play in Reading and explained why they had needed him so badly. Under the pressure of wartime quotas, he wrote, the men in the mills and factories around Reading were working sixty to seventy hours a week. Sunday was their only off day, and since the area offered little in the way of harmless entertainments, most of the men spent their off days and much of their salaries in one of the 250 drinking clubs in and around the city. The result of all this Sunday drinking was a high percentage of absentees from work on Monday mornings. The absences caused slowdowns in production, which led to quotas being missed.

With the objective in mind of finding something that would outdraw the drinking clubs, the steel companies chose baseball. And since he possibly was available, they chose Joe as their guaranteed drawing card. He traveled to Reading almost every Sunday that season. Every time he played he drew a large crowd. The ten or twelve or fourteen thousand men who came to watch him play did not spend their Sundays drinking liquor, or at least they drank less than when they sat in the drinking clubs all day long. Since they drank less, they felt better the next morning and the alarming Monday absentee rate dropped quickly. As it dropped, production rose.

The attraction of Joe's playing had had a real and measurable effect on the war effort, and now the letter came, asking if Joe could come back for one last visit. "We have arranged, at the request of Father Leatherhouse of St. Paul's Cathe-

dral, to present Mr. Jackson with a little token in return for
the service he has provided to the enjoyment of the 10,000
spectators at our Sunday games. In fact, the working men of
our city come for miles to see Mr. Jackson work and they
have decided to make him a little present."

Joe's copy of this letter is still pasted into one of the scrapbooks kept by Katie. It could have been shown as evidence
that he was performing a useful function, that he wasn't the
selfish, unpatriotic coward some of the writers were making
him out to be. But he never revealed the letter and never
answered the attacks which, because of their wide circulation
and his fame, made some people think of Joe as the most
famous slacker of World War I.

15

WHILE JOE WAS AWAY at the Delaware shipyards, all semblance of unity on the White Sox ballclub disappeared. The resentment over low salaries was growing, particularly among those who received the least. The players believed Comiskey was making money and felt they should be paid at least as well as players on other clubs.

The 1917 World Series had capped a very profitable year for Comiskey. His players were the champions of all of baseball, but it would have been difficult to tell from their salaries, which remained among the lowest in the major leagues. For the 1918 season, first baseman Chick Gandil got $4,000. Swede Risberg, the shortstop, $2,500. Ray Schalk, an eventual Hall of Fame catcher in his eighth year with the White Sox, got $7,083.33. Lefty Williams, winner of seventeen games in 1917, got $3,000 for the next year. Eddie Cicotte won twenty-eight games in 1917, high man in the American League. Comiskey paid him $5,000 for 1918, but he did give him an additional $2,000 in the form of a bonus. This meant his salary talks for 1919 would still begin at $5,000. The only .300 hitters on that championship team were in the outfield. Center fielder Happy Felsch hit .308 and got $3,750. And Joe, whose .301 average was the lowest he ever had in his major league career, was still paid $6,000.

Hard feelings splintered the team. One loose-knit group formed around newcomers Chick Gandil and Swede Risberg; these men shared a bitterness against the better-paid players. Many of the White Sox didn't even talk to each other. During infield practice none of the other infielders would throw the ball to second baseman Eddie Collins who had to warm up with catcher Schalk.

As it happened, 1918 was not a good year for baseball. A large percentage of the major-league players had entered the military or had taken jobs in classified work and their places had been filled by less-skilled players. This lowering of quality, coupled with the fact that national interest was focused on the war, caused baseball attendance to drop by forty percent. The owners decided that if they had to suffer bad business, it was better to do so for fewer games, so they shortened the season. They obscured the reason by alluding to a non-existent wartime order from the federal government to cancel games, but it was clear that their motive was simply to cut their losses.

When the owners curtailed the season they still carried the obligation to pay full-season salaries according to the contracts they had signed with their players. But they turned to those same contracts and discovered a simple means of relief. Under the stipulations of the "ten day clause," the owners released every player in the major leagues. Since the players would have been fair game on the open market, the owners quickly reached a "gentlemen's agreement" not to tamper with each other's property so that each could re-sign all his own players the next spring. The owners collectively saved about $200,000 in salaries, even after settling out of court with the few players who sued for their full contractual wages. And at least one writer, taking a hint from the Great Red Scare that was sweeping the country, branded some of the players who wanted their full salaries as "Bolsheviki."

During the war, Comiskey's denunciations of Joe and the other men who'd chosen essential work had been so full of patriotic contempt that some of his fellow owners believed him when he said there would be no room for the "jumpers" on his team when the war was over. When the war did end, the Yankees and the Red Sox offered to buy Joe. Comiskey refused the offers and mailed Joe a contract instead. Joe signed it and sent it back. It set his salary for the 1919 season at $6,000.

While Joe was gone his Chicago fans watched and waited. Some of them were confused by all the public attacks on Joe but when the White Sox played their home opener of the 1919 season his fans acted on their feelings. When the Sox took the field for batting practice, Joe got the biggest ovation. Over five hundred of his fans came out to the game accompanied by a band they had brought along for the occasion. They marched through the stands waving Jackson banners, then sat in their box seats and draped a huge streamer over the railing: JACKSON ROOTERS! They welcomed Joe back the best way they knew. When he came to bat for the first time, the game was interrupted briefly while a delegation of fans approached home plate and presented him with a $200 gold pocket watch as thin as a dime. Joe smiled and thanked them. When he stepped back into the batter's box, the old cry rang through Comiskey Park: "Give 'em Black Betsy, Joe! Give 'em Black Betsy!"

In Chicago and all around the league his fans poured out to see him play again. He responded to their affection by hitting better than he had done for several years. When the writers saw the welcome Joe received and his response to it, they quickly returned to writing about his hitting and dropped the slacker stories as if they'd never been.

Charles Comiskey's response to Joe's triumphant return was less evasive. He was not content to forget his own abusive attacks on Joe's character, he wanted to rewrite them. When he saw that Joe still drew large crowds through the turnstiles everywhere the White Sox played, Comiskey smugly announced he was glad he had not listened to the critics who'd wanted him to get rid of slacker Joe.

And Katie, who seems not to have said anything in public, clipped the reports of Comiskey's response and pasted them into her scrapbooks next to Comiskey's earlier accusations that Joe was a coward who didn't deserve to play baseball.

After their poor showing in 1918 when they dropped all the way to sixth place, the White Sox were not among the pre-season favorites to win the 1919 American League pennant. Their pitching staff was considered thin and the dissension on the team was well known. But powered by the workhorse pitching of Eddie Cicotte and Lefty Williams and the hitting of Joe, Eddie Collins, and one or two others, the Sox got off to a fast start and by the end of April they moved into first place. Except for a few days in mid-June and a day or two in July, they held on to first place all year, though they had to hold off a late rush by Cleveland, whom they finally beat by three and a half games. Joe hit a sharp single in the ninth inning of a game against the St. Louis Browns to drive in the winning run of the game that clinched the pennant.

The pre-season reservations about the team were borne out even though the White Sox won the pennant. The pitching staff was thin — Cicotte (29) and Williams (23) won 52 games between them, which amounted to sixty percent of the team's victories in a season that had been shortened to 140 games. (Subsequent events proved them very wrong and 1919 was a banner year, but before the season had begun the owners shortened the schedule fearing a repeat of the 1918 business losses.) And the other problem, the dissension, grew even worse. The bitterness among the players became more obvious and the rift between players and Comiskey widened when several players asked manager Kid Gleason to intercede with Comiskey on their behalf — they wanted pay raises — and Comiskey ignored the request, refusing to discuss it.

An unhappier, more distressed team never won a pennant. By now the White Sox made no pretense of enjoying their work. Constant bitterness had permanently poisoned the atmosphere. Joe felt it more than most of the other players — in his twelfth year of professional baseball, he still loved the game and spoke sadly of the loss of its fun and pleasure. For the first time in his life, getting ready to play was a chore every single afternoon, whether he was physically injured or not. But he held his disappointment to himself, and his injuries too, and played in all but one of the White Sox games in 1919. He had a successful season.

Joe's .351 batting average was his highest in six years. He led the White Sox and was among the American League leaders in most offensive categories including batting average, runs batted in, hits, doubles, triples, slugging average, and total bases. He was coming off a genuine Joe Jackson season and several newspapers chose him as a probable star of the upcoming World Series. "Joe Jackson is one of the most frequent busters of ballgames known to the game," remarked one New York writer and predicted that Joe would wreck the Cincinnati pitching staff. But Joe did not have the Cincinnati pitchers in mind when he went to Comiskey and asked to be removed from the White Sox lineup for the entire World Series.

The events that led to Joe's strange request and the events that followed its refusal have all been lumped together into the affair known as the Black Sox Scandal of 1919.

At the heart of the Black Sox scandal, and the thing for which it has always been remembered, is the fact that some of the White Sox players conspired with gamblers to lose the World Series intentionally. Because of the scandal and the cover-up that surrounded it, more words have been written about the World Series of 1919 than any other played, yet it remains the series about which we know the least. From its very beginning the entire affair was characterized by confusion, deception, and lies.

Rumors that the fix was in started to circulate on the eve of the series, but they were generally rejected on the grounds that rumors had always circulated at series time and nothing had ever come of them. The series, scheduled for nine games, was played and the favored White Sox lost to the Cincinnati Reds, five games to three. The rumors persisted.

In the final days of the 1920 season, almost a year after the series between the White Sox and the Reds had been played and after repeated denials had failed to put the rumors to rest, the story of the big fix finally broke into the headlines. Then several participants finally talked: to newsmen; to a grand jury; at a criminal trial; and at a civil trial. But the different versions of what had happened were contradictory and mostly self-serving. The confusion caused by these contradictions has never been completely cleared away.

In September, 1920, a grand jury eventually indicted eight of the White Sox for conspiracy: pitchers Eddie Cicotte and Lefty Williams, first baseman Chick Gandil, shortstop Swede Risberg, third baseman Buck Weaver, utility man Fred McMullin and outfielders Happy Felsch and Joe Jackson. The indicted men included five starting players and two of the leading pitchers on the team. These eight players have been known ever since as the Black Sox. When they finally went to trial they were found not guilty by a jury. Nevertheless, they were all banned from organized baseball for life by Judge Kenesaw Mountain Landis, newly appointed as the first Commissioner of Baseball. The lifetime ban on the eight Black Sox was Landis's first official act as Commissioner, and he performed it before the criminal trial was over and the jury had reached its verdict.

The sentence imposed by Landis was represented to the public as the salvation of baseball's integrity. As time passed, the topic of the scandal was strenuously avoided by the spokesmen for baseball, but when it could not be avoided it was presented as the one and only instance of corruption in the history of the major leagues. Landis's stern sentence was offered as proof that the game was clean again: the guilty men had been discovered and removed. Even though they had been found innocent in the eyes of the law, they were not pure enough for the high moral standards of the National Pastime.

Then a fearful silence settled over the whole affair.

With few exceptions, none of the many participants ever spoke publicly again about the scandal. Even those whose contact with the scandal had been merely circumstantial seemed bound by an oath of silence or restrained by an unnamed dread that any mention of it would cause further disaster. Fifty-eight years after the event, Harry "Nemo" Liebold, a surviving member of the 1919 White Sox, a man whose integrity had never been questioned and who had never been accused of any involvement in the fix, agreed to give a telephone interview about other players and many aspects of the game, but at the first mention of the 1919 World Series he hung up the phone without another word.

It is certain there was a conspiracy to fix the 1919 World Series, but most of the specific details are missing. Though it seems clear that first baseman Chick Gandil and pitcher Eddie Cicotte were leaders among the conspiring players, it is not certain if they thought up the fix or if the proposition was brought to them by gamblers.

We also do not know who all the gamblers were, or what their relationships were to each other within the conspiracy. Much of the confusion that has always surrounded the affair was caused by the fact that Cicotte and Gandil entered into deals with at least two different groups of gamblers and perhaps even three. Furthermore, two of the gambler groups, thought to be separate and unrelated by the players, were possibly in league with each other and whether in league or not, both probably were financed by Arnold Rothstein, the Big Bankroll in the world of the racketeers.

The White Sox did lose the World Series, but the conspiracy was a messy and amateurish affair. Almost everything that could be bungled was. So many gamblers around the country heard of the fix that the betting odds on the favored White Sox dropped before the fixers could place their most profitable bets. Arnold Rothstein, who had some reservations about the possibility of actually fixing the Series, hedged his bets and didn't profit as much as he could have. Some of the smaller fixers, betting on individual games rather than on the outcome of the Series itself, went broke when the White Sox won the third game.

Our lack of detailed information about the players' roles is the most tantalizing. Some observers have offered Comiskey's tightfistedness as an explanation for the players' motivations, but nobody has ever offered the details of how the games were fixed. Only the pitchers seem to have had some more or less clear idea of what they were supposed to do to cause their team to lose. For the others there appears to have been no planning or coordination, not even a discussion about how to throw the games while under the scrutiny of hundreds of writers and thousands of fans without giving themselves away. The players themselves were so confused that afterward, in the statements some of them gave, they couldn't even agree on which games they had played to lose and which to win.

In the public version of the Black Sox story Joe's role is the most confusing because it seems to make the least sense. At first Joe did the same as all the other men associated with the White Sox and denied all the rumors and accusations. But when the scandal broke into the headlines in 1920 and he was named as one of the accused players, he changed his course of action. He followed the lead of Eddie Cicotte and voluntarily appeared before the grand jury that had been convened to investigate corruption in baseball. In the alleged pieces of his testimony that were leaked to the press, he named his co-conspiritors and described some of the things he'd done to throw the games.

Though he later retracted his confession, which, as it happened, was among the documents later stolen from the grand jury files, it was never forgotten. Most of the writers and later commentators assumed his retraction was merely a legal maneuver planned by Joe's lawyers. Even many of Joe's supporters believed he was guilty and said later he should be forgiven because he was only an ignorant country boy who'd been taken in by thieves and city slickers. But the question of what Joe had actually done to throw the games was generally ignored.

The grand jury testimony leaked to the press had attributed to Joe the admission that he had made poor fielding and throwing plays and had held back at the plate. Since the leaked versions of his testimony differed from one paper to another, there was no agreement on exactly what he said he'd done, but more interesting was the fact that none of the misplays attributed to him were found in the official box scores and play-by-play accounts of the games. In fact, his performance in the series — he was the leading hitter — seemed to give the lie to his own confession.

16

What you are about to read is the most accurate version of Joe Jackson's role in the Black Sox scandal ever published. It has been drawn from several sources, the most important of which are Jackson's grand jury testimony given in September 1920; the 1700-page transcript of the 1924 civil suit in which Jackson sued White Sox owner Charles Comiskey for back wages on a three year-contract; the "secret diary" kept by Comiskey's secretary, Harry Grabiner; letters to Jackson from Comiskey and Baseball Commissioner Kenesaw M. Landis; the scrapbooks created by Katie Jackson; contemporary newspaper articles; several chapters of *Baseball: The Golden Years* by Harold Seymour; the account of the 1919 World Series as it appears in *Spalding's Official Baseball Guide for 1920*; Chick Gandil's version of the fix, published in 1956; and Jackson's own remarks about the affair, which were told to friends or appeared in print from time to time.

Our focus is on Jackson. This account does not intend to present the story of the scandal in all of its complex details. For those that are presented, in addition to the sources listed above, I have drawn on two books about the scandal, *Eight Men Out* by Eliot Asinoff and *The Great Baseball Mystery* by Victor Luhrs, and an unpublished analysis by Attorney David Carlson, "Strike Four: Joe Jackson, The Black Sox, and the 1919 World Series."

This story is at odds with the traditional version of Jackson's role, and it differs radically from the official version maintained by organized baseball. If anyone has *evidence* to refute this story, let them produce it. Perhaps a smoking gun lies somewhere in the Commissioner's files. Short of that, however, I maintain that *Jackson was literally innocent of guilty involvement in the Black Sox scandal.* Furthermore, I contend that organized baseball, for reasons of its own or perhaps through relying on misinformation, has both perpetrated and perpetuated a lie. Unless Jackson's guilt can be substantiated, baseball should be big enough to admit it made a mistake and correct it. Despite the claims put forward by recent baseball commissioners, there is no statute of limitations—legal, intellectual or moral—on correcting an injustice.

* * *

It began in Boston. The White Sox were in town on their last eastern swing of the 1919 season. Katie had stayed home in Chicago, so he was on his own. One evening after dinner, he decided to take a stroll around Kenmore Square. He couldn't know it then, but a series of events was about to be set in motion which would change his life forever.

He set out alone, with no particular destination in mind.

After a few minutes, someone approached from behind and fell into step beside him. It was Chick Gandil, the team's first baseman. He'd never had much to do with Gandil, so this was a little unusual. They walked along in silence for a block or two, then Gandil, with no preamble, began to talk. He said an arrangement had been made with some gamblers. If the White Sox got into the World Series, which looked likely, the gamblers were prepared to pay $10,000 to each player who'd throw the games.

He looked at Gandil and told him no. Gandil said nothing, he just walked away. But it was too late. Either Gandil had already assured the gamblers that Shoeless Joe Jackson was in on the fix, or he soon would. Whenever it was, the gamblers believed him.

Gandil must have been surprised, for if he was willing to tell Jackson about the fix, he must have assumed he'd say yes. Joe's refusal was a problem, but it was not the only one on Gandil's mind. He wanted the gamblers to make a down payment on their deal. When the gamblers delayed and no advance was forthcoming, Gandil made another deal with a second group of gamblers, this time for a flat fee of $100,000. He also told the second group that Joe joined the fix.

A few days later the team was back in Chicago. After practice, Joe was crossing the small wooden bridge leading to the White Sox clubhouse when Gandil came up behind him and began to ralk rapidly in a voice just above a whisper. This time he offered Joe $20,000 and Joe said no again. Gandil looked him in the face, assured him that the fix was going to happen, adding, "You might as well say yes, or say no and play ball, or anything you want." Without another word Gandil hurried on to the clubhouse and left Joe alone on the bridge.

An invitation to join a fix scheme was not as shocking to a major leaguer in 1919 as it would be today. Fixes were not every day affairs, but they were common enough for every big leaguer to have heard of them. And gambling, always a precursor to a fix, for otherwise there would be no way to profit from it, was uninhibited. Well-known professional gamblers did business at every major league park and betting was routinely transacted in public, but almost nothing was done about it. Some owners said it was good for the game because it helped to fill the stands. Even the owners who opposed gambling did little, for to combat gambling would require the admission that it existed and this would be contrary to the owners' traditional policy. They feared that any admission of corruption, or even the hint of it, would undermine and perhaps destroy the game's position as the national pastime and weaken the hold it had on the public imagination as the purest symbol of wholesome competition. And most of them knew that the drama that attracted the fans to their ball parks depended on the unshakable assumption that the games were completely honest and every player always tried his best. So they were loath to admit any imperfections at all. Their standard response to alarms of corruption began with denial and ended with cover-up.

In 1908, for example, John McGraw, manager and later part owner of the New York Giants, was accused of offering a bribe to some Philadelphia pitchers to throw games to the Giants. The accusation was denied by McGraw and National League spokesmen, but the matter was not investigated. At the end of the season two National League umpires, one of them the "Great Arbiter" Bill Klem, filed reports that charged a member of the Giants with offering them $3,000 to let the Giants beat the Chicago Cubs in the famous play-off for the 1908 pennant.

The official spokesmen tried to deny this charge too, but Klem was a respected baseball man and his accusation could not be ignored. The National League created a special committee to investigate the charges against the Giants. The man selected to chair the committee was John T. Brush, the owner of

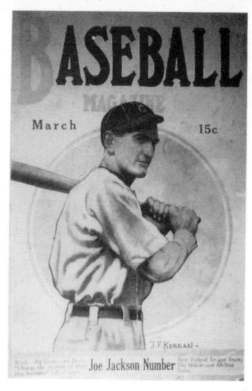

Front cover of *Baseball Magazine*, March 1916.

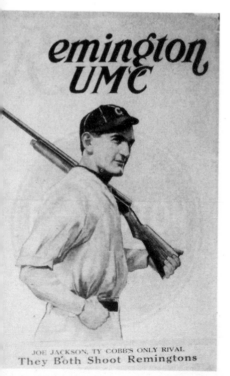

Back cover of *Baseball Magazine*, March 1916.

Studio portrait, 1915.

Detail of studio portrait, 1915.

Joe with Bill Carrigan, manager and part-time catcher for the Boston Red Sox, 1915 or 1916.

Caught unawares with a mouthful of chewing tobacco.

Endorsement ad, 1916.

Endorsement ad, 1916.

Famous White Sox Slugge: Buys Second Oldsmobile

TO followers of the great American game (baseball, not poker) it is hardly necessary to introduce Mr. Joe Jackson. For the benefit of the uninitiated, however, he is a star member of the Chicago "White Sox" team in the American League and one of the greatest batsmen in the game today.

In the picture below he is shown with Mrs. Jackson in the Oldsmobile

Pacemaker which he recently purchased from the G. Bingham Bache Motor Company of Savannah, Georgia. Although he has owned a great many motor cars of various makes, Mr. Jackson seems now to have found what he considers the ultimate in automobiles for this is his second Pacemaker and he says: "The Oldsmobile Eight for me every time."

An advertisement from a Savannah newspaper following the 1917 World Series.

Waiting to take batting practice, probably at the start of the 1918 season.

With a new white bat he called "Blond Betsy," at the start of the 1919 season.

Advertising flyer circulated by the promoter of a New York semi-pro team for which Joe played briefly after being banned from organized baseball. 1922.

BASE BALL FANS ATTENTION!

can we turn down

'Shoeless' Joe Jackson

GREATEST OF ALL OUTFIELDERS

without further hearing? Are you sure he was not "FRAMED UP?" Some may think they have him BURIED ALIVE in scandal. His answer is his remarkable COME-BACK.

JOE JACKSON comes of too sturdy a stock to be disposed of through any "buried alive" process. He is willing to be vanquished only by his peers—if he has any—in a fair game, on the Base Ball Diamond—and not otherwise.

JOE JACKSON challenges any base ball players, amateur or professional, to beat him on his own ground "put up or shut up!" And JOE JACKSON comes back, as he has ever declared, for

A Square Deal
to the FANS
to the Owners
to the Managers
to the PLAYERS—to the Umpires

"Square Deal" Ed. Phelan, President
New York Semi-Professional Base Ball Association
Park Row Building, New York City

(Endorsed)   J. J. FISHMAN
86 Elliott Avenue, Yonkers, N. Y.
Correspondence and Suggestions Solicited

Joe's Waycross, Georgia, semi-pro team. He managed and played the outfield. He is standing, fourth from the left. Early 1930s.

Promotional flyer for a game featuring Joe's semi-pro team. Note the "Menu." Arlington, Georgia, early 1930s.

Promotional flyer for Joe's semi-pro team, Douglas, Georgia, early 1930s.

One Big Day!
in Arlington on Tuesday, Aug. 7

Barbecue, Brunswick Stew, and two ball games with 'Shoeless' Joe Jackson's crew from Americus. This is the day that you young married people can tell your children about in the after years.

The pigs are grunting, the kids are bleating, the bulls are bellowing, chickens cackling and lambs are cutting up now, but "Oh Boy" see 'em Tuesday.

Don't miss, for everybody else will be at Arlington that day, Tuesday, August 7th.

————MENU————

At 11 o'clock. A speaker who makes leaves rattle.
At 11:30 o'clock. The Blakely Brass band who knows how to make you forget the boll weevil.
At 12:45 o'clock. Appetizer.
At 1 o'clock. "Hush your fuss." Suckling pig, veal, mutton, kid, nanny goats, chickens, pickles, cake and red lemonade.
At 2:30 we begin carving on 'Shoeless' Joe Jackson's Americus bunch in a double header.

All the above you get for a "measly" dollar bill if you are a man or woman; half that for boys and girls. Easily $10 worth of food and entertainment.

ROOT, REAR, AND RAVE FOR ARLINGTON ON THAT DAY!

Red Lemonade and' Dinner Free

BASE-BALL

SHOELESS JOE JACKSON CLUB
VERSUS
DOUGLAS A. & M.

The famous Joe Jackson will positively play in this game. Everybody wants to see "Brown Mule" Smith in action against this club. Shoeless Joe is one of the best ball players of all time and will give our people a chance to see how Major Leaguers perform. This will be a big day in Douglas, stores will close and everybody coming to the game.

DOUGLAS
THURSDAY, APRIL 2nd.
A. & M. CAMPUS

Joe with one of his cars,
late 1930s.

Front window of "Joe Jackson's
Liquor Store," West Greenville,
probably in the 1940s.

Joe's business card for the
liquor store.

Joe's autograph, printed in pencil and witnessed by the man who received it. (Courtesy the Joseph Ades Collection)

One of the last photos of Joe, in the kitchen of his West Greenville home, circa 1950.

the Giants. After a brief lapse of time Brush submitted a report to the league president which recommended no further action be taken. Do nothing and the public will forget. Later, the Giants' team doctor, a close personal friend of McGraw, was identified as the go-between, and he was barred from baseball, but the names of the men behind the bribe attempt were never made public.

Another baseball figure around whom charges of corruption often flew was Hal Chase, called Prince Hal because he had no peer as a first baseman. Many people were convinced he was as adept at throwing games as he was at playing the infield. One of these was George Stallings, his manager on the New York Highlanders (Yankees). Toward the end of the 1910 season Stallings accused Chase of throwing games. The charges were denied by everyone, but since they had been made publicly by Chase's own manager, they could not be ignored. Ban Johnson held an official hearing after which he issued his findings: "Stallings utterly failed in his accusations against Chase. He tried to besmirch the character of a sterling player and has utterly failed to injure his character. Anyone who knows Hal Chase knows he is not guilty."

Among those who attended the hearing and presented testimony were Frank Farrell, owner of the Highlanders, and Chase himself. Stallings, whose charges against Chase supposedly were the subject of the hearing, was not even invited to attend. He had spoken out because he wanted to rid his team of a player who was throwing games. He wanted the league or owner Farrell to take some action. But the league did nothing other than to clear Chase. And owner Farrell, once alluded to by the *New York Times* as the "dictator of the poolroom syndicate" and one of the four members of the "secret gambling commission" that funneled graft payments from illegal gambling operations into the pockets of Tammany Hall, took a different action. He fired Stallings and made Hal Chase manager in his stead.

Chase managed the Highlanders from second place to sixth in one season and his managing career was short. By 1913 Frank Chance, the "Peerless Leader" of the old Chicago Cubs, was manager of the team. Before the season was over he too accused Chase of throwing games. Farrell and Chase denied the charges again, but suddenly, with no explanation, Farrell traded Chase to another team.

After a fling with the Federal League, Chase was eventually signed by the Cincinatti Reds. His manager was no less a fabled hero than Christy Mathewson, one of the most respected of all players. In August 1918, after restraining himself for as long as he could, Mathewson accused Chase of throwing games and suspended him without pay. Six months later, in January 1919, the president of the National League conducted a secret five-hour hearing into the latest charges. Mathewson could not attend because he was in the army in France, so his affidavit was read instead. But three of Chase's Cincinnati teammates and a Giants pitcher did testify. They all swore that Chase had offered them money to throw games. John McGraw, Mathewson's old manager, also testified against Chase. One month later, in February 1919, the president of the National League issued his verdict: "Player Chase is not guilty of the charges brought against him." John McGraw, agreeing to pay him the back wages due on his suspended Cincinnati contract, immediately signed Chase to play for the New York Giants.

These episodes from the careers of Chase and McGraw were not everyday events, though they are representative of the moral climate of big-league baseball in general. But Joe would not have had to look to other teams for examples. He undoubtedly knew about, and perhaps participated in, a fix that involved virtually the entire 1917 White Sox. In September of that year, fighting for the pennant, the White Sox had back-to-back doubleheaders with the also-ran Detroit Tigers. To guarantee that the Tigers would not make too great an effort, the White

Sox players contributed money to a pool and gave the Tigers about $1,100. The transaction was apparently arranged by White Sox manager Clarence Pants Rowland. The White Sox won all four games, and went on to win the pennant, as already noted, by a margin of 3½ games over the Cleveland Indians. (This particular piece of corruption did not come to light until 1927, and is treated below in Chapter 18.) It was in this atmosphere that Joe heard and refused Gandil's proposition.

Gandil told the truth when he said the fix would happen with or without Joe, and soon gamblers from coast to coast had heard about it. As the rumors proliferated and even appeared in print, Joe was among the growing number of people who knew they might be true. On the morning of the opening game of the Series, in the crowded lobby of the Sinton Hotel in Cincinnati, Joe bumped into Bill Burns, whom he'd known as an American League pitcher. In answer to Joe's casual question, "How is everything?" Burns suddenly began to talk about some of the details of the fix. Joe didn't know enough about the scheme to understand what Burns told him, but it was the *first corroboration* he got that the fix was actually in. That's when he went to Comiskey and asked to be benched.

We do not know how much Joe told Comiskey, but at the least he must have mentioned the rumors and his fear of being implicated. "Tell the newspapers you just suspended me for being drunk," Joe said, "or anything, but leave me out of the series and then there can be no question."

Among the details we do not know are the roles assigned to the fixed players. There seems to have been little attention paid by anyone to the tactics that would be used to actually throw the games. We do know, however, a good deal about Jackson's role. He refused to join the conspiracy, but his name was used anyway. When he realized he might be implicated despite his refusals, he went to an officer of the team and asked to be benched for the Series.

Comiskey refused. He said the team wouldn't be the same without Joe. He laughed off the rumors and reminded Joe that similar stories circulated almost every year and told him not to worry. But we don't know if Comiskey questioned Joe to learn if he knew more, or promised to protect Joe if anything came of his fears. So Joe played in the 1919 World Series. Afterward he always pointed to his record as proof that he had played to win.

Some of the Black Sox did do things to lose intentionally, particularly pitchers Cicotte and Lefty Williams. Cicotte received $10,000 before he pitched the opening game, which Cincinnati won, 9 to 1. On his way to the park a stranger had jokingly told Cicotte that a man with a rifle was looking for him. Cicotte pitched poorly and made what appeared to be a dumb play when he cut off a throw to the plate, allowing another Cincinnati run to score.

On the night before he was to pitch the eighth and final game of the Series, Lefty Williams received a death threat over the telephone. He got the first Cincinnati batter on a pop-up, but the next four men got hits and Cincinnati had a 3-to-0 lead when Williams was taken out of the game in the first inning.

The version of Joe's role in the series which shows him holding back at the plate and intentionally fumbling in the field is the opposite of what actually happened. After his request to be benched, Joe knew Comiskey would be watching him very closely, so he played with more effort and less fun than usual. The only laugh he could remember from the whole series occurred one morning as he got out of a taxi in front of Comiskey Park and two kids pushed their way through the crowd and came right up to him. One of them pointed down at his feet and said triumphantly to the other, "See, I told you the big sonofabitch wore shoes!"

Since those who believed that Joe was crooked could neither account for nor explain away his record, they mostly ignored it. Some made a joke of it and claimed that Joe had tried to play poorly but that his natural physical instincts were stronger than his brain. He was, they said, too dumb to be a good fixer.

A few others took the position that he had played to lose, but had cleverly chosen his spots. He batted poorly when a hit would have helped and hit well when it didn't count. In light of what Joe accomplished in the series, this theory appears to be based on the assumption that he could get a hit whenever he wanted.

In the World Series of 1919 Joe got more hits than any player on either team. He drove in six runs and scored five. He had sixteen put-outs, one assist, and no errors. On the face of it, any relationship between his record and the accusation that he had played to lose seemed farfetched. It seemed so absurd to Robert Ripley, himself a former sports cartoonist, that he once featured it in *Believe It Or Not*: "Joe Jackson, while trying to throw the Series of 1919, made 12 hits and batted .375." His .375 average led all players on both teams and his twelve hits set a World Series record.

* * *

Soon after the last game of the Series ended Joe was sitting in a chair in his hotel room when Lefty Williams came in. He had been drinking. He held two envelopes in his hand. "Here," he asked Jackson, "do you want one of these?"

"No, what is it?" Jackson answered. Williams pushed an envelope at him and Jackson said, "Go on, what is it that you got?"

"Why, it's money."

"I don't want your money," Jackson answered, and refused to take the envelope.

Williams said the gamblers had sent Jackson's share of the

payoff. He grumbled drunkenly about the amount—only $5,000 when $10,000 had been promised—but he said it was better than nothing and offered the envelope to Jackson again. Jackson refused and Williams threw the envelope down.

Lefty Williams, another Southerner, was one of the few men on the White Sox with whom Jackson spent time off the diamond. Occasionally the two men and their wives traveled as a foursome. Joe believed that Gandil or some of the others were capable of double-crossing him, but he was surprised at Williams and told him so. They got into a shouting match, which ended when Jackson stormed out of his own room, shouting back at Williams that he was going to talk to Comiskey in the morning.

When Jackson returned to his room he found the envelope full of money where Williams had left it and put it in his pocket. The next morning he went to Comiskey's office at the ball park.

Comiskey always kept the front office locked. When a player wanted to talk to him, he had to knock on a wooden shutter and someone inside the office would raise it. When Joe knocked on the shutter that morning Harry Grabiner raised it. Joe told him he wanted to talk to Comiskey. "It is important that I should see him, some information that I got out of Williams in regard to the World Series."

Comiskey, whom we know from Harry's Diary was at that very moment hearing the details of the fix from two of the guilty players (Gandil and outfielder Happy Felsch), refused to see Jackson. "Go home," Grabiner said. "We know what you want," and slammed the shutter in his face. Jackson waited in the outer office for more than an hour, then left.

Comiskey wouldn't speak to Jackson that morning because his cover-up was already underway. He knew from Jackson's earlier effort to be kept out of the Series that he was trying to stay clear of any involvement, presumably because he had refused to participate. Felsch and Gandil, on the other hand, were admittedly crooked and would presumably follow any plan Comiskey devised to whitewash the fix if the rumors grew stronger. But Jackson, acting out of innocence, was liable to say anything, even the *truth*, including his attempt to be benched. If he said this, and he was believed, Comiskey's hypocrisy would be revealed. So he insulated himself from Jackson and, when the scandal broke open a year later, he made every effort to neutralize Jackson's potential to harm him. He did this by destroying Jackson's credibility.

Joe's request to be benched was not the only indication Comiskey had had that something was wrong. In an unusual move, a well-known gambler named Monte Tennes had informed the White Sox after the first game that a fix was in progress. Comiskey had reason to take this tip seriously because Tennes, owner of the largest gambler's wire-service in the country, was in a position to know what he was talking about. Furthermore, after the first game Comiskey's own manager, Kid Gleason, had come to him with the accusation that some of the players were playing to lose. After his team lost the second game, Comiskey had even gone so far as to inform the National Commission, the governing body of baseball, that something was wrong with the way his team was playing. And of course, like everyone else in the country, he had heard the rumors.

When the series ended Comiskey would have been content to forget whatever he had heard and seen and let the rumors fade away as they had always done. Crooked or honest, the suspected players were valuable property and he was not prepared to lose them. But the situation changed when the most damaging accusation to date appeared in print the day after the series. It was in an article by Hugh Fullerton, who was still one of the most respected baseball writers in the country.

"Yesterday's game," wrote Fullerton, "in all probability is

the last that ever will be played in any World Series. If the club owners and those who have the interests of the game at heart have listened during this series, they will call off the annual interleague contest. . . . Yesterday's game also means the disruption of the Chicago White Sox as a ball club. There are seven men on the team who will not be there when the gong sounds next spring, and some of them will not be in either major league."

This prediction of calamity for the World Series did not, of course, come true, nor was Fullerton correct either in the number of players eventually implicated or the timing of their expulsion. Nevertheless, it was by far the boldest of the public statements that had yet appeared. Fullerton's reputation and assertiveness carried great authority and the article sent a shudder through all of baseball. Other owners feared that the internal corruption that had plagued the game was about to be made public. Comiskey was afraid that Fullerton might expose the guilty White Sox and force the men who governed baseball to take action against them. If the case against them was proved, the guilty men would be banned from baseball and Comiskey would lose their athletic services and their value as property.

Also, if Fullerton had proof to support the charges in his article and planned to use it, it would be senseless for Comiskey flatly to deny all the rumors. If he did that he would not only suffer the losses, but would be revealed as a hypocrite and a man who placed his own profits above the integrity of the game. So he had to learn how much Fullerton actually knew. But he had to wait until Fullerton returned from a two-week vacation. Then he invited him in for an off-the-record discussion. Comiskey's worst fears were relieved when Fullerton admitted that he was operating only on rumors. His hunches were correct, as Comiskey knew, but Fullerton still lacked proof.

Comiskey himself had learned much about the fix in the days immediately following the series. A midwestern gambler named Harry Redmon had sent out word that he'd been double-crossed out of several thousand dollars and that he was willing to tell what he knew about the fix to someone who would make up his losses. Manager Gleason, two other White Sox officials, and perhaps Harry Grabiner (Comiskey's secretary) met with Redmon. Though some of his details were wrong, the story Redmon told them contained all the basic features of the fix as they are still known to this day. He named all the White Sox players who eventually were indicted, he named most of the gamblers who were indicted, including former player Hal Chase (Chase seems to have ignored the indictment and later he was cleared by Commissioner Landis), and he also implicated Arnold Rothstein, who was not indicted, though after his death several years later Rothstein's own files revealed that he had invested $80,000 in the scheme to fix the series. Redmon essentially told the truth, but he never received a penny from Comiskey.

According to Harry Grabiner's diary, the meeting with Redmon took place on Sunday, October 12, 1919. Three days after the series ended, the White Sox management knew almost as much as they would ever know about the fix, but Comiskey made no attempt to share this knowledge with Fullerton when he invited him in for a confidential discussion. Instead, he asked Fullerton to investigate the matter through all the newspaper resources at his command and proposed a partnership in which they would share information. Fullerton agreed, and Comiskey waited for his report. If Fullerton collected proof of the players' guilt he would bring it to Comiskey, who could join in the public revelation and thus be viewed as a man who wrecked his own club in the name of honest baseball. If, on the other hand, Fullerton and his many colleagues found no proof, Comiskey would know it was apparently safe to continue the policy of denial and wait for the rumors to disappear.

After a couple of weeks Fullerton reported that neither he nor his colleagues had developed any firm evidence. Comiskey thanked Fullerton and publicly announced that he was offering a $20,000 reward, later reduced to $10,000, for evidence that would prove beyond doubt that a fix had occurred. But he did not tell Fullerton or anyone else that he had hired a private detective to investigate his own suspected players and to gather any evidence he could find of corruption on other teams. If things got too hot, perhaps Comiskey would be able to prevent the other owners from taking action against the guilty White Sox by threatening to expose the corrupt players on their teams.

Fullerton, based on the evidence of his later articles, seems never to have suspected what Comiskey was really up to or how Comiskey had used him.

A few days after Comiskey refused to see him, Joe got on the train with Katie and went home to Savannah. He was smarting over the insult of the slammed office shutter and he couldn't understand why Comiskey hadn't talked to him. It almost seemed that Comiskey didn't want to know what had happened. Joe was perplexed by this strange turn of events, including the fact that he still had the $5,000 in his pocket and didn't know what to do with it.

From his home in Savannah, Jackson carried on a brief correspondence with Comiskey. (See Appendix B.) It began with Joe's inquiry about his World Series check, which he had not yet received, but soon veered off into the question of the rumors that continued to surround the White Sox players. Joe offered to come back to Chicago, or anyplace else, and tell Comiskey what he knew. Comiskey never took him up on it.

The correspondence soon returned to business as usual when Comiskey sent a one-year contract for $7,000 for the 1920 season. Joe sent it back unsigned with a counter proposal for a three-year contract at $10,000 per year. Furthermore, he wanted the contract to be "ironclad," which meant the "ten-day clause" was deleted. (This clause allowed the club owner to dissolve a ball player's contract with ten days' notice without giving any reason.) The negotiations didn't seem to be getting anywhere. Spring training was scheduled to start in March, and Comiskey wanted to have Joe signed by then, but he had more pressing problems on his mind when he took an unprecedented step.

At the end of February 1920, Harry Grabiner travelled to Savannah for the apparent purpose of getting Jackson's signature on a new contract. It was the only time in Jackson's career that a contract was brought in person. Grabiner phoned Joe from the railroad station. Joe was surprised that he was in town and told him he couldn't meet with him. His youngest sister Gertrude was very sick in the hospital, he had been up most of the night, and he was too worried and tired to talk about business. Grabiner was insistent and Joe finally drove to the station and picked him up. They drove around Savannah, which Grabiner had never seen, and stopped for a few minutes to visit Gertrude in the hospital. Grabiner, however, was focused on his task. While he was on the road making personal visits to the implicated players who lived in the South, Comiskey himself was on the west coast for the same purpose. (By February 1920, resulting partially from the work of the private investigators he had hired, Comiskey, and Grabiner too, knew most of the story of the fix.)

Grabiner was all business. But before getting to the contract, he brought up the "rumors" about the World Series, most probably the real reason for his unique visit. Comiskey, who was about to re-sign some players he knew were crooked, and others whom he had strong reason to suspect, apparently wanted Grabiner to discuss the situation so everyone would have the story straight. Furthermore, as an inducement to go along with his cover-up scenario, Comiskey took the most uncharacteristic step of all: he offered the suspect players *raises* for the 1920 season.

Grabiner said they'd made an investigation and "had the goods on three men: Cicotte, Gandil, and Williams." He also said they knew he, Jackson, had discussed the fix with Gandil and that he had received $5,000 from Williams.

Jackson denied discussing the fix and reminded Grabiner that he had tried to talk with Comiskey right after the Series and then offered to return to Chicago: "What's the matter with you people up there anyway, that you didn't have me come up and give you that information that I knew?"

To Jackson's denial of having discussed the fix, Grabiner replied, "Well, just let it go at that. Whether you did or whether you didn't, let's talk contract."

But Joe was not ready to let it go. He asked Grabiner what he was supposed to do with the $5,000 that Williams had given him. "Why, keep it." Grabiner answered, and turned the conversation back to the new contract. Jackson kept the $5,000. (In comparison to his $6,000 salary in 1919, it was a considerable sum.)

Joe still wanted a three-year ironclad contract at $10,000 per year. Grabiner said, "Well, I'll tell you what I'll do for you; I'll give you a three-year ironclad contract at eight thousand dollars a season instead of ten thousand for one." By ironclad he meant that the ten-day release clause would be left out of the contract. He reached into his inside jacket pocket, drew out a folded contract, and held it out to Joe. "Now, you can take that," Grabiner said, "or we'll kick you out of baseball. You know we can do pretty well as we please with ballplayers."

Joe thought it over for a while. He wanted to drive back to the house so Katie could read the contract as she had always done, but Grabiner urged him to keep driving around. Finally he asked Grabiner to read it to him—"You know I can't read, Harry"—and Grabiner did. He read it as if the release clause had been removed. Joe pulled over to the curb in front of his own house. He still wanted to go in so Katie could read the contract and sign it as she had signed all his others for him. But Grabiner stayed in the car. Joe knew that Katie wanted him to hold out for $10,000. But he was afraid to push Grabiner. He was uneasy about all the things that had happened and what Grabiner and Comiskey knew about him, particularly the $5,000. The situation perplexed him. Under pressure from Grabiner he awkwardly put his name on a three-year contract which he could not read.

The aura of corruption taken on by the White Sox in 1919 did not fade away in 1920. Though they were in first place much of the time, rumors persisted throughout the season that some of the players were still throwing games. Just as they had in the World Series, the rumors about Joe seemed absurd. He started the season as if he was out to prove something. He began to hit in the very first game and didn't stop.

Coming into New York in July he was batting in the .390s. Babe Ruth, on his way to a phenomenal fifty-four home runs and already the acknowledged slugging king, paid a small tribute to the man whose batting style he had copied; he gave Joe one of his new bats. Ruth wished him well with the bat, but made Joe promise he wouldn't use it against the Yankees.

Joe liked the feel of the new bat. It was as long as Betsy, but thinner in the handle, thicker in the barrel, and, at fifty ounces, two ounces heavier. He rubbed in a few coats of tobacco juice and used it for the first time in a game against the Red Sox. The first time up he hit a home run deep into the right field bleachers, four hundred fifty feet away. He didn't use Ruth's bat frequently, but it seemed to touch off one of his hitting streaks. By the end of July he was batting over .400.

1920 was Joe's last season. In some ways it resembled

1911, his first. He was a batting demon in the American League. The fans came out to cheer him everywhere he played and they left the ball parks well satisfied. But, also like 1911, everywhere he played some rumors were sure to surface. In his first years the rumors said he was a coward. Now in 1920 they said he was a crook. As the season wore on, the rumors grew and the pressures grew with them. By mid-September the White Sox were in a three-way fight for the American League pennant with New York and Cleveland. It was an exciting and close race, but it had competition for the fans' attention. The rumors of corruption which had circulated so freely all year suddenly broke out in a scandal. Gamblers had apparently tampered with a National League game between the Phillies and the Cubs. The Cook County district attorney called for a grand jury investigation and the grand jury convened on September 21. Two days later the White Sox, trailing the Indians by two games, opened a three-game series in Cleveland. In the first game, Joe hit two doubles and a single to lead the White Sox to a victory.

On the same day the grand jury investigation suddenly switched its focus from the Cubs-Phillies game to concentrate on the World Series of 1919, and newspapers around the country carried an alarming headline that pushed the Red Scare, the Palmer Raids, and the Wall Street Explosion out of the headlines. BARE FIXED WORLD SERIES! the new headline blared, and right beneath it were the words of the assistant state attorney: "The last World Series...was not on the square. From five to seven players on the White Sox team are involved."

No names had yet been mentioned publicly, but the pressure increased on the guilty players and on those involved in any way. Joe did not feel guilty, but he felt uneasy about two things: Comiskey and Grabiner might think he was implicated because they knew he had received the $5,000 and had kept it. In the next game Joe hit one single in four times at bat and Chicago lost 2 to 0.

The White Sox won the crucial third game, 5 to 1. Joe hit two more doubles and a home run, bringing his three-game total to seven hits in twelve tries. It was the kind of series Joe had been famous for in the early days in Cleveland. There could have been a poetic rightness to it. He was closing out his best season since 1912. He had hit as only Joe Jackson could, and though the pennant was at stake his old Cleveland fans still loved him. They would not have begrudged him his triumph if it had remained untainted. But this was 1920, not 1912. Sometime during the game the news arrived in League Park that the names of the eight suspected White Sox had been made public. Joe Jackson was fifth on the list.

Some fans began to taunt the players, and a few singled out Joe. In Cleveland, where he had been the batting wonder of the age and the idol of the fans, he was cursed as a crook. In the fifth inning, after he'd hit his home run over the right field wall, he surprised everyone in the park, perhaps himself included, by making an insulting gesture while rounding second base. He repeated it as he crossed the plate. Now the main body of the crowd, which may have been unaware of the news and the curses aimed at Joe, became angry and booed and jeered him for the rest of the game. Thousands of veterans, in town for an American Legion convention, recalled their own resentment at him, which dated back to World War I, and chanted with disdain, "Shipyard! Shipyard!"

After the game the White Sox returned to Chicago for a series against the Tigers. James T. Farrell, whose boyhood world revolved around the White Sox, was at the Sunday game. He had read the accusations made against the players but he did not want to believe them. He recalled that game and its mood in *My Baseball Diary*:

> It was a muggy, sunless day. I went to the park early and watched
> the players take their hitting and fielding practice. It looked the
> same as always. They took their turns at the plate. They had their
> turns on the field. They seemed calm, no different, no different
> than they had been on other days befor the scandal had broken.
> The crowd was friendly to them and some cheered. But a subtle
> gloom hung over the fans.

The White Sox, behind the pitching of Eddie Cicotte,
won the game. Afterward, Farrell joined the crowd gathered
near the steps of the White Sox clubhouse. It was customary
for a small group to gather to watch the players leave, but on
this day over two hundred men and boys waited. After a
while the players began to emerge, one or two at a time.
"And then Joe Jackson and Happy Felsch appeared. They
were both big men. Jackson was the taller of the two and
Felsch the broader. They were sportively dressed in gray silk
shirts, white duck trousers and white shoes. They came down
the clubhouse steps slowly, their faces masked by impas-
sivity."

A few of the fans called to the two men, but they started to
walk away and made no response. The crowd slowly followed them. Farrell moved with the crowd, following about
five feet behind the players. Suddenly one of the fans called
out, "It ain't true, Joe!" Neither player turned to acknowledge the cry, even when the crowd took it up and men and
boys repeatedly called, "It ain't true, Joe!"

The crowd followed the players under the stands and out
onto a soccer field behind the right field bleachers. Farrell
waited near the exit and watched. "Many others also waited,"
he wrote. "Soon Felsch and Jackson drove out in their
sportive roadsters, through a double file of silent fans."

While the White Sox were playing the Tigers on that over-cast breathless Sunday in Chicago, a factory worker and small-time Philadelphia gambler named Billy Maharg, in a last-minute and futile attempt to collect the $10,000 reward offered by Comiskey for hard evidence about the fix, told his story to a reporter. It bacame Monday's headline: GAMBLERS PROMISED WHITE SOX $100,000 TO LOSE.

Maharg's story implicated himself, Sleepy Bill Burns, several gamblers, including Arnold Rothstein and his associate, former world featherweight boxing champion Abe Attell, and eight White Sox. Maharg never collected Comiskey's reward, but he did force Comiskey's hand.

In the year that the rumors hung over the White Sox, Comiskey had collected enough information to know that they were true. On the advice of his lawyer, Alfred Austrian, Comiskey had hired private investigators, who successfully collected information on the suspected players. As Harry Grabiner had put it as early as February 1920, Comiskey "had the goods on three men." He also had supportive evidence from Joe and other sources. But he suppressed all his information and continued to deny all the rumors so he could protect his investment in his valuable players, whose bungling of the fix probably confirmed his low opinion of them as men.

When Maharg talked, Comiskey's game of denial was over, but he acted quickly in his new role. Before the grand jury had time to indict them, Comiskey himself served the suspected players with checks for their pay to date and for-mal notices of indefinite suspension: "Your suspension is brought about by information which has just come to me, directly involving you . . . in the baseball scandal . . . result-ing from the World Series of 1919." He assured them they would be reinstated if found innocent and banned for life if guilty. He closed by explaining that he was acting for the good of the public, "even though it costs Chicago a pennant."

Comiskey released the suspension notice to the press and presented himself as the innocent, unknowing victim: "COMISKEY HARD HIT BY PERFIDY OF HIS PLAYERS . . . Shock So Great Friends Fear for His Health."

Now, with the advice of Alfred Austrian, he planned how to feed the players to the grand jury in the manner which would best maintain his image as the honest man who had wrecked his own championship team because it was corrupt.

Each new revelation about the fix increased the pressure on the suspected players. After Maharg's statement made the headlines and the grand jury indicted the eight players, Manager Gleason saw that Eddie Cicotte was about to crack, so he steered him to the White Sox office where Comiskey and Alfred Austrian were waiting. Cicotte was frightened and he talked quickly. He admitted that he'd been paid $10,000 before the series began and that he had played to lose. He didn't tell Comiskey and Austrian anything they hadn't already known. But that did not surprise them. Their main concern with Cicotte was not to get information from him, but to convince him to follow their advice.

Cicotte was a veteran of fourteen major-league seasons. He had seen how other owners had protected corrupt players in the past and he may have assumed there was a chance for him, too. But he underestimated the seriousness of an appearance before a grand jury and he misunderstood his relationship with Alfred Austrian. He knew Austrian was the White Sox's lawyer and assumed that meant he was his lawyer too. But he was wrong. Austrian's only client in the matter was Charles Comiskey, whose property and reputation were at stake.

Believing Austrian was helping him, Cicotte followed his advice. Austrian said Cicotte's only chance was to admit his guilt, say he was sorry, and hope for the best. Austrian also convinced him that the public and the court would especially resent his betrayal of Comiskey and that he ought to express his regret at this aspect of his treachery.

Cicotte had no more love for Comiskey than the other players, probably less. (Like them, he had endured the low pay and general meanness of the White Sox operation, but he had an added resentment. In 1917 he had had an agreement with Comiskey that called for a bonus if he won thirty games. After he won twenty-eight, Comiskey refused to let him pitch on the grounds he had to rest for the World Series.) But Cicotte was frightened and he thought that to have any chance at all to remain in baseball, he needed Comiskey's help. So he agreed to everything and let himself be taken to the grand jury by Austrian.

When he got to the grand jury room, Cicotte was asked to sign a waiver of immunity. If he signed, it would mean that anything he said could be used to incriminate him and that he was liable to be prosecuted. Austrian neither cautioned him nor explained what the waiver meant. Cicotte didn't know what it was, but he signed it. Then he told his story to the grand jury. When he named his fellow conspirators, he relied on the word of Chick Gandil and said Joe Jackson had been in on the plot.

Outside the grand jury room Cicotte spoke to the press. Mindful of Austrian's advice, he said he had done it for his wife and kids and was particularly sorry he had sold out Mr. Comiskey.

The news of Cicotte's grand jury confession spread rapidly. When Joe heard that Cicotte too had accused him, he headed for Comiskey Park. In the light of past baseball scandals, most notably the case of Hal Chase, Jackson had good reason to believe that Comiskey would know how to handle the court hearings and manage to save the guilty men. As for his own situation, he would remind Comiskey of the things he had done to stay clear of the conspiracy, but when he got to Comiskey Park, Comiskey refused to see him. Instead, he was referred to the office of Alfred Austrian, Comiskey's lawyer.

A forceful and shrewd man, Austrian was the senior partner in one of Chicago's most powerful and prestigious law firms whose other clients included the Chicago Cubs. As he had never met Jackson before, he introduced himself and began immediately to talk about the grand jury hearings. Like Cicotte before him, Jackson assumed Austrian was *his* lawyer. Austrian said nothing to make him think otherwise. Jackson told Austrian what he knew about the fix, stressing his request to be benched before the series and his offer to talk to Comiskey after the series was over. He tried to convince Austrian he was innocent.

For Austrian, however, the question of Jackson's guilt or innocence was less important than Jackson's potential to expose Comiskey. The very points in Jackson's favor tended to prove that Comiskey had evidence of the fix much earlier than he claimed, that he lied to the public, and that he had re-signed players he knew were corrupt. If Jackson told his story and it was believed, Comiskey's reputation would suffer and legal complications might follow. Without doubt, Ban Johnson would use Jackson's story in his effort to drive Comiskey out of baseball. As Comiskey's lawyer, Austrian's task was to convince Jackson that the truth would harm him and that his only chance was in confessing his guilt and acting contrite.

Austrian listened to Jackson's story, then gave his opinion. The truth, if in fact Jackson was telling the truth, would not be believed. First of all, his own teammate Cicotte had named him. Second, Maharg, one of the admitted fixers, had also named him. Why would they do this if it was not true?

Joe had never met Maharg in his life. He tried to explain that Maharg didn't know what he was talking about; he'd said Jackson was part of it because Gandil had told him so. As for Cicotte, he didn't know why he'd named him, unless he'd heard it from Gandil too. What Jackson did not know was that Cicotte had rehearsed his testimony with Austrian and Illinois State Attorney Hartley Replogle, the man conducting the grand jury, before he went before the grand jury.

Austrian said it sounded weak, difficult to believe. Then he assured Jackson that whatever reasons the others had for implicating him, he had implicated himself beyond any question by receiving and keeping the $5,000. There was no way he could explain that.

Perhaps Jackson explained how Williams had tossed down the money after Jackson refused to accept it. Perhaps he told how he'd gone to see Comiskey the next morning and was refused an audience. Perhaps he also told how he'd asked Comiskey's secretary Harry Grabiner what to do with the money and was told to keep it. The details of this crucial meeting between Jackson and Austrian are scant. While Austrian kept detailed notes of his pre-testimony meetings with Cicotte, and later with pitcher Lefty Williams, he claimed under oath that he kept no such notes on his three-hour meeting with Jackson, a remarkably convenient oversight, for such notes could have demonstrated the truthfulness of Jackson's assertion that he had been talked into lying to the grand jury. In any event, the $5,000 worried Jackson, but he still felt the true story would be believed.

Austrian said he doubted it, and suggested that Jackson find out by phoning the judge in charge of the grand jury and telling him the truth. Austrian dialed and handed the phone to Jackson.

Jackson told Judge McDonald he was innocent.

The judge said he had already heard Cicotte and thought Jackson was a liar. Jackson hung up, more confused than ever. He tried to think, but he must have felt trapped.

Austrian hammered away. He repeated that Jackson's story, true or not, was not believable. The judge didn't believe it. If the case went to trial, a jury wouldn't believe it either. Whether he had done it or not, the best way out, the only way out, was to admit it and say he was sorry. If he did that, the club would stand behind him.

Then Austrian reminded Joe of the gamblers who, unlike the fans, would not forgive. If Joe told the truth, that is, that he had refused the offer and had played to win, the gamblers would think he had double-crossed them, for they believed he had accepted the offer. And they knew he had taken their $5,000. In light of the death threat made against Lefty Williams, Joe saw it could be dangerous for him if the gamblers thought he had deceived them.

The meeting in Austrian's office lasted for several hours. Sometime toward the end, still under the mistaken assumption that Austrian was acting in his behalf, Jackson agreed to follow Austrian's advice. They went over the details of the story Jackson would tell to the grand jury. He would say he was guilty, repeat Cicotte's version of the fix, and blame everything on Gandil, who had retired from baseball right after the Series. Austrian must have thought it best to underline the fact that Gandil had been the instigator. (In his testimony Jackson did call Gandil the "instigator," probably the only time in his life he ever used that word.) Jackson would say that Gandil had talked him into it and then double-crossed him over the money—he promised $20,000 and only paid $5,000. Joe would present himself as the ignorant yokel who'd been taken by the sharpers. Poor old Shoeless Joe.

As soon as Jackson agreed and the script for his testimony was worked out, Austrian personally rushed him over to the grand jury before it adjourned for the day. Austrian seems to have feared that if Jackson had a night to think over what he was about to do, he would change his mind. Even worse, he might go out and get his own lawyer.

At the court house, Austrian introduced Joe to Judge McDonald, but he didn't tell Joe that McDonald, Comiskey, and Austrian had been friends for over twenty years. He also neglected to mention that he, Austrian, had been offering to support McDonald in his attempt to be named Commissioner of Baseball. After a brief discussion in the judge's chambers, at which Repolgle was also present, Austrian left. As Joe was not his client, Austrian apparently felt no obligation to give him any self-protective legal advice or even explain the waiver of immunity he signed before he went in front of the grand jury.

Despite the rumors and distortions that have been published ever since, Jackson's grand jury testimony hardly constituted a confession. If there is a more enigmatic and puzzling document in the history of baseball, it has yet to come to light. In addition to the fact that he was coached and advised by Austrian to say he was guilty and ask for forgiveness, the most amazing aspect of his testimony is its self-contradictory nature, for Jackson told *two completely different stories* and nobody ever asked him why. On the one hand, he admitted his guilt, but on the other he said he was invited into the fix twice, and turned it down both times.

The transcript of Jackson's testimony is twenty-seven pages long. He is questioned by Hartley Replogle, an Assistant State Attorney and a man who was eager to please Comiskey. (See Appendix A for the complete transcript of Jackson's testimony.)

Replogle began by establishing the fact that Jackson had knowingly signed a waiver of immunity. That, of course, was a cruel kind of joke. Jackson was functionally illiterate, a fact that was public knowledge. He signed the waiver, which he obviously could not read, on the advice of Austrian, whom he had reason to believe was acting as his lawyer.

After Jackson identified himself, Replogle got right down to the business of Jackson's guilt.

Q: Did anyone pay you any money to help throw that series in favor of Cincinnati?

A: They did.

Q: How much did they pay?

A: They promised me $20,000 and paid me five.

Q: Who promised you the twenty thousand?

A: Chick Gandil

* * *

Q: Who paid you the $5,000?

A: Lefty Williams brought it in my room and threw it down.

* * *

Q: When was it that this money was brought to your room...?

A: It was the second trip to Cincinnati. That night we were leaving.

Q: That was after the fourth game?

A: I believe it was, yes.

Taken at face value, these answers are a clear cut admission of guilt. Jackson's words are just what Replogle expected to hear. But closer inspection reveals a small but curious inconsistency having to do with the supposed date on which Williams threw down the money.

In the prepared story, it seems Austrian tried to incriminate and compromise the players as much as possible. In this way he hoped to underline their treachery and Comiskey's innocence. For this reason, the script would say that Williams received the money and gave $5,000 of it to Jackson *during* the Series. But the script writers got confused about the game sequence. Neither was very knowledgeable about baseball. Austrian testified under oath that he never went to the ballpark and had no interest in the game itself. Replogle's questions and comments in his interrogation of Jackson reveal a man who is hardly a baseball fan. Close analysis of this small error reveals an opening to the probable truth.

In Jackson's testimony he says he got the money after the

fourth game, and fixes the date by placing it on the night they left Chicago to return to Cincinnati for the second time. However, the sequence in this nine-game series was two games in Cincinnati, three in Chicago, two in Cincinnati, and if needed, two more in Chicago. Therefore, since Jackson said Williams gave him the money the night they left Chicago, he must be referring to the fifth game, not the fourth. Later, in testimony during the 1924 civil suit Jackson pressed against Comiskey for back wages, and in interviews given in the 1940s, Jackson maintained Williams gave him the money *after the series was over*. Oddly enough, this assertion is corroborated by Williams himself in his own 1920 grand jury testimony. This seemingly insignificant error is worth looking at because it demonstrates the scripted nature of the grand jury testimony given by the players.

Because the owners erroneously believed business would be bad in 1919, they shortened the season to 140 games. The result for the players was less money, at least for those whose owners, such as Comiskey, calculated their salaries on a per game basis. This subject was broached during Williams' grand jury appearance, before which he too had a "meeting" with Austrian. Williams' deep seated bitterness against Comiskey for the way he had been treated caused him either to forget Austrian's script or to throw caution to the wind, for he suddenly blurted out an important fact in the middle of the following exchange.

Q (Replogle): What was your [1919] salary on the White Sox team?

A (Williams): I believe it would figure out approximately a little over $2800. It was a short season and I was getting $500 a month, but we didn't play quite six months. [*Note. Williams won 23 games in 1919.*]

With the bitterness still in his mind, Williams was asked the next question:

Q: Was there any plan to lose any of the first four games or were you just to lose the Series?

A: Just to lose the Series. We were supposed to lose the first two games and after the first two games we were supposed to get our money, *but I never got a nickel until the last two games were played.*

The way Williams blurted out the information about when he received his pay-off, an out-of-context remark, lends his words great credibility. The question was about the plans made by the players and the fixers for throwing the series, but Williams, with his anger still aroused at the recollection of how he'd been financially exploited by Comiskey, quickly veers off into the issue of money. In his mind, the mistreatment he'd gotten from Comiskey is of the same order as the mistreatment he received from the fixers, who also short-changed him. When he finally blurted out that he didn't get any money from the fixers "*until the last two games were played,*" he was speaking the truth. He also contradicted his previous testimony, in which he repeated Jackson's statement about the fourth game. But this was not what Replogle wanted or expected to hear, for it gave the lie to the prepared script, so he ignored it and quickly went on to the next question. This seemingly unimportant discrepancy about the date Williams received the pay-off money bears directly on Jackson's assertion that he was coached by Austrian, for clearly Williams, too, told a story manufactured from bits of truth and bits of fiction that could only harm himself and help Comiskey.

Returning to Jackson's testimony, we find an exchange that had probably been agreed on beforehand as a way to establish the fact that Jackson had played honest ball on the field, even though he had "agreed" to be in on the fix. In this way, as part of the bargain forced on Jackson by Austrian, Jackson could throw himself on the mercy of both the court and the public and seek forgiveness on the grounds that he had played honest ball.

Q: Did you make any intentional errors yourself that day?

A: No, sir, not during the whole Series.
Q: Did you bat to win?
A: Yes.
Q: And run the bases to win?
A: Yes, sir.
Q: And fielded the balls at the outfield to win?
A: I did.

A few minutes later, Jackson discussed one of the most revealing plays in the Series. Cincinnati was at bat in the top of the fifth inning of game 4. There was no score. Cicotte was pitching. With one out, he misplayed a ball lined back to the mound, allowing the batter to reach second base. The next batter hit a single to Jackson in left field. The runner on second rounded third and Jackson threw to the plate, but Cicotte deflected the ball, allowing the run to score. Cincinnati won, 2-0.

Q: Did you see anything wrong about that game that would lead you to believe there was an intentional fixing?
A: The only thing that I was sore about that game, the throw I made to the plate, Cicotte tried to intercept it.
Q: It would have gone to the first base if he had not intercepted it? (*Note. Replogle, with little knowledge of baseball, presumably meant home plate.*)
A: Yes.

The description of this play, as it appears in the 1920 edition of *Spalding's Official Baseball Guide*, gives no hint of intentional misplay: "Duncan smashed a hot one to Cicotte, who recovered the ball but threw wild, and reached second on the error. Kopf followed with a single to left and Duncan ran to third. *Jackson made a throw in the direction of the plate and Cicotte deflected the ball out of Schalk's reach*, so that Duncan scored and Kopf reached second." (Italics added.) But to some of the fans at the game, including James T. Farrell, who was then fifteen, the play looked odd. "I remember this play vividly even now. There was Joe Jackson. He fielded the ball on one bounce, and got off *a quick, accurate throw.* As the ball sailed in, *I knew that the Cincinnati runner would be out if he tried to score.* He didn't. He merely made a stab at going on. And...there was the figure of Cicotte near third. He tried to stop Jackson's throw. The runner scored and Kopf reached second. I wondered why Cicotte had done this. The play didn't seem right, especially for a player as smart as Cicotte. I spoke to [my brother] Earl about this play. We both agreed that it was a boner." (Italics added.)

To remove any doubt about the physical actions on the diamond during this play, we need only look at the sworn testimony of James C. Hamilton, the Official Scorer of the 1919 World Series. (Hamilton testified at the 1924 trial in Milwaukee about any suspicious plays he may have seen.):

A: There was only one incident....
Q: Did Joe Jackson have anything to do with that play?
A: He did.
Q: What was it?
A: He threw a ball from center field to the plate; the ball was *apparently going to Schalk to catch the runner at home plate.* Cicotte intercepted it by jumping in the air, knocked it down and booted it and the runner scored....The throw, to my eye, would have gone to the home plate....*It was a good throw.* [Italics added.]

The significance of this play, the most blatant intentional misplay of the series, cannot be overstated. Cicotte was indisputably a ringleader of the fix, so there is no doubting *his* intention: his misplay clearly reveals his state of mind. But it also reveals Cicotte's understanding of Jackson's state of mind. If Cicotte *knew* that Jackson was in on the fix, why would he take the risk of performing such an obvious "mistake," when it clearly would have been easier for Jackson to have made a slightly off-target throw from 300 feet away with no one being the wiser? The obvious answer, of course, is that Cicotte *did not believe Jackson was fixed* and presumed he would make an honest throw to the plate.

Considering the facts that Cicotte had already received $10,000 and was one of the players in repeated direct contact with the fixers, we can be sure of his intention to lose the Series. But his split-second decision to intercept Joe's throw may have been prompted by another player, namely Chick Gandil. In a generally unreliable article published in *Sports Illustrated* in 1956, "This Is My Story of the Black Sox Series," Gandil, admittedly corrupt, offered the following insight into the play: "When the next batter singled to left center, and Jackson threw to the plate to try to cut off a run, *I yelled to Cicotte to intercept the throw*." (Italics added.) Gandil offers as an excuse his opinion that there was no play on the runner at the plate, though no other observers of the play agree with his assessment. While Gandil's description of his own role would seem to shift part of the blame for the intentional misplay to himself, his words are in fact revealing of his state of mind at the moment he called to Cicotte to cut off the throw; like Cicotte, *Gandil acted as if he too believed Joe was playing honest ball.*

About halfway through his testimony, Jackson's answers begin to tell a very different story about his involvement in the fix:

Q: Weren't you in on the inner circle?
A: No, I never was with them, no sir. It was mentioned to me in Boston. As I told you before, they asked me what would I consider, $10,000? and *I said no*, then they offered me twenty. [Italics added.]

Q: Who mentioned it first to you?

A: Gandil.

Q: Who was with you?

A: We were all alone.

Q: What did he say?

A: He asked me would I consider $10,000 to frame up something and I asked him frame what? and he told me and *I said no*. [Italics added.]

Q: What did he say?

A: Just walked away from me, and when I returned here to Chicago he told me that he would give me twenty and *I said no again*, and on the bridge where you go into the club house he told me that I could either take it or let it alone, they were going through. [Italics added.]

Q: What did they say?

A: They said, "You might as well say yes or say no and play ball or anything you want." I told them I would take their word.

Q: What else did you say?

A: Nothing.

Q: Did you talk to anyone else about it?

A: That's all I talked to.

Once again, in the face of a blatant contradiction, Replogle never even blinked. He did not ask Jackson how he could first admit involvement and then strenuously deny it a few minutes later. Jackson's words left such a strong impression on the grand jury foreman, Harry Brigham, president of the North American Can Company, that he later testified under oath that in his opinion Jackson never confessed to any involvement in the fix at all.

In response to questions about the gamblers and fixers, Jackson revealed how little he actually knew about the fix. (Burns had been a pitcher in the American League in the early years of Jackson's career; Attell, former lightweight boxing champion of the world and an underling of Arnold Rothstein, was one of the fixers.)

Q: Go back to Attell and [Bill] Burns, just what do you know about them?

A: All I know is what Gandil told me over there, I talked to Bill [Burns] myself later.

Q: What did you talk to Burns later?

A: It was the day the World Series started.

Q: What did you say to him and what did he say to you?

A: I met him in the lobby of the hotel, we sat there; I can't remember the name of the hotel.

Q: Sinton Hotel?

A: Sinton Hotel, yes.

Q: That is in Cincinnati?

A: Yes. I said, "How is everything?"

Q: What did he say?

A: He said "Everything is fine."

Q: Then what happened?

A: He told me about this stuff and I didn't know so much, I hadn't been around and I didn't know so much. He said, "Where is Chick [Gandil]?" I said, "I don't know." He walked away from me. I didn't know enough to talk to him about what *they* were going to plan or what *they* had planned, I wouldn't know it if I had seen him, I only knew what I had been told, that's all I knew. [Italics added.] [*Note. Given the apparent meaning of the last sentence, there must be a typo in the transcript and the next to last phrase ought to read "I wouldn't know it if I hadn't seen him."*]

In another passage of his testimony, Jackson said that until the day the World Series began, he had never talked about the fix with anyone other than Gandil, so the results of this chance encounter with Burns were momentous. The conversation with

Burns was the first time Jackson received any corroboration of Gandil's assertion that a fix was in the making. Remember, rumors and gossip of fixes were relatively common. Everyone in baseball knew about the corruption, including Joe, but until he heard Burns, Jackson could not know if Gandil was for real or not. Now that he knew a fix was actually in operation, what did Jackson do? He did exactly what he was banned from baseball for *not* doing, he informed his club.

In a 1949 interview with Furman Bisher, Jackson maintained he went directly to Comiskey. We do not know everything that he told him, but Jackson did say he mentioned the widespread rumors of a fix that surrounded the Series and asked to be benched so afterward there could be no question of his involvement: "Tell the newspapers you just suspended me for being drunk, or anything, but leave me out of the Series and then there can be no question."

Another version of Jackson's approach to the White Sox prior to the start of the series is given by Eliot Asniof in *Eight Men Out*. Asinof says Jackson went to White Sox manager Kid Gleason and asked to be benched because he didn't feel well enough to play. Asinof attributes Jackson's action to his feeling of guilt for having agreed to join the fix, but that is unsubstantiated conjecture. The fact remains that Jackson went to the club before the series began and at least asked to be benched. There remains, of course, the possibility that he told the club much more. In any event, his request was denied and he played.

Replogle's line of questioning is most interesting for the questions he did *not* ask. Here, for example, with Joe's account of his chance meeting with Burns, was an opportunity to follow up and perhaps uncover more about the fix. But Replogle did not want Joe to tell what he did as a result of this meeting, namely, tell Comiskey, so the subject was immediately dropped.

In other answers, Joe was mindful of Austrian's advice. He

used his very word and called Gandil the "instigator." At the end of one answer, he added, "I tried to win all the time." But before his testimony was completed he showed he was contrite by admitting, "I was ashamed of myself."

Joe emerged from the grand jury room accompanied by two bailiffs. When a reporter asked if he was in custody, Joe replied the bailiffs were his protection: "Risberg threatens to bump me off if I squawk. . . . I'm not going to get far from my protectors until this blows over. Swede's a hard guy." Joe may or may not have said these words. If he did, it was more likely he was afraid of the gamblers who, under the impression that he had agreed to join the fix, might now conclude that he had double-crossed them.

The news articles that described Joe's grand jury appearance are interesting for their content, but their style is more revealing. Though the Black Sox scandal was the biggest baseball story ever and received more front-page coverage than any other event in the history of the major leagues, many of the writers could not forget that they were writing about old Shoeless Joe, the yokel gone bad.

One article purported to be an interview with Joe following his grand jury appearance. In it Joe told of his conversation with the judge. "I got in there and I said: 'I got five thousand and they promised me twenty thousand . . . I never got the other fifteen.' I told that to the judge. He said he didn't care what I got, that if I got what he thought I ought to get for crabbing the game of the kids I wouldn't be telling him my story. I don't think the judge likes me. I never got that fifteen thousand that was coming to me. Before we broke up I climbed Gandil and McMullin and Risberg about it. They said to me, 'You poor simp, go ahead and squawk. Where do you get off if you do?' "

A paragraph or two later this writer has Joe respond to the

rumors that the third game, which the White Sox won 3 to 0, was honestly played: "Let me tell you something," said Joe. "The eight of us did our best to kick it and little Dickie Kerr [the only honest starting pitcher on the Chicago staff] won the game by his pitching."

In the second inning of the game he was talking about, Joe had leaned into a fastball and hit a line drive single to left field for Chicago's first hit. After a hit by center fielder Felsch, Joe scored the first run of the game on Gandil's single. In the sixth inning Joe hit another single. His performance in that game would seem to give the lie to his later assertion that he had tried to lose it, but the writer paid no attention to that. He probably paid no attention to Joe's words either, if in fact he had an interview with him. The words he put in Joe's mouth were just a new version of the old yokel stuff. Now his fellow crooks called him a poor simp, and Joe is made to mouth the insult himself.

One of the most famous lines to come out of American sports was supposedly addressed to Joe as he walked down the steps of the courthouse on his way from the grand jury room. The best-known version of that scene was written by Hugh Fullerton, the same man who had predicted in the spring of 1911 that Joe would fail because he was ignorant.

Fullerton's widely syndicated article first appeared in the *New York Evening World* on September 30, 1920, the day after Joe's grand jury appearance. More than any other single story, it created the public version of Joe's infamy and established the image of him that has been remembered.

Though he never talked to Joe (he once admitted this under oath), Fullerton felt no inhibition in writing about him. First he revived some of the shoeless yarns: "A major league club was forced to hog tie him to get shoes on him and he had wailed that he couldn't hit unless he could get toe holds." Then he quickly traced Joe's rise: "The unknown, the rough, uncouth mill-boy became one of the idols of the kids of America. In Cleveland, when he swaggered along the streets, crowds of small boys followed him, crowding close to him and perhaps dreaming that someday they too would play baseball 'like Joe.' When he was sold to the Chicago club there was a revolt of the fans in Cleveland. The kids had been deprived of their idol and refused to be comforted even when Tris Speaker came [to Cleveland] to occupy the pedestal. In Chicago they swarmed to him. . . . The ignorant mill-boy had become the hero of millions. Out on the hot prairies teams of 'Joe Jacksons' battled desperately with the 'Ty Cobbs.'"

Since it was the point of the whole article and the fulfillment of his own prediction, Joe's fall is shown with greater detail:

There came a day when a crook spread money before this ignorant idol and he fell. For a few dollars, which perhaps seemed a fortune to him, he sold his honor, and when the inevitable came, when the truth stood revealed, Joe Jackson went before a body of men and told the story of his own infamy. While he related the sordid details to the stern faced, shocked men, there gathered outside the big stone building a group of boys. Their faces were serious. More serious than those who listened inside to the shame of the nation's sport. There was no shouting, no scuffling. They did not talk of baseball or of anything else. A great fear and a great hope fought for mastery within each kid's heart. It couldn't be true. After an hour, a man, guarded like a felon by other men, emerged from the door. He did not swagger. He slunk along between his guardians, and the kids, with wide eyes and tightened throats, watched, and one, bolder than the others, pressed forward and said "It ain't so, Joe, is it?" Jackson gulped back a sob, the shame of utter shame flushed his brown face. He choked an instant, "Yes Kid, I'm afraid it is," and the world of faith crashed around the heads of the kids. Their idol lay in dust, their faith destroyed. Nothing was true, nothing was honest. There was no Santa Claus. Then, and not until then, did Jackson, hurrying away to escape the sight of the faces of the kids, understand the enormity of the thing he had done.

Fullerton's article was a bravura performance, perhaps the best piece he ever wrote. It seemed so real that few questioned its authenticity. But Joe always denied it. "I guess the biggest joke of all," he once said, "was that story that got out about 'Say it ain't so, Joe.' It was supposed to have happened . . . when I came out of the court room. There weren't any words passed between anybody except me and a deputy sheriff. . . . He asked me for a ride and we got in the car together and left. There was a big crowd hanging around in front of the building, but nobody else said anything to me."

Joe's walk down the courthouse stairs carried him out of organized baseball and into American legend. The little boy's words, real of fictional, entered the language.

17

THE BLACK SOX were indicted by the grand jury at the end of September. In mid-November Judge Landis was named the first Commissioner of Baseball. The change from the three-member National Commission to a single Commissioner was caused by long-standing resentment among the owners. Most of the resentment was over the decisions handed down by the Commission in cases involving the disputed ownership of players. Sometimes when a young player had signed two different contracts with two different clubs or when a player's contract had been declared void for some technicality, it happened that two clubs put forth a claim of ownership for the same player. The National Commission settled these disputes. No matter how they decided, the owner who lost was sure to feel cheated.

The National Commission had been formed as baseball's governing body when the National and American leagues came to terms with each other in 1902. By design, its first two members were the presidents of the two leagues and its third member, the chairman, was to be chosen by them. In the seventeen years of the National Commission, two of its members were constant: Ban Johnson, American League president, and August Herrmann, president of the Cincinnati Reds and the only chairman the Commission ever had. Herrmann's National League affiliation may have appeared to favor the National League clubs in disputes, but in actuality Herrmann was greatly influenced by the strongman of the Commission, Ban Johnson.

Ban Johnson, a hard-drinking, self-righteous former newsman, was the founder of the American League. As time passed, his self-image inflated until he believed his decisions were not only final and binding, but were above question. He expected the owners to do what he said and make no complaints.

In the early years Charles Comiskey had been one of Johnson's staunchest allies, but the great egos of the two drove them apart. Each wanted to view himself as the Founding Father of the American League or, at least, as a unique power in major-league baseball. Their enmity flared into open antagonism when the National Commission, led by Johnson, ruled against Comiskey in a player-ownership case. Comiskey was furious and set out to destroy Johnson.

Out of his hatred for Johnson, Comiskey supported the plan to replace the National Commission with a single Commissioner, a man chosen from outside baseball who would have power over the owners and the league presidents. If Comiskey couldn't drive Johnson out of the game, he would at least humiliate him and reduce his power.

But Ban Johnson did not quit. He hired private investigators to collect information which he could use to his own advantage, and he fought back. When he couldn't save the National Commission, he tried to put his man into office as the new Commissioner. The man he supported for the job was Judge McDonald, the judge who eventually presided over the grand jury that investigated baseball corruption. Without Johnson's intervention, the grand jury, which had been called to investigate charges of a fixed game in the National League between the Cubs and the Phillies, probably would not have turned its attention to the 1919 World Series. Johnson, aware of the fix and Comiskey's cover-up, wanted to expose the scandal, wreck the White Sox by banning the guilty men, disgrace Comiskey by exposing his hypocrisy, and drive him out of the game. At one point Johnson sent a go-between to Comiskey, offering to buy his endangered team.

Behind the scenes the major-league owners had split into two groups: Ban Johnson and his supporters on one side and all the anti-Johnson men, including Comiskey, on the other. Their battle was for control of major-league baseball and the ownership of the White Sox, one of the most profitable of all franchises. But the public was led to believe that the only issue in selecting the new Commissioner was the corruption of a few players, and so the coming of Judge Landis as the ruler of baseball was greeted with the anticipation that he would clean it up.

Kenesaw Mountain Landis was named to commemorate the site of the Civil War battle in which his father, Dr. Abraham Landis, lost a leg to a Confederate cannonball. Years later, when his father's commanding officer in that battle became secretary of state, he brought Kenesaw Mountain to Washington, D.C., as his private secretary.

Landis's legal education was scant. "Because I'm a lawyer," Landis once remarked, "persons naturally think I'm a college graduate. But I'm not and I'm proud of it. I just keep my mouth shut about where I acquired my knowledge of the law." But his political connections were strong. After managing one of Frank O. Lowden's Illinois gubernatorial campaigns, Landis was appointed judge of the United States District Court for the Northern District of Illinois by President Theodore Roosevelt.

Landis became a household name when he fined Standard Oil $29,240,000 for using illegal railroad rebates to suppress competition, but his ruling was overturned on appeal and the government never collected the fine.

There was never any telling what Landis might do when he sat on the bench. Sometimes he let obviously guilty men go free on the grounds that they had been underpaid or unduly tempted. But at other times he was severe and the papers called him "the lean clean whip of the government" and "the scourge of the disloyal."

When World War I began he favored military conscription. His words were carried by the national press: "We are a nation of cowards! A population which will sit back and let a militia fight for it is not worth fighting for. The men who are exposed to conscription are those who would not volunteer for service under any circumstances." When the United States entered the war, Landis went after pacifists and antiwar defendants with added vehemence.

In 1918 he presided over the "Chicago Trial," in which over one hundred members of the Industrial Workers of the World were charged with violating several wartime emergency laws. When they were found guilty, Landis imposed over two million dollars' worth of fines and handed down maximum sentences, which ranged from one to twenty years. When a defense attorney admitted under pressure from Landis that an appeal would be filed, the judge recalled all the defendants and added fines of twenty to thirty thousand dollars for each man.

Big Bill Haywood, leader of the IWW and the most famous of the defendants, wrote his autobiography while serving his Leavenworth sentence. After recalling the hardships suffered by his fellow defendants during the trial, he acknowledged that it had been difficult for Landis too: "During that season his time was much occupied and he could not go to as many ballgames as had previously been his custom." The judge must have resented it bitterly. That season his beloved Chicago Cubs won their first pennant in eight years and he had missed most of the season. In 1923, five years later and four years after the end of the war, President Coolidge commuted the sentences of the "war obstructors." Landis denounced him bitterly.

Landis sat on his last political trial after the war was over. The defendants were Victor Berger, Socialist congressman from Milwaukee, and five other socialists. The charge was conspiracy to obstruct the war effort, but the greater issues were the defendants' politics and national origin. The defense requested a change of venue; Berger was a German-Austrian émigré and Landis, they claimed, hated all Germans and German-Americans. They alleged that Landis had once said, "One must have a very judicial mind, indeed, not to be prejudiced against the German-Americans in this country. Their hearts are reeking with disloyalty."

Landis scoffed at the charge that he was prejudiced and refused the request for a change of venue. When Berger and the others were found guilty he gave them the longest sentence the law would allow — twenty years in Leavenworth.

The United States Supreme Court eventually reversed the decision and disqualified Landis for "prejudicial conduct before the trial." The defendants were released and never tried again. "It was my great disappointment to give Berger only twenty years," Landis told an American Legion convention. "I believe the law should have enabled me to have had Berger lined up against a wall and shot."

He was also an avowed Prohibitionist. When Prohibition became the law of the land he quickly became known as one of the harshest judges in the country on speakeasy operators. Though he himself drank illegal whiskey at the Chicago dinner parties he attended, Landis was not hindered by that in the performance of his judicial duties. He is said to have closed over six hundred Chicago speakeasies in two years and sent many of their operators to federal prison.

Two weeks after he became Commissioner of Baseball, in November 1920, Judge Landis addressed the issue of the indicted players. Their trial had not yet taken place, and would not for almost a year, but Landis issued his own verdict and sentence: "There is absolutely no chance for any of them to creep back into Organized Baseball. They will be and remain outlaws. . . . It is sure that the guilt of some of them at least will be proved."

Landis's ability to enforce his words was guaranteed when the owners voted to give him complete control of baseball. They bound themselves to honor all his decisions and punishments. They even waived their rights to go to court or complain in public. Several years later an owner finally challenged that decision and took Landis to court. But a federal judge ruled that the owners had in fact endowed the Commissioner of Baseball "with all the attributes of a benevolent but absolute despot and all the disciplinary powers of the proverbial pater familias." By their own hands the owners had set a despot in authority over the game and entertainment business they liked to call the National Pastime.

Unlike Landis, the criminal case against the Black Sox moved slowly and the suspended players had time on their hands. Soon after the grand jury hearings were over in the fall of 1920, Joe joined several of the other indicted players and formed a barnstorming team — they called themselves the Black Sox. Since they'd been ordered not to leave the state while waiting for their trial, they played most of their games in Illinois, though they did play a few in neighboring states. The men on the Black Sox were willing to play anywhere and against anybody, but they ran into the power of organized baseball. Frequently their requests to rent diamonds were refused, and sometimes their advertised appearances on publicly owned diamonds in parks or playgrounds were canceled by local authorities on what were called "moral grounds."

While waiting for the trial to begin, Joe and Katie lived in their Chicago apartment. Since he was stuck in Chicago and in need of income to replace some of his White Sox salary, Joe opened a small poolroom across from the University of Chicago, where he drew most of his customers from the student population.

Before the case came to trial, a new Illinois Attorney General was elected to office. When he assigned a prosecutor to the case, it was discovered that much of the case file was missing, including the testimony of the players and their signed waivers of immunity. The original indictments were dismissed and a second grand jury was impaneled. This time around, Jackson had a lawyer. He retracted his original grand jury testimony, but he and his colleagues were still re-indicted.

The trial finally began at the end of June, 1921. Seven players and ten gamblers stood indicted on a variety of conspiracy charges. The eighth player, Fred McMullin, had been dropped from the case due to lack of evidence. Most features of the case had changed. Three assistants of the former district attorney, who had helped prepare the original case for the prosecution, now reappeared as attorneys for the defense.

All the players showed up, but only a few of the gamblers actually appeared in court. Some just disappeared, and Hal Chase, whose name frequently came up as one of the original designers of the fix, simply ignored the indictment and stayed in California. The trial itself was as big a news event as the original exposé. The defendants and their attorneys, who numbered in the dozens, kept the trial lively. The court room was packed with fans every day. One afternoon the "Clean Sox" (the name given to the unindicted White Sox), led by manager Gleason, visited the court to wish the Black Sox well publicly.

The district attorney opened his case by announcing that the original confessions, the immunity waivers, and some of the testimony had been stolen from the files. This threw the court into confusion and long arguments about the admissibility of unsigned carbon copies of the confessions. It also reduced the State's case; all the district attorney could offer now was the testimony of two of the confessed fixers, Billy Maharg and Sleepy Bill Burns, the man brought back from Texas by Ban Johnson. Unlike the players, Maharg and Burns were granted immunity.

Neither Burns nor Maharg knew the whole story, but their version of the affair became the best known: the players, specifically Cicotte and Gandil, offered to fix the series for $100,000; through the treachery of the players and the machinations of other gamblers, some of whom worked for Arnold Rothstein, Burns and Maharg had been double-crossed when the White Sox won the third game of the series; neither of them gave any testimony that placed Joe in direct conversation with them about the fix.

At the conclusion of its case the State asked for jail sentences of five years and $2,000 fines. The jury deliberated for less than two hours and found all the defendants innocent of all charges. The Black Sox and the jurymen had dinner in an Italian restaurant. The next day Judge Landis issued his final decision on the Black Sox: "Regardless of the verdict of juries, no player that throws a ball game; no player that undertakes or promises to throw a ball game; no player that sits in a conference with a bunch of crooked players and gamblers where the ways and means of throwing games are planned and discussed and does not promptly tell his club about it, will ever play professional baseball."

Landis' all-encompassing edict was meant to cover every possible loophole, and served as the basis for Jackson's expulsion. Despite a widely held misconception, Jackson was not banned for anything he did on the diamond in the 1919 World Series, a point substantiated by Comiskey himself, who swore under oath he never saw Jackson play dishonest baseball, including in the 1919 World Series. Jackson was banned for not telling his team about the plot to throw the Series into which he'd been invited.

18

AFTER THE TRIAL Joe and Katie closed out their Chicago apartment and went home. The northern papers and some in the South said Joe went home in disgrace. But he didn't act as if he felt disgraced and he didn't hide. At first he worked with Katie in the dry-cleaning business they had started, the Savannah Valet Service. As soon as it got warm Joe accepted some of the many offers he had received to play semipro ball. The first offer took him to the New York City area, where he apparently earned between one and two hundred dollars for each game he played.

While he was playing in the New York area in the summer of 1922, the promoter of the team he played for organized a campaign to have Joe reinstated. He collected several thousand signatures on a petition that asked Commissioner Landis to clear Joe "in view of his acquittal by jury in a duly constituted court of Justice."

As part of his effort to collect signatures, the promoter arranged some public appearances for Joe. At one of these, in a New York dance hall, Joe surprised most of his listeners. They had expected him to act contrite and humbly to ask Landis for forgiveness. Instead, Joe said what was on his mind: "Of course, if Commissioner Landis sees fit to reinstate me, I will greatly appreciate it. But if he does not, then I don't care what he says. As long as I have strength I will play the game, even though I have to do so by myself."

At the end of the summer the petition was sent to Landis. He ignored it.

The next baseball season Joe stayed in the South. He was glad to be back on southern ballgrounds — they looked familiar and he felt at home. All over the South, fans welcomed him back. He frequently played with pickup teams or in exhibition games, but sometimes he signed on with teams in leagues, such as the South Georgia League, which had teams in Americus, Albany, Arlington, and three other small cities in Georgia.

The South Georgia League was outside the control of organized baseball and perfectly free to ignore Landis's rulings. Nevertheless, the owners had adopted a rule that prohibited them from signing any of the players on Landis's blacklist, which included over fifty players by the mid-1920s. Some fifteen of these players were blacklisted for life, the rest for a season or two. None of them had any recourse, for the major-league owners had granted Landis full power to blacklist any player if, in his opinion, such a move was for "the best interests of the game."

When the Americus club announced it had signed Joe for the coming season, the president of the South Georgia circuit said it couldn't be done. But the Americus owner, J. Rufus Lane, truly wanted Joe and he argued his case shrewdly. When his opposition claimed that Joe's presence would taint all the other players in their league and prevent them from ever moving up into organized baseball, Lane produced a telegram from the secretary of the National Association of Minor Leagues, which reminded everyone that organized baseball had nothing to do with the players in the South Georgia League. Then the opposition declared their league would get a bad reputation if Joe was allowed to play on one of their teams. Lane answered this charge by pointing out that Joe had gone to trial and had been found innocent. It was the kind of argument that appealed to logic and a sense of fair play, but Lane must have known it would not hold weight, for he immediately followed it with a reference to something his fellow owners would understand — money. He assured them that Joe would be the biggest attraction their league had ever had, and would make money for them all. The rule against blacklisted players was rescinded and Joe joined the Americus team.

When Americus signed him and fought to keep him on the team, Joe became a news item around the South and on the sports pages of the northern papers too. Interest centered on the moral issue of whether he should be allowed to play. In the *Atlanta Journal* one writer attacked Joe, calling him "an ignorant, illiterate fellow" whose very presence would taint baseball in Georgia. He assured the readers that the Georgia fans would not come out to watch a man like Joe play ball.

The league and the cities in which Joe now found himself playing were a long way from the American League and places like Chicago, Cleveland, or Philadelphia. As to prestige, even cities like Savannah and New Orleans were far off. In the face of such a drastic and sudden come-down in the many-leveled world of baseball, Joe might easily have turned inward to dwell on self-pity. But it was not in his style to sulk. In fact, his response was just the opposite.

Joe was rejuvenated by his return to playing in the South. The fans cheered him wildly, and all around the league they took up the old cry: "Give 'em Black Betsy, Joe, give 'em Black Betsy!" Perhaps Joe responded to the loving welcome of the fans, perhaps he just felt good to be home again. And, too, perhaps he wanted to demonstrate that even at the age of thirty-six he was still the same Joe Jackson on a baseball diamond. Whatever the reasons, he threw himself into the games with exuberance.

He started hitting in his very first game for Americus and never stopped. One week his totals for five games were two home runs, four triples and five doubles. He got sixteen hits in twenty-seven times at bat for a weekly average of .727! At the end of the season he led Americus to victory in the South Georgia League little world series. In the six games he got eleven hits in twenty-two times at bat. It seemed that every time he unleashed Black Betsy a blue darter whistled to some part of the field.

The players in the South Georgia League were crack semiprofessionals, but they were surely not as good as the major leaguers against whom Joe had once played. Some of his critics made light of his hitting by saying he was too good for the pitching he faced, that he had too much talent and experience. There was some truth to what they wrote, but in their eagerness to minimize Joe's performance, they missed the point of it all. Joe was simply playing as well as he could. His swing was still an action of grace and power, and though he may have had an easy time against the semipro pitchers, he was only doing what he had always done: standing at the plate and banging out the best the pitchers could offer. He drew record crowds around the league and the fans who came out to see him play went home well satisfied. Joe always gave them their money's worth and something to remember. Frequently, as with other teams in other leagues, the fans came out to see him hit and went home talking about his fielding.

In one of the little world series games he hit a grand-slam home run, but after the game the fans buzzed about the catch he'd made in the sixth inning. The batter sent a high drive to deep center field and the Americus fans groaned because it looked like a sure home run. But Joe took off after it, racing over the sparse outfield grass with his back to the plate. The ball soared through the air and Joe raced over the ground. With his back still to the plate, he caught up with the ball in deep center and caught it over his shoulder. The local writers acclaimed it as "the most sensational and spectacular play ever seen on a minor league diamond." In an earlier game he had raced in and caught a sinking line drive behind second base for a shoestring catch that saved the game. In an exhibition game played in Montgomery, Alabama, he made a racing, diving backhanded catch of a line drive which stood the Montgomery fans on their heads. The writers who made little of Joe's phenomenal hitting said nothing about his fielding or throwing. While they could argue that he overpowered the pitchers with his talent and experience and was nothing more than a big fish in a small pond when it came to batting, there was no way they could cheapen his performance in the field. A great catch is a confrontation between a fielder and a ball and has little to do with the quality of the other players.

The pattern established early in his big-league career held true. Some of the writers attacked Joe, others defended him. But the fans made their own decisions. Shoeless Joe belonged to them; when he came to town they went out to greet him. He was always featured in advertisements for games against the Americus team, which soon became known as "Shoeless Joe Jackson's Americus bunch." These games were more than mere athletic events, they were social events that involved whole towns. Frequently they were preceded by band concerts and barbecues, and crowds of two thousand men, women, and children were not uncommon. One poster told the fans, "This is the day that you young married people can tell your children about in the afteryears."

Even when the quality of the pitching in the South Georgia League was taken into account, Joe's hitting was spectacular. He seemed to get a hit almost every time he went to bat. Some of the writers in the northern papers, who followed Joe's career sporadically, had to admit that he still could hit. Before his first Americus season was over he was featured in a comic article about a fictional White Sox scout who claimed he'd discovered and signed the best-looking prospect he'd ever seen: "Man, he is a wonder. He can catch flies like a frog and cover more ground than a circus tent. He can run like a scared rabbit and hit, buddy, that boy sure can sock. I never seen such form at the plate. . . . Why, this guy is so recently from the cotton fields that spiked shoes hurt his feet and he takes his practice in tennis shoes and he bats with an old crooked bat that he holds with the crooked part toward the catcher. Why, man, he'd be a riot." When asked where he found this wonder, and what his name was, the scout answers, "Playing with Americus. I signed him for the White Sox. His name is Joe Jackson."

As soon as the little world series was over, offers poured in for exhibition games. Everyone wanted to see Joe play again.

Some promoters wanted the whole team, others wanted only Joe. "Must have you at once," a promoter from Fall River, Massachusetts, wired, "will make up what you lose." Other telegrams offered flat guarantees of up to two hundred dollars per game for Joe, or a percentage of the gate receipts. The Georgia Hussars wired, "Name lowest guarantee for which you will play." Joe received more offers than he could accept, and he continued to be in demand until he retired from active play. The promoters knew he could always draw a crowd, and the fans knew he'd always show them something to please.

For the first decade of his legal career, Milwaukee Attorney Ray Cannon arranged his schedule so he'd be free during the baseball season, which he spent as a right-handed pitcher in fast semi-pro leagues in Ohio and Wisconsin. Perhaps it was through his own baseball connections that he met Oscar "Happy" Felsch, a Milwaukee native, who became his client. In May 1922, Cannon wrote to Joe Jackson: "At the request of Oscar Felsch I am writing you concerning the cause of action which in my opinion you have against the Chicago American League Baseball Club, for back salary under a written and special contract."

Cannon specified the claims he was putting forth for Felsch: back salary for 1920; $1,500 that Comiskey had promised each player if the White Sox won the 1917 pennant; and his $700 share of the White Sox 1920 second-place money. Concerning the last item, Cannon added, "I have already compelled them to pay Felsch his share."

From his home in Savannah, Jackson had been trying himself to collect his second-place money. He'd written to American League President Ban Johnson, who turned the matter over to Commissioner Landis. (See Appendix C.) In April he had received Landis' ruling: "In view of *the crime in connection with the World Series of 1919*, of course the money about which you inquire cannot be paid to you." (Italics added.) Once again, Judge Landis took the position that baseball "law," as laid down by himself, superseded the American legal system, which had found Jackson not guilty. Jackson accepted Cannon's proposal by return mail.

Joe's civil suit, which ultimately pitted him and Ray Cannon against organized baseball, did not go to court for a year and a half. During that time a series of events unfolded which demonstrated Landis' special venom toward Jackson, the lengths to which organized baseball would go to prevent any improvement in the ballplayers' bargaining position, and Comiskey's willingness to use any means at all to win a fight.

Soon after taking Joe's case, Cannon wrote to Johnson seeking Joe's second-place money. In light of the fact that he'd gotten Felsch's with little trouble, he expected no problem. Johnson, in fact, was willing to settle the matter, but the question had to be put to Landis. Perhaps Landis saw Joe as Johnny Reb, or still remembered the news stories about "Slacker Joe." Whatever his reasons, Landis refused to release Joe's share.

The complexities of the civil suit were soon compounded. As a result of his own baseball experience and his knowledge of the mistreatment players received from major league owners, Cannon took unusual action. In October 1922, he announced the formation of a Baseball Players Union. A *New York Times* editorial opined that this was sure to make the owners nervous.

Before the year was out, a Milwaukee Attorney named George Hudnall was appointed special prosecutor to oversee a grand jury investigation of Ray Cannon. Neither Hudnall nor his firm had a criminal practice, making this appointment unusual. What he did have, however, were strong Republican party ties, and Cannon was a well-known Democrat who would go on to serve several terms in the U.S. House of Representatives. The political connections were important because the men around Comiskey and Landis, including Alfred Austrian, were nationally prominent Republicans.

By February 1923, the grand jury returned a two count

indictment against Cannon. One was for allegedly misinform-
ing clients about the severity of their legal problems (they faced
misdemeanors and he supposedly told them they faced felonies
and charged them accordingly) and the other was the charge
that he had bribed the district attorney with a case of imported
champagne. (This was during prohibition, but no charge of
violating the Volstead Act seems to have been brought.) An odd
part of the bribery charge, in which there are normally two
parties, the giver and the taker, was the absence of an
indictment against the district attorney.

In a letter to Jackson, Cannon offered an explanation for the
indictment and revealed the connection between Hudnall and
Comiskey: "Comiskey has deliberately framed on me, and has
with his money caused a grand jury in Milwaukee County to
return indictments against me. The detectives that he employed
in Chicago were the same detectives that employed a detective
agency in Milwaukee to shadow me, and *his own personal
lawyer in your case* [Hudnall], is the lawyer that was made the
special prosecutor before the grand jury, and the one who
signed the indictments against me, so you can see for yourself
what methods he will resort to in order to gain a point." (Italics
added.)

At some point in the investigation of Cannon, Hudnall was
replaced as special prosecutor. In December 1923, about a week
before Joe's case came to trial, the indictments against Cannon
were dropped at the request of the new prosecutor on the
grounds of insufficient evidence. But Comiskey's purpose had
been served. This harassment had succeeded in diverting
Cannon's attention while he was preparing Joe's case for trial.

Cannon rejected a settlement offer of $2,500 made by
Comiskey and the trial began in January 1924, at the Milwaukee County Courthouse. (The case was heard here because
the White Sox were a Wisconsin corporation.) Joe's suit rested
on two points. The first was his contention that he'd been
tricked by Grabiner into believing the ten-day clause had been
deleted from his contract before he signed it. The significance

of this claim lies in the fact that if the clause was legally part of the contract Comiskey would have the absolute right to terminate the contract at his own convenience, without even giving an explanation. If the clause was in effect, Joe would have no grounds on which to sue for breach of contract. But if it was illegally in the contract—that is, if Joe had signed as a result of Grabiner's misrepresentation—it would be inoperative and Comiskey would have to provide valid reasons for having terminated the contract.

The second point was the verdict in the Black Sox trial. Though Landis had declared Joe and the others guilty and had banished them for life, in the eyes of the law they were innocent men. If Comiskey wanted to argue that Joe's guilt in the Black Sox affair was sufficient cause to break his contract, then he would have to provide evidence that would outweigh the verdict in the Black Sox trial.

The White Sox were defended by Hudnall's Milwaukee firm and several lawyers from Austrian's office, though Austrian himself participated as a witness. While Joe was on the witness stand answering a series of questions about the name of a hotel, one of Comiskey's lawyers casually produced a document, held it up, and asked, "You were sworn to testify before the grand jury at Chicago on the twenty-eighth of September, nineteen-twenty, were you not?"

Joe answered, "Yes."

Before the interrogation could continue, one of Joe's lawyers, quick to understand that Comiskey's lawyer was holding a transcript of Joe's grand jury testimony, jumped up and objected on the grounds that all proceedings before a grand jury are "privileged, impressed with secrecy by law, a secrecy which must be held inviolable in court."

The judge, citing Wisconsin case law, allowed them to be used. The only pertinent issue was their potential to impeach Jackson by demonstrating that he was lying or had lied under oath. (That is, if the story he told in Milwaukee did not agree with what he had said to the grand jury in Chicago, one of the two stories must be perjury. The irony of the situation lay in the fact that Comiskey was now trying to use the false story pressed on Joe in 1920 to cheat him out of the money due on his contract.) The judge also ruled that though the jury could consider the fact that Joe had been indicted by the grand jury in Chicago, it must disregard a statement by Joe's lawyer that Joe had been tried on that indictment and found innocent.

Comiskey's lawyers now proceeded to read excerpts from Joe's grand jury testimony, asking Joe if in fact he'd made the sworn statements attributed to him. He denied some and admitted others. The fact that he had repudiated his grand jury testimony was never made clear to the Milwaukee jury. His lawyers' requests for copies of the grand jury documents being read from by Comiskey's lawyers were sidestepped.

When asked by Cannon how he had obtained the grand jury material, Hudnall could offer no explanation. When Comiskey was on the witness stand himself, he denied any knowledge of the grand jury records and said Austrian had obtained them. Austrian, also under oath, blandly claimed he'd received the material from the prosecutor's office after the Black Sox trial, an explanation that seemed to make no sense, since the prosecutor's office did not have these materials...that's why the original criminal indictments had been dismissed and a new grand jury impanelled.

Though the possibility was raised that these may have been the very records stolen from the grand jury files, neither Joe's lawyers nor the judge pressed the matter very forcefully. If they had, they might have discovered that the events of 1920, when rumors of baseball corruption were universal, had made allies of Charles Comiskey and Arnold Rothstein, each of whom was afraid that the grand jury testimony might prove harmful to him. Comiskey, who may have still harbored the hope that he could save his players if he could somehow suppress their grand jury testimony, was chiefly concerned that their testimony or the testimony of others may have exposed his role in the cover-up. Rothstein, whose name was mentioned frequently as the banker of the fix, feared that the testimony might contain evidence of his involvement.

While he was still under oath, attorney Alfred Austrian admitted that Rothstein had come to his office for a discussion, but he was not pressed to divulge the contents of that discussion. It seems likely that this was when they made their plan to offer $10,000 to the outgoing district attorney, or perhaps to one of his staff members, for the removal of the grand jury records. The stolen materials surfaced briefly in New York, where they were offered for sale to a newspaper by one of Rothstein's agents. The offer was declined. Then the materials disappeared until they turned up a few years later in the hands of Comiskey's lawyers. After the trial they were not seen again for sixty-five years.

During the three weeks of the trial the jury heard much conflicting testimony. From the grand jury records they heard Joe quoted as answering both yes and no when asked if he had done anything to fix the World Series. To confuse matters even further, Comiskey admitted under oath that in all the years Joe had played for his club, from 1915 to September 28, 1920, he did not know of one dishonest move ever committed by Joe on a ballfield.

Because many of the people involved in the fix were called to testify, the transcript of this trial provides the clearest version of what Jackson actually did, By 1924, when the immediate fallout from the Black Sox scandal had begun to settle, some of the participants felt freer to tell the truth. When they did, strong evidence emerged to support Jackson's claim of innocence.

Burns and Maharg testified that Jackson did not attend any of the planning meetings. Furthermore, neither of them ever spoke to Jackson about the fix. They testified they only spoke to Jackson's teammate, Lefty Williams, who said he was representing Jackson. Williams himself testified that he never asked for or received Jackson's permission to use his name with the fixers.

Following are two excerpts from the 1924 sworn testimony of Bill Burns and Lefty Williams. Their answers explain how Jackson's name got involved and why the gamblers believed he was in on the fix.

Burns, one of the first gamblers in contact with the corrupt players, was questioned by Hudnall:

Q: Who were the eight [players], who mentioned them?

A: Well, Cicotte and Gandil mentioned several; and they were all there *except Jackson; and Williams was kind of representing Jackson.* (Italics added.)

Q: How do you know Williams was representing Jackson?

A: Well, they mentioned to Williams.

Q: Who mentioned to Williams?

A: Gandil.

Q: What did he say?

A: He wanted to know if he was representing Jackson, and he said he was,—anything that Williams agreed to, why, it would be all right with Jackson.

Q: When you speak of the eight players do you mean the seven who were there, and Jackson?

A: Yes, sir.

It should be said that *nobody places Jackson at any of the planning meetings between the players and the gamblers.* Burns, and Maharg too, took the word of Williams and Gandil that Jackson was in. This accounts for Jackson being named by Maharg when he broke his story in September of 1920. (As for meetings held by the players without the fixers present, only Cicotte and Jackson himself place Jackson at such a session, but these assertions came in their grand jury testimony, for which both had been rehearsed by Alfred Austrian.)

Lefty Williams testified in 1924 by deposition. He was examined by one of Comiskey's lawyers, who read from Williams' 1920 grand jury testimony in the following exchange:

Q: You took care of him [Jackson], is that the idea?

A: He made the remark whatever we done would be agreeable with him. [*Note well. This is what Williams said in his scripted grand jury testimony. Soon he would dramatically change his story.*]

Q: Did you give Jackson his $5,000?

A: I did—I didn't give it to him, I throwed it on the bed, and I says, "There is your dough, there is the dough that we got."

In response to a question about the date of a meeting at the Warner Hotel in Chicago prior to the start of the Series, Williams said:

A: I could not exactly say the date, and I went down to the Warner Hotel, and I met Eddie Cicotte, Chick Gandil, Buck Weaver, and Happy Felsch and myself and two strangers. They introduced them as Sullivan and Brown, said they were from New York, they were the fellows going to try to put over this deal.

* * *

Q: Would you know these men if you were to see them now?

A: I believe I would. So we had this meeting, and they asked me what I thought. I said, "For $5,000 I wouldn't throw no World Series." I said, "That is not enough money for an ordinary working man to do a dirty trick." They said, "What do you think?" I said, "In my estimation I wouldn't consider nothing under $10,000." They said, "What does Mr. Jackson think, $10,000?" I said, "Whatever they do is all right with Mr. Jackson." I said, "I figured if I wouldn't get in on it it would be done anyway, and I haven't got any money, and I might as well get what I can get." It was agreed upon, and we all left.

Two things are of importance in these passages from Williams' 1920 grand jury testimony. The first is that Jackson is *not* at the meeting. The second is Williams presentation of himself as spokesman for Jackson. However, Jackson denied he gave Williams the right to represent him, and Williams' assertion is not corroborated by anyone else in the entire plot. What's more, under cross-examination by Ray Cannon in 1924, *Williams admitted he used Jackson's name without permission.*

Q: (Cannon) Did you yourself have any talk with Joe Jackson before or during the World Series with reference to the throwing of the Series to the Cincinnati team?

A: No, sir.

Q: Did Joe Jackson tell you at any time prior to or during the World Series that you could use his name in dealing with the gamblers?

A: No, sir.

Q: In reference to throwing the games?

A: No, sir.

Q: Did you have any talk with him in that connection at all?

A: No, sir.

Q: At any time?

A: No, sir.

Q: To your knowledge did Joe Jackson know his name was being used by anybody for the purpose of dealing with the gamblers?

A: No, sir.

Q: In throwing the 1919 World Series?

A: Not to my recollection, his name was never mentioned.

After admitting that he'd never gotten Jackson's permission to use his name, Williams tries to take back everything with his last answer, but it is only his weak attempt to deny his own treachery.

A puzzling aspect of Williams' payment to Jackson, in light of the fact that Jackson was not in on the fix, is *why* he gave him the money. There are several possible reasons. One, for example, could have been Williams' fear that Jackson might have found out in the future that his name had been used and that Williams had received his (Jackson's) share of the pay-off. In such an event, Jackson might have made a claim on the money. But I believe Williams acted out of remorse for having betrayed

Jackson, perhaps his closest friend on the team. We know from his own testimony that he received the money a day or two before the Series ended, but he didn't give the $5,000 to Jackson until after the Series was over. We can imagine him wrestling with the problem before he decided what to do. If his motivation was to make some amends, his action backfired in a way he could not have imagined. The best thing he could have done for Jackson was to have kept all the money himself, for it was the money that helped seal Jackson's fate.

The special verdict reached by the jury consisted of its answers to a series of questions posed by the court. When asked, "Did the plaintiff Jackson unlawfully conspire with Gandil, Williams and other members of the White Sox, or any of them, to lose or 'throw' any of the baseball games of the 1919 World Series to the Cincinnati Baseball Club?" the jury answered "No." The jury also found that Joe had relied on Grabiner's word and that Grabiner had intentionally misled him by reading the contract as if the ten-day release clause had been left out. It ruled that Joe was fairly entitled to a compensation from the White Sox of $16,711.04.

But before Joe could feel vindicated or even express some satisfaction, the judge overturned the jury's verdict. Then after citing discrepancies between Joe's grand jury testimony (as read to the court by Comiskey's lawyers) and some of the statements made by Joe on the witness stand in his own courtroom, the judge put Joe in jail for perjury. Joe's stay in jail was brief, and it appears he accepted an out-of-court settlement offered by Comiskey to forestall an appeal, but Joe never forgot the outcome of his suit. He became convinced that anything he did or said to try to clear his own name would somehow be turned against him. He didn't make another public statement about the Black Sox for twenty-five years.

Two years after the ironic conclusion of his suit against Comiskey, Joe's sense of being victimized, his feeling that he was being used as an example, was underlined by the Cobb-Speaker affair. Toward the end of 1926, the baseball world was stunned by the sudden announcement that Ty Cobb, playing manager of the Detroit Tigers, had retired from the game. A month later Tris Speaker, manager and star center fielder of the Cleveland Indians, followed. No explanations were offered in either case and since the two men were among baseball's biggest stars, rumors circulated freely. Finally Commissioner Landis announced that Cobb and Speaker had left baseball in the face of an accusation. Dutch Leonard, a former big-league pitcher, had charged that a game between the Tigers and the Indians had been fixed in the Tigers' favor and that, knowing this, Cobb and Speaker had bet on the outcome of the game. The game in question, won by the Tigers, was played on September 25, 1919, the same week that the Black Sox fix was being planned. It was never made clear why Leonard waited so long to make his charges.

The case against Speaker relied mostly on the word of Leonard, but the case against Cobb was supported by a letter Cobb had written to Leonard in October 1919, in which Cobb expressed regret that he hadn't been able to raise the cash quickly enough to place a bet. He was "considerably disappointed in our business proposition," Cobb wrote, "because we had $2000 to put into it and the other side quoted us $1400, and when we finally secured that much money it was about two o'clock and they refused to deal with us."

When Cobb and Speaker had been confronted privately with Leonard's accusation, they had chosen to retire silently from baseball rather than fight the accusation. But when Landis made the accusation public, both men asked to be reinstated so they could confront Leonard's charges and try to clear their names. In the hearings that followed, Speaker pointed out that there was no evidence against him save Leonard's words, though he could offer no cogent reason why Leonard would want to destroy his reputation.

In his self-defense, Cobb had to account for the letter. He admitted that he had written it, but he tried to explain away its incriminating content by saying he had merely responded to a request from Leonard to find out how much money had been bet on the game.

Landis took the case under advisement and promised a decision in due time. But before he could make a ruling on the Cobb-Speaker affair another scandal broke into the headlines. Swede Risberg, one of the Black Sox, claimed that back in 1917 the Detroit Tigers had thrown a four-game series to the White Sox. Almost fifty players and former players appeared at the hearings that followed Risberg's charges. Joe received an order from Landis to attend the hearing, but he refused. Later he explained, "It was none of my business. I owed nothing to baseball. I had given them my word once and they wouldn't take it."

Of all the players who testified, only Chick Gandil supported Risberg's version of the 1917 events, which included the delivery of over a thousand dollars from the White Sox players to the Detroit players. Several of the men who had been members of those teams admitted that money had changed hands, but they claimed it was a gift to the Detroit players for beating Boston, the White Sox rival for the 1917 pennant.

In public Landis made a show of patiently conducting the hearing into all the charges of corruption, but in private he complained: "Won't the goddamned things that happened before I came into baseball ever stop coming up?" Afraid that they might not, he announced a statute of limitations on past corruption. After a due pause, he ruled that the charges raised by Risberg against the Tigers and the White Sox and the charges made by Leonard against Cobb and Speaker had not been proved. Nothing was done to any of the players accused by Risberg. Cobb and Speaker returned to baseball, though neither of their original teams wanted them back. Speaker went to Washington, Cobb went to Philadelphia, where he closed out his career playing for Connie Mack.

In 1933, at the age of forty-five, Joe stopped playing baseball. But he had a chance to remain in the game when he was offered the managership of a Greenville team in one of the semiprofessional industrial leagues, a descendant of the old mill teams for which he had played almost thirty years earlier. Some of the league officials were afraid, however, that Joe's presence might cause problems with organized baseball, even though their league was not part of organized baseball. Their fears were based on past actions taken by Landis.

Perhaps they had the Dickie Kerr case in mind. Kerr, then a rookie, was the hero of the 1919 Clean Sox. He won the two games he pitched in that World Series and many claimed he salvaged what little was saved of the White Sox honor. To reward his series performance and his thirteen wins in the regular season, Comiskey paid him $4,500 for 1920. In 1920 Kerr won twenty games, but Comiskey refused to increase his salary. Kerr complained and said he would sign with a Chicago semipro team that had offered him $5,000 for a shorter season. But he declined the semipro offer and came back to the White Sox for the 1921 season. With the Black Sox gone, the team was only a remnant of its former self: they won sixty-two games that year and Dickie Kerr won nineteen of them. Comiskey again refused to raise his salary and Kerr accepted an offer to play semipro ball in Texas for more money. That season his Texas team played a game or two against another semipro team, the touring Black Sox, which included on its roster several of the men who had been banished. Comiskey reported the incident to Landis and Dickie Kerr, the hero of the 1919 White Sox, was suspended from organized baseball for one year.

Kerr was suspended because, in the eyes of organized baseball, he had been contaminated by his contact with some of the Black Sox. The men who operated the semiprofessional leagues in Greenville were well aware of the problem of contamination and its possible consequences. Joe, the most famous of the Black Sox, was potentially the biggest contaminator, so they felt they ought to clear his participation with Landis before they signed him. This led to a major effort to clear his name. Mayor John Mauldin of Greenville headed a drive that collected over five thousand signatures on a petition addressed to Landis. In mid-December, amid a flurry of news reports, Mauldin mailed the petition and an application for Joe's reinstatement to the Commissioner's office.

Most of the press treated it as a quaint and lost cause, but a few writers felt it was time to end Joe's punishment, whether he'd been guilty or not. They canvassed recognized baseball men for their opinions on the petition, but they were answered only by what one of them called a "terrified silence." Then on December 21, the *New York World Telegram* published an interview with Ed Barrow, business manager of the New York Yankees, who was described as the one major-league official who "had the gumption and the human sympathy to come out in favor of the reinstatement of Joe Jackson."

Barrow's support was mostly for the wrong reasons. He said he believed that Joe was "starving down there, eking out a bare and brutal living pressing pants." It was understandable that Barrow should believe this, for most of the frequent references to Joe which continued to appear in the national press stressed that he had failed in life just as he had morally failed in baseball. He was usually described as poor, almost destitute.

In the early 1930s, shortly after the start of the Depression, while Joe was still playing semipro ball, the Associated Press sent out a story about him that ended "The former star gets only $5 a game now and $7.50 for a doubleheader. 'Say it ain't so, Joe.' " Katie clipped this article from the newspaper and pasted it into one of her scrapbooks beside a contemporary letter from a baseball promoter who offered Joe a minimum of $150 a game or 40 percent of the receipts if he agreed to a series of games in the Piedmont region. On the next page Katie pasted an article about the Savannah Valet Service.

The stories about Joe's life as a pants presser were based on the business Joe and Katie owned, the Savannah Valet Service, a dry-cleaning establishment that employed over twenty people in its two store fronts and its cleaning plant. While the wire services offered yarns about Joe's poverty, he was in fact a reasonably prosperous businessman. He also owned a $10,000 home and two automobiles. While these figures do not add up to wealth, they must be seen in the context of the Great Depression. By most standards, and certainly by the materialistic ones used by the writers, Joe was successful. He was earning more money than he had when he played in the major leagues. But as always, most writers wrote what they wanted about Joe, as if he were a fictional character whose exploits they were inventing. Like most other readers of the sports pages, Barrow read of those exploits and believed them.

He also believed the earlier yarns, so as part of his defense of Joe's reinstatement Barrow offered an excuse for Joe's crime: he had fallen into temptation in 1919, Barrow explained, because he was "a man of such small mentality."

But Barrow's basic reason for supporting Joe was compassion. "I believe he has done a long and sufficient penance," Barrow said, "and that it would be the human thing to lift the bars and let him run that club in Greenville. After all, it is not in Organized Baseball and no harm would be done to anybody."

Before the ink was dry on the Barrow article, it was attacked by Westbrook Pegler, whose syndicated column appeared in almost two hundred newspapers with a total readership of twelve million. Pegler believed the appeal should be automatically denied. While arguing that eternal banishment was the smallest sentence the Black Sox deserved, he expressed his regret that Joe and the others had not been sent to jail. At the very least, he complained, the government should have prosecuted them for income tax evasion.

Pegler lectured his readers on the wages of sin, reminding them that good citizens "will turn on a man who throws a ballgame and crush him." By the time he reached the end of the column his rage had turned to frenzy: "I am against the proposal to reinstate Jackson feeling that he and the others should be made horrible examples. Show them any consideration and you will set an example which might lead to grafting in public office . . . and the degradation of government, particularly in Chicago, New York and Illinois. . . . The question of Jackson's reinstatement simply comes to this. . . . Will the citizens condone misconduct in the high places of American life or will they not?"

Pegler's view that the Black Sox should be held up perpetually as horrible examples was shared by Judge Landis, who was absolutely adamant in his refusal to reinstate any of them. Landis was unrelenting toward all the Black Sox, but he seems to have had special animosity toward Joe. Described by a friendly biographer as "a man who never forgot and rarely forgave," Landis must have remembered that Joe Jackson was both a southerner and one of the most publicized "slackers" of World War I.

Three weeks after Christmas Landis issued his ruling on the petition for reinstatement: "This application must be denied."

Down in Greenville, despite Landis's ruling, Joe got the job anyway. The next year he sold Savannah Valet and his house and he and Katie moved back to Greenville. After a brief try at the restaurant business — they ran a big barbecue place out on a highway — they bought a liquor store in West Greenville, the part of town that had once been Brandon Village. Their old neighbors and friends welcomed Joe and Katie back. The business was successful and it gave Joe time to follow baseball.

Over the next seven or eight years he managed several local teams, ending with Woodside Mill in the King Cotton League. After he retired from managing he was offered the chairmanship of the protest board of the Western Carolina Semi-pro League. He accepted, and held the post for the rest of his life.

The faith demonstrated by his neighbors and fellow southerners was shared by fans around the country, many of whom wrote to let him know they thought he was innocent. From 1920 on there was a steady trickle of mail, but whenever an article about him appeared a rush of mail was sure to follow. In the summer of 1942, *Sporting News* published a feature on his life since the scandal. The article was written by Scoop Latimer, sports editor of the *Greenville News* and the same writer who had first published the nickname "Shoeless Joe" back in 1908 when Joe was playing for the Spinners.

Latimer interviewed Joe on his fifty-fourth birthday. When Latimer arrived at Joe's house, Joe was still resting in bed. He had had a heart attack and his doctor ordered rest. But Joe got out of bed to greet some neighborhood boys who came over to give him his birthday present, a replica of Black

Betsy. Joe had given the original to the mayor of Greenville a few years earlier. While Latimer interviewed Joe, the boys helped celebrate Joe's birthday by eating the cake and homemade ice cream Katie served them.

Joe reminisced. Among other things, he denied that anyone ever said, "Say it ain't so" to him and maintained his innocence in the scandal: "Regardless of what anyone says, I'm innocent of any wrongdoing. I gave baseball all I had. The Supreme Being is the only one to whom I've got to answer. If I had been guilty of 'laying down' in the Series, I wouldn't be so successful today, for I'm a great believer in retribution. I have made a lot more money since being out of baseball than when I was in it. And I have this consolation . . . the Good Lord knows I am innocent of any wrongdoing."

Joe still loved baseball. He said he would follow it again if he were a young man starting out. When asked why, he answered, "There's a lot of pleasure to be found in the game." It was a revealing answer. As boy and man he had played baseball for forty years. For part of his life it had been his profession. It had brought him to national fame and later into national disgrace. Yet the first thing in his mind when he praised the game was the pleasure it offered him as a player.

Among the letters Joe received were a few dated between December 1943 and January 1944, during the Second World War. Up in an army hospital in Michigan a wounded soldier named Charlie was in critical condition. He had lost both legs in battle and he was fighting for his life. One afternoon he told his buddy Jack about the times his father used to take him to see Joe Jackson play in Chicago and how Joe had become his idol. Over twenty years later Joe was still his idol.

Jack traced Joe to Greenville and sent a letter to the *News* suggesting that a note from Joe would do a lot to cheer up

Charlie. Joe heard about the request and responded. A few days later he got a letter from Jack.

Dear Joe:

I could say thank you and let it go at that, but I can't. If you live a hundred years, you'll never make a man more happy than you did this day. I've seen men die and it mattered not, but today I saw a legless kid laugh over the gift and Christmas card marked Shoeless Joe Jackson and I couldn't keep back the tears. . . .

I'm no ball fan. I've heard about you but gave it no thought. For the rest of my life I'll remember you, not as a ballplayer, but as a man, a man who found time to bring happiness to an unlucky kid. From this Christmas and always may God go with you, Joe Jackson, as he does with the great.

When you hear bells ring, and all those songs in the street and everyone knows that Christmas is here, remember that we, Charlie and I, will be thinking of you. Charlie will be seeing you in uniform and tossing the ball before cheering thousands. I'll be thinking of you as a busy man who took time out to make a beautiful Christmas for my friend Charlie.

The next mail brought a letter from Charlie's brother, who still lived in Chicago. Charlie was not yet able to write his own letter, but his brother assured Joe that his message had improved Charlie's morale beyond everyone's expectations. "To Charles and all of us you will always remain the immortal Shoeless Joe Jackson. God bless you, Joe. We have never lost faith in you."

Joe and Katie also had a more personal interest in servicemen. They never had children of their own, but they were virtually parents to one of Joe's nephews, who lived with them from infanthood until the day he joined the navy.

Bringing up his nephew was the closest Joe got to having a son, but his special relationship with all kids, begun when he was a young man, never faded. In Greenville the boys followed him around and visited when he was ill. Even after the Black Sox scandal kids from all over the country, and from Canada and Cuba too, wrote to him. And not only boys. One Fathers' Day he received a card from a girl who called him "my second favorite daddy."

When Joe turned sixty, in 1948, the event was celebrated with a "Joe Jackson Night" at the Brandon Mill ballgrounds.

The old diamond had been reversed. Center field was where home plate used to be, and a concrete grandstand squatted on the spot where the center field dump had been, the dump from which Joe had heaved his mighty show-outs. The old textile league had also changed and Brandon Mill was playing in the Western Carolina League. All these things had changed, but the people's affection for Joe had not. On a rainy night twenty-five hundred of them turned out to show how they felt.

The grandstand was packed and the sidelines were crowded. Sitting in a drizzle waiting for the pre-game birthday ceremony, the crowd took up a spontaneous chant: "You got a tough break, Joe! You got a raw deal!"

A great ovation met Joe as he walked out to home plate. He said a few simple words of thanks and then he was given some presents: a radio, a lounging robe and slippers, a Good Luck floral horseshoe from the Greenville professional team, now in the South Atlantic League. There were other gifts too, and then someone passed a hat. The fans tossed in coins as they or their parents had for Joe's Saturday Specials.

Joe accepted the gifts graciously, but he was reticent about taking the money. He didn't like the idea of anybody thinking he was broke and in need of a handout. When he was assured of the spirit in which the hat had been passed and the coins contributed, he graciously accepted the silver too.

The big birthday party for Joe was picked up by the wire services as a human interest story and accounts of it appeared in newspapers around the country. As soon as the papers hit the newsstands, it seems, birthday cards and letters began to pour in. Some were from boys who had read about him and wanted his autograph, but most were from older fans, men and women who had seen him play. Since no address had been published in the news stories, the letters were addressed to "Shoeless Joe Jackson, Greenville, South Carolina" and on the envelopes carried such notes to the mailman as "Baseball Immortal," "Former Chicago White Sox Great Left Fielder," "Ex-Ballplayer," and "Member of the 1919 Chicago White Sox Baseball Club." One was written by a kid in Illinois on the back of a World War II "War Shipping Administration Statement of Cargo Availability" form. And one was from a lawyer in Nashville, Tennessee, who wrote, "I am going to call to your attention one time when you appeared at bat forty years ago, which you have perhaps forgotten."

The lawyer went on to describe a game in Chattanooga in which Joe had hit a ninth-inning home run. His recollection of the game, seen when he had been "a young boy," matches the contemporary box score with two exceptions. He recalled the wrong pitcher on the mound for Chattanooga, and he remembered the score being 1 to 0 before Joe's home run when in fact it had been 3 to 2.

He recalled that the first Savannah batter in the top of the ninth reached first base. With Savannah one run down, he continued, "naturally, the play during those days was for the next man to sacrifice. I saw Bobby Gilks walk out from the bench in his citizen's clothes when you went to the plate and evidently tell you to hit the ball and not lay it down or sacrifice. The first ball pitched you knocked at least one hundred feet over the right field fence. . . . I was then a boy and this performance made a great impression on me and I followed your career throughout the years."

Joe's lawyer-fan could not resist a comment about Judge Landis, who had died a few years earlier. "Ordinarily I feel that perhaps unkind things should not be said about a man after he is dead, but . . . he [Landis] disregarded the findings of the jury and the judgment of the court in your case and thereby deprived you for life from making a comfortable living." Joe's ability to earn a living came to mind easily. The news wire stories about the "Joe Jackson Night" stressed the facts that Joe was still feeling ill from a recent heart attack and that he was destitute. The lawyer wrote that the article he had read left "the inference that you have but little if any property and since you . . . may not be able to work for some time, you may need help. I understand of course, that you are not a pauper or an object of bounty, and I trust that you will receive this letter in the same spirit in which I write it and will accept the enclosed check for $50 in the same spirit which prompts me to send it to you. If so, you never have received and will not receive a gift to which you are more welcome. . . . If you will accept it, I just hope the . . . check will do you one tenth as much good as it does me to give it to you."

The lawyer's impulse to repay Joe in some small way for the pleasure he had given him over the years was an honest one. It grew out of respect. Joe was still the hero of his boyhood. But his gift was misdirected.

Joe bitterly resented the stories that presented him as a broken-down old ballplayer headed for the poorhouse. The fact that the story about his being broke was a total lie did not make him feel better. It made him feel worse. He felt it as another attempt by the press to make him into something that he wasn't. He had worked hard and made good money in the twenty-eight years he had been banished from baseball, and now the writers were at it again, telling everyone who cared to read their articles that Joe Jackson was a poor failure. He sent the $50 check back by return mail. He also sent a letter.

We do not have a copy of the letter Joe sent, but in response to it the lawyer from Nashville answered, "I thoroughly understand and fully appreciate the spirit or motive which prompted you to return the check. You may be fully assured that my feelings are not hurt one wit on account of the fact that you declined it. I am glad to know that you are feeling much better."

In 1949 Joe finally told a public version of the fix, but it was simplified and watered down. Perhaps he'd forgotten all the things that had actually happened, or had gotten them confused and jumbled together in his mind. Perhaps he had become vulnerable himself to the lies that were told about him, for in a comment on his early career he mistakenly recalled that in 1911 he'd been ahead of Cobb a few weeks before the season ended.

But by this time the details of the fix were not what mattered most. The hundreds of people who wrote to him were more concerned with memory and faith. They could not forget Joe; they wanted to believe.

A man from Ozone Park, New York wrote: "You may think it odd of me, someone you don't know, to write you, but I just felt I had to write you to let you know how I feel. . . . I wish something could be done to correct the great mistake and injustice done to you. . . . I know I speak for many thousands of people. Best of luck and health to the greatest ballplayer that has ever been."

An old fan from Ohio sent Joe a photograph of a surgeon and an Ohio Supreme Court justice, both of whom had been among Joe's Royal Rooters when they'd welcomed him back from the shipyards in the spring of 1919.

The man who'd been the Savannah bat boy in 1909 wrote from Arizona to say he well remembered "what a grand fellow you were and how you could plaster that ball." The current bat boy of the New York Yankees, on the advice of someone on the team, wrote to ask for batting tips.

The letters came from Hobby's Garage in Kentucky; a retirement home in Florida; a V.A. hospital in Illinois; a mother in Brooklyn who wrote about her son; a court clerk in Pennsylvania; a farmer in Alabama; an old man in Connecticut who asked what he could do to help clear Joe's name.

Many of the letters came from boys requesting Joe's autograph, but most were from fans who had seen him play, who remembered and still could see Joe gliding over the grass or setting up in the batter's box with Black Betsy on his shoulder: "You were my idol when I was a kid trying to play ball," wrote an old man from Texas. "The first real bat I ever owned was a Joe Jackson model . . . so after all these years it is good to hear you defend yourself. We believed in you all the time, Joe, and I hope you all the best, for no one will ever pinch hit for you in the hearts of us oldtimers who seen you play."

A major effort to clear Joe Jackson's reputation was launched in February 1951. The South Carolina State Senate and House of Representatives passed a "concurrent Resolution memorializing the Commissioner of Baseball to reinstate 'Shoeless Joe' Jackson as a member in good standing in professional baseball." The Resolution quickly summed up most of the arguments that have been made in Joe's favor:

Whereas, nearly thirty-two years have elapsed since the scandal of the 1919 World Series; and

Whereas, though the story has frequently seen print, fact and fancy have been so confused that today it still is not known what actually took place; and

Whereas, Joe Jackson was acquitted of all charges of conspiracy by a jury of 'twelve good men and true'; and

Whereas, though set aside by the Judge, a jury verdict against the Chicago White Sox was awarded him for the balance of his contract; and

Whereas, the fact that his fielding average for the Series of 1919 was perfect and the fact that in that series he set a record of twelve hits for a World Series (a record that still stands though once tied) offer strong evidence that he was no party to a conspiracy to "throw" the series; and

Whereas, he has suffered lifelong ignominy as a result of the scandal of 1919 and his subsequent banishment from organized baseball; and

Whereas, persons actually convicted of crimes are not barred from the pursuit of their trades and professions upon their return to private life; and

Whereas, thirty-two years is far too long for any man to be penalized for an act as to which strong evidence exists that it was never committed by him; and

Whereas, Joe Jackson has been active in civic matters, particularly in programs for the benefit of young boys, since his return to private life; and

Whereas, the General Assembly of South Carolina believes him to have been innocent of any conspiracy to "throw" the World Series of 1919; and

Whereas, though he is now too old to participate in baseball, the General Assembly feels that he should be exonerated by baseball as he was exonerated by juries in both criminal and civil courts.

Judge Landis, Joe's old nemesis, died in 1944. In the Spring of 1945 the owners elected Albert "Happy" Chandler, former Governor of Kentucky and a sitting U.S. Senator, to succeed him. But by 1951, in light of some of Chandler's actions, many owners regretted their choice. When Branch Rickey had sought approval to bring Jackie Robinson into organized baseball and thereby break the tacit ban against African-American players that had been in place since 1884, Chandler overruled the majority of owners and sided with Rickey.

Around this same time, Chandler further angered the owners by siding with the players in a battle over the players' pension fund. As Curt Flood recalled this episode in his excellent autobiography *The Way It Is*, "For one mad moment, Chandler behaved, Heaven help us, like a neutral commissioner.... [He] went to bat for the hired hands.... He implied the owners were trying to welch. As far as I know, this was the only occasion on which any Commissioner of Baseball has ever permitted facts to undermine his relationship with the owners. In 1951, Chandler was replaced...."

Chandler's job was in jeopardy and the Commissioner's Office was in a state of siege when the South Carolina Resolution arrived. Years later, Chandler said he never even saw it, and this is probably true.

We are left to wonder what Chandler would have done in response to the Resolution if he had been solidly entrenched as Commissioner. In his later years, when Jackson's name was back in the news, Chandler made several public statements that indicate he would have taken some positive action.

In 1984 he told *Sports Collectors' Digest*: "I think Joe Jackson had bad treatment and that baseball people are obligated to do something about it. It's an injustice that ought to be corrected by the baseball people. I don't think he ever did anything in connection with that scandal and he was an outstanding baseball player. This effort [to clear his name] is a mission of mercy and I hope it succeeds."

A few years later, when the film *Eight Men Out* was showing, Chandler spoke up again in Jackson's favor, this time in the *New York Times*: "It's been a long time. This injustice needs to be corrected. They gave him shabby treatment. I'd support his reinstatement. He wasn't a well-educated man but a great player. He deserves to be in the Hall of Fame."

Several months after the South Carolina Legislature sent its appeal to the Baseball Commissioner, Joe broke onto the sports pages once again. Up in Cleveland, a thousand miles away, the fans were talking about his reputation.

The Cleveland baseball writers and the Cleveland Indians ballclub had decided to create a Cleveland Baseball Hall of Fame. Ballots were printed on which the fans could vote for the charter members of the new Hall — their choice for the best man who ever played for Cleveland at each position. The ballot listed the names of several legendary players — Cy Young, Larry Lajoie, Tris Speaker — but Joe's name was not included. The fans, particularly the old-timers, protested his exclusion. They said Joe had never been suspected of anything but being the best hitter in baseball during the years he'd played for Cleveland. The argument made sense to the men who'd made the ballot and Joe's name was included.

When the fans' votes were counted, Joe was among the top four vote-getters and was chosen as one of the charter members of the Cleveland Hall of Fame. He was invited to attend the formal induction ceremonies in early September, but he was too ill to go.

Though he was not there in person, the presence of his name was enough to provoke indignant responses in the press. One writer chastised the Cleveland fans for honoring a man of "impugned baseball integrity."

As if in answer to the grumblings in the press, the men behind the Cleveland Hall of Fame decided to create a ceremony for Joe that would replace the official induction ceremony he'd missed. They told their story to Ed Sullivan, whose "Toast of the Town" television variety show had millions of Sunday-night viewers. Sullivan was interested and Joe was booked for the "Toast of the Town" show of December 16.

The scenario would be simple. Ed Bang, an old-time Cleveland writer who had covered Joe's career with the Naps, would introduce him to the national television audience. Tris Speaker, who had replaced Joe as the star of the Cleveland outfield, would present him with a gold clock, the emblem of his membership in the Cleveland Hall of Fame.

But when Ed Bang phoned to tell him the good news, Joe thanked him and declined the invitation. He gave no reason. He only said he did not care to go. After failing to convince him, Bang asked him to call if he changed his mind.

When Joe's family and friends heard about the Ed Sullivan show, they tried to make Joe change his mind. Katie wanted him to go, and his sisters and brothers agreed. Even his friends said it would be a chance to clear his name. But Joe had his doubts. Every other attempt to clear his name had failed. The usual result was a rush of articles about what a yokel and a crook he was. He did not want that to happen again.

But his family and friends persisted and Joe finally agreed. Since he was still weak from a recent heart attack, his doctor agreed to travel with him. The arrangements were made for Joe and Katie to take the long trip north again.

Joe's scheduled appearance on national television was publicized and his fans around the country waited to watch the show. But just as he had done in 1908 when his first trip north to Philadelphia had been announced, he disappointed his fans. Ten days before the show, on Wednesday, December 5, 1951, Joe had another heart attack and he died.

Shoeless Joe Jackson was buried in Woodlawn Memorial Park in Greenville. Among the hundreds at his funeral were a handful of major leaguers and dozens of men from the local mill teams and semipro teams throughout the South.

There were so many flowers the funeral director and his staff didn't know what to do with them all, so they piled them up in a tangled heap on top of Joe's grave. One woman made a large baseball and a six-foot bat out of white flowers, but they got lost in the heap.

Soon after Joe died, several articles appeared calling for his reinstatement, but when nothing happened the articles ceased. That was almost thirty years ago. From time to time a plea for his reinstatement still appears, for there are many people who would like to see his name cleared and his banishment lifted so he can take his place in the Baseball Hall of Fame. But perhaps it is too late.

As a player there is no doubt he belongs in the Hall of Fame. But it might be a disservice to the memory of the man to take his name out of banishment, for it was in his banishment that he achieved his greatest feat: under the weight of a great slander he played baseball as long as he was able and he carried himself with dignity.

If Shoeless Joe Jackson is no better than the men enshrined in the Baseball Hall of Fame, men like Cobb, Comiskey, Landis, and McGraw, he is also no worse. But they have become legendary figures known for their heroic deeds and he has become a symbol of failure and corruption. As he told an old Greenville friend the day before he died, "I don't deserve this thing that's happened to me." In truth, Joe Jackson's greatest crime was his innocence.

The Legend Continues

As I Write This, Joe Jackson has been dead for forty years and it is seventy-one years since he was thrown out of baseball. But paradoxically, his name is known to more people today than ever before.

When the original version of this book was first published in 1979, Jackson was an all-but-forgotten figure in the shades of baseball history. Since then, he has made a remarkable comeback. This book had something to do with the resurgence of Jackson's legend, but I think it really began with the early 1980's release of *The Natural*, starring Robert Redford. This film. of course, was based on Bernard Malamud's novel of the same name, and Malamud himself on several occasions revealed that Shoeless Joe was the main model for Roy Hobbs, though the shooting incident was based on the career of Eddie Waitkus. Those who knew the genesis of the fictional Roy Hobbs were disappointed with the Hollywood ending tacked on to Malamud's novel, in which the forces of evil win out in the end as they did in Jackson's case.

Around this time, I was contacted by a New Jersey school teacher named Ray Allen who had read my book and wanted to do something to clear Jackson's name. This contact led to the formation of The Shoeless Joe Jackson Society (114 Robin Hood Road, Greenville, South Carolina, 29607), a small, loose-knit organization originally dedicated to the goal of clearing Jackson's name in the Baseball Commissioner's official registry of players and/or getting him installed in the Hall of Fame, two related but separate goals. In light of the so-called "Rose Decision," however, in which the directors of the Hall of Fame ruled that no player on the Commissioner's Ineligible List could be inducted into the Hall, the Society's efforts have been refocused solely on the Commissioner's Office.

Spokespeople for the Society include Lester Irwin, a nephew of Katie Jackson who coaches baseball in Greenville; Attorney David Carlson of Chicago; baseball writer Paul Green of Ridgeway, Wisconsin; and Ray Allen.

Among those who have publicly supported the Society's goals, in print or on the air, are the late former Baseball Commissioner A.B. Happy Chandler; Harvard Law School Professor Alan Dershowitz; *Sports Illustrated* writer Nick Dawidoff; *Sporting News* columnist Art Spander; actor D.B. Sweeney, who portrayed Jackson in *Eight Men Out;* and Ted Williams, who expressed sympathy for Jackson's plight in an interview he gave at the Hall of Fame. (See Appendix H.)

In the late 1980s, the release of two Hollywood films, *Eight Men Out* and *Field of Dreams*, elevated Jackson's "comeback" to a new plateau. Millions of people who had never heard of him before knew him now, but they were left with a mixed message about who he really was.

* * *

It is the evening after the first game of the 1919 World Series. Shoeless Joe Jackson is lying on the bed in his hotel room, one arm resting on his face. There's a knock on the door; Joe says come in.

It's Fred McMullin, the White Sox utility infielder. He closes the door and stands near it. He reaches into the inner pocket of his sports coat, pulls out an envelope and says, "I've got something for you, Joe."

Jackson doesn't look up, nor does he acknowledge McMullin's presence in any other way. All he does is say in a dull monotone, "On the dresser."

McMullin places the envelope on the dresser top, turns to Jackson and says, "Swede said he'd appreciate it if you'd ease up a little on the field." After a suggestive laugh he adds, "You looked awfully good out there today."

Jackson remains impassive. McMullin departs without another word, closing the door behind him.

It is a compelling scene, revealing at once Jackson's complicity in the fix and his ambivalent attitude toward his own corruption. The envelope, we are meant to understand, contains Jackson's pay-off money. The message from Swede Risburg, apparently the enforcer in this conspiracy, is meant to allude to Jackson's paradoxical on-field performance: he has agreed to enter the scheme, yet he seems to be playing to win.

The problem with the scene is that it never happened. It is a complete fiction. Nevertheless, it has been seen, absorbed and believed as *fact* by millions of moviegoers who saw the 1988 film *Eight Men Out*.

The scene is mentioned here as an example of the kinds of distortions and disinformation to which Jackson was and still is subjected. One of the first requirements for setting the record straight is to clear away such disinformation. The errors of fact contained in this scene are numerous. There are a lot of things we do not know about the Black Sox scandal, but some things we *do* know. For example, there is neither evidence nor hint, in all the accounts of this event, to even suggest that McMullin was the player who delivered the money to Jackson. Lefty Williams testified that *he* delivered the money, a fact corroborated by Jackson's testimony. Furthermore, according to the sworn testimony of both men involved in the scene, Jackson *did not take the money*. Williams offered the envelope, Jackson refused to take it, Williams tossed it down and Jackson stormed out of his own room, threatening to tell Comiskey the next morning.

It is difficult to understand why the film chose to substitute McMullin for Williams; it doesn't seem to aid the development of the plot in any way. But the distorted portrayal of Jackson's response, "On the dresser," at least has the excuse of revealing character, in so far as the film intended to present that character in a negative light. This intention to draw Jackson as a guilty man, and thus bolster the case against him, is also demonstrated in the timing of the scene—on the evening after the *first* game. As we've seen the fourth game is the earliest time mentioned, and that in the fictional portions of Jackson's and Lefty Williams' grand jury testimony. In fact, Williams threw down the money after the Series was over.

The timing of Jackson's receipt of the money is important: he is more damned if he got it *during* the Series than after. In an apparent effort to remove any doubt about his guilt, the film, based on no fact, gives him the money after the first game.

Docudramas like this film are always open to the charge of distortion; in the name of dramatic tension and narrative continuity, they invent episodes and dialogue; it is an artistic necessity inherent in the genre. But what are we to make of omissions of fact, omissions that could have been included in one or two seconds, omissions so glaring they distort both the historical conduct of the on-screen character and the audience's perception of him?

This film makes a plea for Buck Weaver. Among other arguments in his favor, he is shown jumping up at the Black Sox criminal trial to demand a separate trial of his own. As proof of his innocence, he offers his outstanding .324 World Series batting average. By contrast, the film completely *suppresses* the fact that Jackson got twelve hits to set a World Series record and had a batting average of .375. Presumably, this information, part of the same factual record as Weaver's accomplishments, would have raised ambiguities in the film's depiction of Jackson as an indisputably guilty man.

The Joe Jackson of *Eight Men Out* is an illiterate ignoramus whose greed and arrogance lead him to be easily corrupted. His guilt is never questioned. By way of contrast, in *Field of Dreams* (based on William Kinsella's novel *Shoeless Joe*) we find a very different version of Jackson. In this 1989 film, he is shown as a decent and caring man, a player whose intense love for the game transforms him into a metaphor for all that is best in the game itself. Furthermore, as the personification of baseball, he is the "instrument" through whom the film's protagonist, Ray Kinsella, is reconciled with his dead father.

Field of Dreams was filmed in the cornfields of Dyersville, Iowa, about twenty-five miles west of Dubuque. The tract of land on which the dream field was built was owned by two different farmers. When shooting was completed, one farmer plowed the land under and put it back to corn. The other, Don Lansing, was moved by the same voice that moved Ray Kinsella (Kevin Costner) in the film: He kept the field, including the grandstand, and with the help of his sister, Betty Boeckenstedt, opened it to the public. Don and Betty charge no entrance fee, all they ask of visitors is to sign a guest book.

This Field of Dreams quickly became a tourist attraction and a baseball shrine. As the James Earl Jones character told the Costner character in the film, "This field, this game is part of our past. It reminds us of all that once was good, and it could be again. Oh, people will come, Ray. People will most definitely come." And come they have, from all over the country, by the thousands each week during the baseball season. They play pickup games, snap photographs, and talk about baseball; Jackson is the most popular player. And before they leave, most of the visitors walk into the tall corn at the edge of the outfield where Shoeless Joe disappeared.

* * *

Support for Jackson has come from many diverse sources. In the past few years, the legislatures of four states have passed resolutions urging the Commissioner of Baseball to reinstate Jackson: Hawaii, Illinois, Louisiana, and South Carolina (in a repeat of an earlier petition). In addition to the activities of the Jackson Society, independent "crusaders" have sprung up. One, a Long Islander named Jack Parks, was so taken with Jackson that he built a shrine to Shoeless Joe in his basement. Canvassing shopping malls on weekends, Parks singlehandedly collected over 8,000 signatures on a Jackson petition. Like others before him, the response Parks received from the commissioner was less than satisfying.

From time to time, other individuals have queried the commissioner about Jackson's status, but official responses have been curt, misinformed, and usually illogical. For reasons of their own, commissioners absolutely refuse to even look at the Jackson case, this despite the numerous letters, petitions, and legislative requests they continue to receive. It almost seems as if the commissioners fear that a look into the facts of the Jackson case will somehow hurt baseball. Of course, whatever the outcome of such an honest inquiry, the opposite would be the case. Baseball could only gain in admiration if it would confront the issue, whatever the outcome. If, after a review,

Jackson was reinstated, baseball would be closer to its own self-image as the symbol of the best in American life. After all, the issue is justice and fair play. (For a sampling of how commissioners have handled such inquiries, see Appendix J.)

My own feelings about Jackson's role in baseball history and his place in popular mythology have undergone several changes. When I began this book in the mid-1970s, I believed he was a guilty man. I saw him as a prototype of the innocent country boy corrupted by the big city. But the evidence that came to light about his actual role in 1919 soon led me to the inescapable conclusion that he was literally innocent.

When I completed the original version of this book, I believed his unique legend was best served by leaving him in official disgrace. As the eternal outsider, his legend transcended the world of baseball and placed him firmly in our national mythology. Now I doubt the rightness of this conclusion. More than ever in an age typified by corruption in high places, the Baseball Hall of Fame is perceived as a shrine to all that is best in baseball and, by extension, all that is best in American life. By virtue of his character off the field and his achievements on it, Shoeless Joe Jackson deserves to be in the Hall of Fame. In fact, the Hall remains incomplete without him.

Appendix A

Jackson's Grand Jury Testimony

A good deal has been written about Joe's grand jury testimony. At the time, numerous newspapers published leaked versions of what they called his "confession." They claimed Joe confessed to trying as hard as he could to throw the games, thus setting a precedent of belief that has been followed ever since. Apparently relying on these accounts, subsequent writers repeated them. In his 1963 account of the scandal, Eight Men Out, Eliot Asinof, for example, says: "he [Jackson] told the jury how he hadn't played good baseball..." Twenty-five years later, in a book about the Carl Mays–Ray Chapman tragedy, Mike Sowel writes, "Jackson said he 'helped throw games by muffing hard chances in the outfield or by throwing slowly to the infield.'" Other examples are too numerous to cite. A reading of this transcript will show that not only did Jackson not say the self-incriminating things about his on-field performance attributed to him, but that he said just the opposite.

255

BEFORE THE GRAND JURY OF COOK COUNTY

September. A.D. 1920 Term.

In the Matter of the)
Investigation of Alleged)
Baseball Scandal)

September 28, 1920

1:00 o'clock P.M.

Present: Mr. Hartley L. Replogle, Assistant
State's Attorney, on behalf of
The People.
Hon. Charles A. McDonald, Chief Justice
of the Criminal Court

BASEBALL INQUIRY	Tuesday, September 28, 1920
GRAND JURY	3:00 o'clock, P.M.

JOE JACKSON

Called as a witness, having first been duly sworn, testified as follows:

EXAMINATION BY
Mr. Replogle

Q: Mr. Jackson, you understand that any testimony you may give here can be used in evidence against you at any future trial; you know who I am, I am State's Attorney, and this is the Grand Jury, this is the Foreman of the Grand Jury. Now, I will read this immunity waiver to you so you will know just what it is:

"Chicago, Illinois, September 28, 1920. I, Joe Jackson, the undersigned, of my own free will make this my voluntary statement and am willing to testify and do testify before the Grand Jury with full knowledge of all the facts and of my legal rights, knowing full well that any testimony I may give might incriminate me, and might be used against me in any case of prosecution or connected with the subject matter of my testimony, and now having been fully advised as to my legal rights, I hereby with said full knowledge waive all immunity that I might claim by reason of my appearing before the Grand Jury and giving testimony concerning certain crimes of which I have knowledge.

(Whereupon the witness signed the foregoing document).

Q: What is your name?

A: Joe Jackson.

Q: Where do you live, Mr. Jackson?

A: You mean in the City here?

Q: Where is your home?

A: Greenville, South Carolina.

Q: What is your business?

A: Baseball player.

Q: How long have you been playing professional baseball?

A: Since 1908.

Q: Where have you played professional baseball?

A: Why, I started out in Greenville, South Carolina; went from there to Philadelphia, Philadelphia Americans.

Q: How long were you with them?

A: I went in the fall of 1908, and went to Savannah, Georgia.

Q: How long were you there?

A: Finished the season there, and I was called back by the Athletics; from there went to New Orleans, in 1910; 1910 in the fall I came to Cleveland and stayed with Cleveland until 1915, and I have been here ever since.

Q: Did you play with the White Sox from 1915?

A: About the middle of the season I was there.

Q: Are you married or single?

A: Married.

Q: Have you any children?

A: No, sir.

Q: Is your wife in Chicago at the present time?

A: Yes, sir.

Q: Where is your Chicago address?

A: Trenier Hotel, 40th and Grand Boulevard.

Q: You were playing professional ball with the White Sox in the season of 1919, were you?

A: Yes, sir.

Q: You played in the World Series between the Chicago Americans Baseball Club and the Cincinnati Baseball Club, did you?

A: I did.

Q: What position did you play in that series?

A: Left field.

Q: Were you present at a meeting at the Ansonia Hotel in New York about two or three weeks before—a conference there with a number of ball players?

A: I was not, no, sir.

Q: Did anybody pay you any money to help throw that series in favor of Cincinnati?

A: They did.

Q: How much did they pay?

A: They promised me $20,000, and paid me five.

Q: Who promised you the twenty thousand?

A: "Chick" Gandil.

Q: Who is Chick Gandil?

A: He was their first baseman on the White Sox Club.

Q: Who paid you the $5,000?

A: Lefty Williams brought it in my room and threw it down.

Q: Who is lefty (sic) Williams?

A: The pitcher on the White Sox Club.

Q: Where did he bring it, where is your room?

A: At that time I was staying at the Lexington Hotel, I believe it is.

Q: On 21st and Michigan?

A: 22nd and Michigan, yes.

Q: Who was in the room at the time?

A: Lefty and myself, I was in there, and he came in.

Q: Where was Mrs. Jackson?

A: Mrs. Jackson—let me see—I think she was in the bathroom. It was [a] suite; yes, she was in the bathroom, I am pretty sure.

Q: Does she know that you got $5,000 for helping throw these games?

A: She did that night, yes.

Q: You say that you told Mrs. Jackson that evening?

A: [I] Did, yes.

Q: What did she say about it?

A: She said she thought it was an awful thing to do.

Q: When was it that this money was brought to your room and that you talked to Mrs. Jackson?

A: It was the second trip to Cincinnati. That night we were leaving.

Q: That was after the fourth game?

A: I believe it was, yes.

Q: Refreshing your recollection, the first two games that you remember were played in Cincinnati?

A: Yes, sir.

Q: And the second two were played here?

A: Yes.

Q: This was after the four[th] game?

A: Yes, sir.

Q: You were going back to Cincinnati?

A: Yes, sir.

Q: What time of the day was [it] that he came to your room?

A: It was between, I would say, 7 and 8 o'clock in the evening, right after the game.

Q: After the fourth game? Do you remember who won that game?

A: Dick Kerr, I believe.

Q: Cincinnati won that game, Cicotte pitched and Cincinnati won; do your remember now? Cincinnati beat you 2 to nothing?

A: Yes, sir.

Q: Were you at a conference of these men, these players on the Sox team, at the Warner Hotel sometime previous to this?

A: No, sir, I was not present, but I knew they had the meeting, so I was told.

Q: Who told you?

A: Williams.

Q: Who else talked to you about this besides Claude Williams?

A: Claude didn't talk to me direct about it, he just told me things that had been said.

Q: What did he tell you?

A: He told me about this meeting in particular, he said the gang was there, and this fellow Attel (sic) [Attell], Abe Attel, I believe, and Bill Byrnes (sic) is the man that give him the double crossing, so Gandil told me.

Q: You say Abe Attel (sic) and Bill Byrnes (sic) are the two people that Claude Williams told you gave you the double cross?

A: Chick Gandil told me that.

Q: Then you talked to Chick Gandil and Claude Williams both about this?

A: Talked to Claude Williams about it, yes, and Gandil more so, because he is the man that promised me this stuff.

Q: How much did he promise you?

A: $20,000 if I would take part.

Q: And you said you would?

A: Yes, sir.

Q: When did he promise you the $20,000?

A: It was to be paid after each game.

Q: How much?

A: Split it up some way, I don't know just how much it amounts to, but during the Series it would amount to $20,000. Finally Williams brought me this $5,000, threw it down.

Q: What did you say to Williams when he threw down the $5,000?

A: I asked him what the hell had come off here.

Q: What did he say?

A: He said Gandil said we all got a screw through Abe Attel. Gandil said that we got double crossed through Abe Attel, he got the money and refused to turn it over to him. I don't think Gandil was crossed as much as he crossed us.

Q: You think Gandil may have gotten the money and held it from you, is that right?

A: That's what I think, I think he kept the majority of it.

Q: What did you do then?

A: I went to him and asked him what was the matter. He said Abe Attel game him the jazzing. He said, "Take that or let it alone." As quick as the Series was over I left town, I went right on out.

Q: Did you ever meet Abe Attel?

A: Not to my knowledge, no sir. I wouldn't know him if I would see him.

Q: Did you ever meet Bill Byrnes (sic)?

A: Yes, sir.

Q: Where did you first meet Bill Byrnes (sic)?

A: When I first came in the American League to play ball I first met him.

Q: Where was he then?

A: He was at Detroit when I met him.

Q: Do you know whether or not he was in on this deal?

A: Well, I knew what Gandil told me, that he and Attel was the men that—

Q: Bill Byrnes (sic) and Abe Attel?

A: Yes.

Q: Were the men that what?

A: And some other gentlemen, I can't recall their names. There was three of them.

Q: A Jewish name, if you know, would you know it if you were to hear it?

A: No, sir, I would not.

Q: Do you know whether or not Gideon of St. Louis was in on this in any way?

A: No, sir, I only know he was with Risburg (sic) [Risberg] and McMullin all this time.

Q: Whom, Gideon?

A: That's all I know. I seen him around with them.

Q: What is his first name?

A: Joe.

Q: Joe Gideon? Do you know whether or not Rawlins of the Philadelphia National League Club was in on this in any way?

A: No, sir, I do not.

Q: You know Rawlins?

A: I only know him by name.

Q: You know Gideon?

A: Yes.

Q: Where did you see McMullin and Risburg together?

A: In Cincinnati one night in the smoking room of a Pullman car.

Q: Where else?

A: And I saw them on the street together in Cincinnati. I didn't see them in Chicago here, because I didn't live in that neighborhood, though I would see Joe at the ball grounds.

Q: You saw Gideon?

A: Yes.

Q: At the ball park during the World's series?

A: Yes, I saw him here one day, I saw him in here.

Q: And you were to be paid $5,000 after each game, is that right?

A: Well, Attel was supposed to give the $100,000. It was to be split up, paid to him, I believe, and $15,000 a day or something like that, after each game.

Q: That is to Gandil?

A: Yes.

Q: At the end of the first game you didn't get any money, did you?

A: No, I did not, no, sir.

Q: What did you do then?

A: I asked Gandil what is the trouble? He says, "Everything is all right" he had it.

Q: Then you went ahead and threw the second game, thinking you would get it then, is that right?

A: We went ahead and threw the second game, we went after him again. I said to him, "What are you going to do?" "Everything is all right," he says, "What the hell is the matter?"

Q: After the third game what did you say to him?

A: After the third game I says, "Somebody is getting a nice little jazz, everybody is crossed." He said, "Well, Abe Attel and Bill Byrnes (sic) had crossed him," that is what he said to me.

Q: He said Abe Attel and Bill Byrnes (sic) had crossed him?

A: Yes, sir.

Q: After the fourth game, did you talk to him then before Williams brought you the money?

A: No, sir; I didn't talk to him then, no, sir. Williams and I talked.

Q: Who was your best chum on the team, who did you go with in the club?

A: Williams and Lind. I hardly ever pal with any of them there except those two.

Q: Who did Gandil pal with mostly on the team?

A: Risburg.

Q: Who did McMullin pal with mostly on the team?

A: I cannot recall who McMullin roomed with.

Q: Who did he go with?

A: You could see him and Charlie together, and Chick, quite a bit.

Q: Chick Gandil and Charlie Risburg?

A: All times, not only on this occasion.

Q: Do you know who was the first man that the gamblers approached, that Byrnes (sic) and Attel approached on your team?

A: Well, I don't know who the first man was.

Q: Who do you think was the man they approached?

A: Why, Gandil.

Q: What makes you think Gandil?

A: Well, he was the whole works of it, the instigator of it, the fellow that mentioned it to me. He told me that I could take it or let it go, they were going through with it.

Q: Didn't you think it was the right thing for you to go and tell Comiskey about it?

A: I did tell them once, "I am not going to be in it." I will just get out of that altogether.

Q: Who did you tell that to?

A: Chick Gandil.

Q: What did he say?

A: He said I was into it already and I might as well stay in. I said, "I can go to the boss and have every damn one of you pulled out of the limelight." He said, "It wouldn't be well for me if I did that."

Q: Gandil said to you?

A: Yes, sir.

Q: What did you say?

A: Well, I told him any time they wanted to have me knocked off, to have me knocked off.

Q: What did he say?

A: Just laughed.

Q: When did that conversation take place, that you said any time they wanted to have you knocked off, to have you knocked off?

A: That was the fourth game, the fifth night going back to Cincinnati. I met Chick Gandil and his wife going to the 12th Street Station. They got out of the cab there. I was standing on the corner.

Q: Do you recall the fourth game that Cicotte pitched?

A: Yes, sir.

Q: Did you see any fake plays made by yourself or anybody on (sic) that game, that would help throw the game?

A: Only the wildness of Cicotte.

Q: What was that?

A: Hitting the batter, that is the only thing that told me they were going through with it.

Q: Did you make any intentional errors yourself that day?

A: No, sir, not during the whole series.

Q: Did you bat to win?

A: Yes.

Q: And run the bases to win?

A: Yes, sir.

Q: And field the balls at the outfield to win?

A: I did.

Q: Did you ever hear anyone accusing Cicotte of crossing the signals that were given to him by Schalk?

A: No, sir, I did not.

Q: Do you know whether or not any of those signals were crossed by Cicotte?

A: No, sir, I couldn't say.

Q: But you didn't hear any of the boys talking about that, did you?

A: No.

Q: After the fourth game you went to Cincinnati and you had the $5,000, is that right?

A: Yes, sir.

Q: Where did you put the $5,000, did you put it in the bank or keep it on your person?

A: I put it in my pocket.

Q: What denominations, in silver or bills?

A: In bills.

Q: How big were some of the bills?

A: Some hundreds, mostly fifties.

Q: What did Mrs. Jackson say about it after she found it out again?

A: She felt awful bad about it, cried about it a while.

Q: Did it ever occur to you to tell about this before this?

A: Yes, where I offered to come here last fall in the investigation, I would have told it last fall if they would have brought me in.

Q: And you are telling this now, of course, of your own free will, you want to tell the truth, is that the idea, of all you know?

A: Yes, sir.

Q: In the second game, did you see any plays made by any of those fellows that would lead you to believe that they were trying to throw the game, that is the game that Claude Williams pitched with Cincinnati?

A: There was wildness, too, that cost that game. Two walks, I think, and a triple by this fellow, two or three men out.

Q: Was there any other move that would lead you to believe they were throwing the game?

A: No, sir, I didn't see any plays that I thought was throwing the game.

Q: In the third game Kerr pitched three, 1 to nothing. Did you see anything there that would lead you to believe anyone was trying to throw the game?

A: No, sir. I think if you would look that record up, I drove in two and hit one.

Q: You made a home run, didn't you?

A: That was in the last game here.

Q: The fourth game Cicotte pitched again? It was played out here in Chicago and Chicago lost it 2 to nothing? Do you remember that?

A: Yes, sir.

Q: Did you see anything wrong about that game that would lead you to believe there was an intentional fixing?

A: The only thing that I was sore about that game, the throw I made to the plate, Cicotte tried to intercept it.

Q: It would have gone to the first base if he had not intercepted it?

A: Yes.

Q: Did you do anything to throw those games?

A: No, sir.

Q: Any game in the series?

A: Not a one. I didn't have an error or make no misplay.

Q: Supposing the White Sox would have won this series, the World's Series, what would you have done then with the $5,000?

A: I guess I would have kept it, that was all I could do. I tried to win all the time.

Q: To keep on with these games, the fifth game, did you see anything wrong with that or any of the games, did you see any plays that you would say might have been made to throw that particular game?

A: Well, I only saw one play in the whole series, I don't remember what game it was in, either, it was in Cincinnati.

Q: Who made it?

A: Charlie Risburg.

Q: What was that?

A: It looked like a perfect double play. And he only gets one, gets the ball and runs over to the bag with it in place of throwing it in front of the bag.

Q: After the Series were all over, did you have any talk with any of these men?

A: No, sir, I left the next night.

Q: Where did you go?

A: Savannah, Georgia.

Q: Weren't you very much peeved that you only got $5,000 and you expected to get twenty?

A: No, I was ashamed of myself.

Q: Have you ever talked with Chick Gandil since that time?

A: No, I never saw him since.

Q: When was the last time you saw him and talked to him?

A: It was on the following morning after the series were over, that day in Comiskey's office, waiting in there.

Q: What did you say to him at that time?

A: I told him there was a hell of a lot of scandal going around for what had happened. He said, "To hell with it." He was about half drunk. I went on out and left that night.

Q: Was Chick Gandil in the habit of drinking?

A: Yes, Chick liked his liquor.

Q: Did you drink much, Mr. Jackson?

A: Now and then, I don't make no regular practice of it.

Q: Do you get drunk?

A: No, sir.

Q: Have you been drunk since you have been with the Chicago White Sox team?

A: Yes, sir.

Q: During the playing season?

A: Yes, sir.

Q: Where?

A: Atlantic City.

Q: You were not playing—

A: Off days.

Q: Did Mr. Comiskey or Mr. Gleason know you were drunk at that time?

A: I don't judge they did, no, sir.

Q: Who was with you when you got drunk?

A: Claude Williams, John Fornier (sic) [Fournier] and myself.

Q: That was some years ago, he played with the Chicago team, is that right?

A: I think it was '18.

Q: You haven't been drunk since you played with the Chicago team?

A: Not what you would call drunk, no.

Q: Did you ever talk to Happy Felsch since that time, about those games?

A: I believe I mentioned it to Happy the other day, too; Yes, I knew I did.

Q: What did you say to him?

A: I told him they would have him down before the Grand Jury before long, the way things looked.

Q: What did he say?

A: He said, "All right."

Q: What day was that, Mr. Jackson?

A: I don't remember what day it was, but one day last week.

Q: Were you playing ball?

A: We were walking across the field, yes, sir. Just before practice, I believe, and we were taking our position for practice that day.

Q: Do you know whether or not Happy Felsch received some of this money?

A: I don't know that he received any more than what the boys said.

Q: What did the boys say about him?

A: They said each fellow got so much money.

Q: Did they say how much?

A: $5,000, I understand, Felsch.

Q: Do you remember whether or not some of them got more than $5,000; in other words, if I was to tell you one man got $10,000, you wouldn't doubt it, would you; you don't know?

A: Yes, I know the man you would refer to.

Q: Do you know how much he got?

A: I know what he said.

Q: Do you know how much he said he got?

A: $10,000.

Q: Who do you think I mean, then?

A: Eddie Cicotte.

Q: When did Eddie Cicotte tell you he got $10,000?

A: The next morning after the meeting we had in his room.

Q: Did you tell him how much you got?

A: I did.

Q: What did you tell him?

A: I told him I got five thousand.

Q: What did he say?

A: He said I was a God damn fool for not getting it in my hands like he did.

Q: What did he mean by that?

A: I don't know, that he wouldn't trust anybody, I guess.

Q: What did he mean, that's what he meant by it?

A: Why, he meant he would not trust them, they had to pay him before he did anything.

Q: He meant then that you ought to have got your money before you played, is that it?

A: Yes, that's it.

Q: Did you have a talk with any of the other players about how much they got?

A: I understand McMullin got five and Risburg five thousand, that's the way I understand.

Q: How do you understand that?
A: Just by talking to different fellows.
Q: To whom?
A: Different fellows.
Q: Did you talk to McMullin himself?
A: Very little I never talked to Mac any more than just hello and go (sic) [so] on.
Q: Did you ever ask him how much he got?
A: Yes.
Q: What did he say?
A: Never made me any answer, walked right out.
Q: Did you ever ask Charlie how much he got?
A: Yes.
Q: What did he say?
A: Asked me how much I got.
Q: What did you tell him?
A: Told him.
Q: What did you tell him?
A: I told him I got $5,000.
Q: What did he say?
A: He said, "I guess that's all I got."
Q: Did you believe him at the time?
A: No, sir, I think he was telling a damn lie.
Q: What?
A: I think he was lying.
Q: Did you tell him at the time he said it he was lying?
A: Yes.
Q: You thought he was lying even at that time, did you?
A: Yes, sir.
Q: When was that time?
A: That was this spring. We were talking in Memphis, he and I were taking a walk.
Q: On your training trip?
A: Yes, sir.
Q: Did you ever talk to anyone else [about?] how much they got?
A: No sir, I didn't.
Q: You never asked Williams how much he got?
A: Williams I have, yes.
Q: What did he say?
A: He said he got $5,000 at that time.

Q: You think he told [or "gave"] you the truth?

A: No, sir, I do not.

Q: What do you say?

A: No, I dod (sic) [did] not.

Q: What do you think?

A: I think that those fellers cut it up to suit themselves, what little they did have.

Q: Who is that?

A: This gang.

Q: What gang?

A: Charlie.

Q: Charlie Risberg?

A: Yes.

Q: Who else?

A: McMullin and Williams.

Q: Who else?

A: Cicotte, they were gambling.

Q: Weren't you in on the inner circle?

A: No, I never was with them, no, sir. It was mentioned to me in Boston. As I told you before, they asked me what would I consider, $10,000? and I said no, then they offered me twenty.

Q: Who mentioned it first to you?

A: Gandil.

Q: Who was with you?

A: We were all alone.

Q: What did he say?

A: He asked me would I consider $10,000 to frame up something and I asked him frame what? and he told me and I said no.

Q: What did he say?

A: Just walked away from me, and when I returned here to Chicago he told me that he would give me twenty and I said no again, and on the bridge where you go into the club house he told me I could either take it or let it alone, they were going through.

Q: What did they say?

A: They said, "You might as well say yes or say no and play ball or anything you want." I told them I would take their word.

Q: What else did you say?

A: Nothing.

Q: Did you talk to anyone else about it?

A: That's all I talked to.

Q: Did you ever talk to Buck Weaver about it?

A: No, sir, I never talked to Buck Weaver, never talked very much.

Q: Did you know [at?] the time Buck was in on the deal?

A: They told me he was; he never told me it himself.

Q: Who told you?

A: Chick told me.

Q: Did Mrs. Jackson ever talk to Mrs. Weaver about it, that you know of?

A: No, sir, not that I know of; no, sir.

Q: Is Mrs. Jackson a friend of Mrs. Weaver's, and did they chum together frequently—or did they?

A: They are all chummy there on the ball ground, sit together there on the stand, most all the ball players' wives sit together.

Q: Who did Mrs. Jackson sit with most?

A: Mrs. Williams and her sit together.

Q: Did Mrs. Jackson talk to Mrs. Williams about it?

A: Not that I know of.

Q: Did Mrs. Williams ever talk to Mrs. Jackson about it?

A: I don't know, they never talked when I was around, I don't know what they did when I wasn't around.

Q: Go back to Attell and Burns, just what do you know about them?

A: All I know is what Gandil told me over there, I talked to Bill myself later.

Q: What did you talk to Byrnes (sic) [Burns] later?

A: It was the day the World's Series started.

Q: What did you say to him and what did he say to you?

A: I met him in the lobby of the hotel, we sat there; I can't remember the name of the hotel.

Q: Sinton Hotel?

A: Sinton Hotel, yes.

Q: That is in Cincinnati?

A: Yes. I said, "How is everything?"

Q: What did he say?

A: He said, "Everything is fine."

Q: Then what happened?

A: He told me about this stuff and I didn't know so much, I hadn't been around and I didn't know so much. He said, "Where is Chick?" I said, "I don't know." He walked away from me. I didn't know enough to talk to him about what they were going to plan or what they had planned, I wouldn't know it if I had [not?] seen him, I only know what I had been told, that's all I knew.

Q: Who was the third party in with Byrnes (sic) [Burns] and Attell?

A: I don't know their names, I know there was three names.

THE FOREMAN: Q: What makes you think that Gandil was double crossing you, rather than Attell and Byrnes (sic) [Burns?]

A: What made me think it was Gandil going out on the coast, so I was told, I was surmising what I heard, they came back and told me he had a summer home, big automobile, doesn't do a lick of work; I know I can't do that way.

MR. REPLOGLE: Q: In other words, if he double crossed you fellows he couldn't come back and face them, and he had plenty of money to stay out there. It wasn't at the time that you thought Gandil was double crossing you, you thought Gandil was telling the truth, is that right?

A: No, I told Williams after the first day it was a crooked deal all the way through, Gandil was not on the square with us.

Q: Had you ever played crooked baseball before this?

A: No, sir, I never had.

Q: Did anybody ever approach you to throw a game before this?

A: No, sir, never did.

Q: Did anybody ever approach you to throw a game since that time, to throw the World Series?

A: No, sir.

Q: Do you have any suspicion about the White Sox, any of the players throw any of the games this summer?

A: Well, there have been some funny looking games, runs, I could have just my own belief about it, I wouldn't accuse the men.

Q: Where at?

A: A couple in New York, this last Eastern trip, looked bad, but I couldn't come out and open and bold and accuse anybody of throwing those games.

Q: Who pitched?

A: Williams got one awful beating up there, 25 to something there.

Q: Who else?

A: I don't remember whether Cicotte started the game there or not.

Q: Do you remember the last series you played in Boston? Last [Lost?] three straight games, did any of those games look suspicious to you?

A: There was a lot of funny pitching, lot of walking.

Q: Who was pitching those games?

A: Kerr and Williams and Cicotte.

Q: Was Kerr in on this in any way, do you think?

A: I don't think so.

Q: Were any of the other six players in it except the ones we have mentioned?

A: Not to my knowledge.

Q: Do you remember the Washington Series here the last time Washington played here, that you lost three straight games?

A: No, sir.

Q: Did any of those games look suspicious to you?

A: I didn't pay any attention to them, looking for errors, and that, I was out trying to beat them.

Q: Was anything whispered around the club that you know of, that you should beat New York and then drop these games for these other teams so that Cleveland would win?

A: No, sir, I never heard that.

Q: Did you hear anything in your ball team to the effect that if the White Sox would take second place and would get part of the World's Series money because you won second place in the pennant race and then get the City Series money, that you would make more money than if you won the pennant and won the World's Series?

A: No, sir.

Q: Did any of the players ever tell you that?

A: No, sir, never told me that.

Q: Did that ever occur to you, yourself?

A: No, sir. I wanted to win, this year, above all times.

Q: Why?

A: Because—I wanted to get in there and try and beat some National League club to death, that's what I wanted to do.

Q: You didn't want to do that so bad last year, did you?

A: Well, down in my heart I did, yes.

Q: Did you hear any of the players that mentioned that proposition to you that I have just mentioned?

A: No, not to me, no, sir; they have not.

Q: Have you heard from Gandil since he has been on the coast, has he written to you?

A: No, sir.

Q: Did you write and ask him for the other $15,000?

A: No, sir.

Q: Why didn't you?

A: I didn't think it would do any good, I didn't pay any attention to that.

Q: Did you ever talk to Claude Williams about it since the series?

A: We have talked about it once or twice, yes.

Q: When?

A: Sometime this summer, I don't remember when it was.

Q: In what city, if you can recall?

A: I think it was here, in Chicago.

Q: Where in Chicago, at the ball park?

A: No, we were out riding in his car.

Q: What did you say to him and what did he say to you?

A: We were just talking about how funny it looked that Gandil didn't come back, and he must have made an awful lot out of it, crossed up the boys. We both decided he crossed them up.

Q: You think now Williams may have crossed you, too?

A: Well, dealing with crooks, you know, you get crooked every way. This is my first experience and last.

Q: Where else did you talk to Williams, outside of the time you were out riding in his car?

A: Somewhere we were at, I believe in Washington.

Q: When was that?

A: That was this summer, I think.

Q: How long ago?

A: I think it was the second Eastern trip.

Q: What did you say to him at that time, and what did he say to you?

A: We just brought up the World's Series, I told him what a damned fool I though (sic) [thought] I was, and he was of the same opinion, so we just let it go at that.

Q: Does your contract with the Sox Baseball team call for $6,000?

A: $8,000

Q: What party (sic) [part] of the money did you get when you were sold by Cleveland to Comiskey?

A: I think they gave me $1,000 out of the sale.

Q: That's all you got out of it, just $1,000?

A: Yes.

Q: Do you know how much Mr. Comiskey paid the Cleveland Club for you?

A: I do not, no, sir.

Q: You knew it was a big sum of money, did you?

A: So they said.

Q: You were satisfied with $8,000 a year, were you?

A: That's all I could get out of them.

Q: Did you get $8,000 in 1919?

A: No, sir.

Q: What did you get in that year, that was last year?

A: '19, I believe they gave me $6,000, last year.

Q: That is for the season, not the year?

A: Yes, just the playing season, yes, sir.

Q: That also includes all your expenses on the trips, doesn't it?

A: Yes, sir.

Q: Railroad fare, board, room and so forth?

A: Railroad, fare, room and board.

Q: You were pretty well satisfied with that, weren't you?

A: They wouldn't give you any more, that's all you could get. I was pretty lucky to get a contract like that with him when I came over here.

Q: What were you getting with Cleveland?

A: I was getting six the last year, and I had been in that automobile wreck, and it looked like I was through as a ball player.

Q: $6,000 is the most you ever got until this year, is that right?

A: (no answer)

Q: Did you ever talk to any of the other men about this, now, that I have not asked you about?

A: No, sir.

Q: Do you know anything more about it than I have asked you?

A: No, sir, I don't believe I do.

Q: Can you think of anything else of importance that I have not asked you?

A: This other fellow, if I could think of his name, I can't think of his name.

Q: Did Cicotte ever tell you who paid him the money?

A: He told me about somebody paying him money, yes; but I don't know their names, except Bill Byrnes (sic) [Burns] and Abe Attell. That's the only two names that I know. I did not attend the meetings.

Q: You say Williams gave you your money; what ball player paid Cicotte his money?

A: These gamblers paid him, I think, all along, from what I learn.

Q: Did Williams ever tell you who paid him?

A: Never did.

Q: Did you ever ask Williams where he got this $5,000?

A: Yes.

Q: What did he say?

A: Up at Gandil's apartment, he said.

Q: Have you ever talked to Byrnes (sic) [Burns] since the World's Series?
A: No, sir.
Q: Do you know where he lives, where he is?
A: No, sir, I do not.
Q: You talked to Gideon this summer?
A: Yes; "Hello, how are you", and something like that.
Q: Do you know whether or not Gideon is in on the deal?
A: No, sir, I do not.
Q: Do you think he was?
A: (no answer)
Q: Does Williams know where you are now?
A: I don't think so.
MR. REPLOGLE: It is an off day, no game today.

(Whereupon the Grand Jury adjourned to Wednesday, September 29, 1920, at 9:30 o'clock A.M.)

After the 1924 trial, Jackson's grand jury testimony disappeared for sixty-five years. It resurfaced in 1989 at the opening show of the new Chicago Historical Society Museum, "Say It Ain't So, Joe." Once again labelled his "confession," the transcript was loaned to the museum by the descendant firm of Alfred Austrian's old firm. Perhaps with an eye to Austrian's questionable behavior with Jackson on that afternoon of September 28, 1920, a partner in the current firm wrote in a cover letter, "As is true today, an employer's lawyer was not required by the rules of legal ethics to provide a Miranda-type warning to an employee suspected of dishonesty." This is a disingenuous statement. Miranda warnings are given by officers of the law at the moment of arrest, informing the suspect of his or her rights to remain silent and to get a lawyer. This coy red herring appears to be an attempt to divert the reader from the real issues, which are:

Did Jackson have reason to believe that Austrian was his lawyer?

Did Austrian have reason to believe that Jackson was proceeding under a mistaken assumption, and if so, did he do anything about it to clarify the matter?

If Austrian was only Jackson's employer's (Comiskey's) lawyer, then under what theory of a lawyer's duties and obligations did Austrian offer to and even force upon Jackson his legal advice?

Lastly, and most concisely, did Austrian tell Jackson he was not his lawyer, that he was Comiskey's lawyer and that therefore a conflict of interest prevented him from even discussing the matter with Jackson, and advise Jackson to retain his own counsel?

Austrian, of course, did none of these things. Instead, he used the situation to entrap Jackson and to direct his actions for the sole benefit of his only client in the matter, Charles Comiskey.

Appendix B

Comiskey-Jackson Correspondence

THE COMISKEY-JACKSON LETTERS

*Following is an exchange of letters between Charles Comiskey and Joe
Jackson between October 1919 and February 1920, reproduced as they
appear in the transcript of the 1924 Civil Suit. Joe's letters were
written by Katie.*

Savannah, Georgia, October 27, 1919

Mr. Charles A. Comiskey:

As I haven't heard anything from the club in Regards to my Saries
check and would like to know why you are Holding it as I kneed the

money Would like to have something from you as earley as possiable. And if possiable send it to me this week.

Joe Jackson,
621 W. 39th Street,
Savannah, Ga.

*   *   *

(On White Sox Letterhead)

Nov. 11, 1919

Mr. Jos. Jackson,
17 Congress St.,
Savannah, Ga.

Dear Friend:

In answer to your recent communication, wish to state that there has been a great deal of adverse talk in which your name has been mentioned, along with several others, referring to and reflecting on your integrity in the recent World's Series. One or two players took the stand and they would gladly return to Chicago at any time to uphold any reflection cast on them.

I wish to advise you that I have nothing whatever to do with the handling or issuing of same, as the National Commission turned over to Manager Gleason the players' share for distribution so would suggest that you take the matter up with him direct.

Would gladly pay your expenses to Chicago and return if you wish to come on in reference to the matter pertaining to the talk emanating from the World's Series.

With kindest regards, I remain,
Yours very truly,
(Original signed by Mr. Comiskey)

*   *   *

Savannah, Ga.
Nov. 15, 1919

Mr. Charles A. Comiskey:

Your letter just came, and I sure am surprised to hear that my name
has been connected with any scandle in the recent World Saries, as I
think my playing proved that I did all I could to win, and I wrote Mr.
Gleason yesterday and as soon as I hear from him I will be onley to
glad to come to Chicago or any place you may say and clear my name
and whoever started this will have to prove his statements, and that
has nothing whatever to do with holding our checks, and as soon as I
hear from Mr. Gleason as to why he is holding the checks I will come
to Chicago if you say. But in the first place the National Commission
is responsible for our money and why is Gleason holding it as I am
under no contract to him, I am not looking to him for the money, and I
don't see why they make a lot of fus because we Lost as it isent the
first time a Series was lost and I am sure I did all I could to win and I
think my Record for the Series Will Show if you Look at it, I diden
know Gleason's address in Philey, so had to write to the Club there and
hope it will be forwarded to him at his home adress.

And let me hear from you as to when you want me to come to
Chicago as I expect to hear from Gleason in a few days.

Joe Jackson
621 W.39th St.
Savannah, Ga.

* * *

(White Sox Letterhead)

Nov. 11, 1919

Mr. Joe Jackson
17 Congress Street
Savannah, Ga.

Dear Friend:
I am formulating plans for the season of 1920 pertaining to the
personnel of the White Sox, and would like to hear from you at your
early convenience as to your playing terms for the coming season.
Kindly give this matter your consideration, and let me hear from you.

Trusting you have been spending a very pleasant winter and wishing you the compliments of the season, I remain,

Yours very truly
(Original signed by Mr. Comiskey)

P.S. Kindly treat this matter confidential

* * *

Savannah, Ga.
Jan. 24, 1920

Mr. Charles A. Comiskey:

Yours received in Regards to my contract. First I Diden get the Nine days pay for the Series that I understand the other Boys got, and also a pare of Shoes and new Glove that was stolen in the Club House when Bill James trunk was stolen. Mr. Gleason had the club House Boy to make a list of the things that was stolen and send to the office. But I never heard anything from it, and unless I get this and a three year ironclad contract for ten thousand a year I cant signe as living expenses are going up all the time and I dont rate myself the class of player Eddie Collins or Buck Weaver, I think that if Eddie is worth fifteen thousand and Buck ten that I am also worth ten thousand a year. I can't live in Chicago at what I am getting and pay a Hundred for a flat. Besides, other living expenses there, as I am going to open up a nother Billiard parlor in Birmingham and can make more By Beeing with the Business all the time then I can at my present Salrie there.

Yours Respectfuley,
Joe Jackson
621 W. 39th St.
Savannah, Ga.

* * *

(White Sox Letterhead)

Jan. 29, 1920

Mr. Joe Jackson
17 Congress St.
Savannah, Ga.

Dear Friend:

Your letter of recent date received, and contents noted. I wish, to advise you that your last season's contract was fulfilled to the letter. You received the amount that was agreed upon in full, namely, $6000.00.

Herewith enclosed please find contract for the season of 1920 for $7000.00, which is a very liberal increase over that of the past season.

I am completing all my plans for the personnel of the club for 1920, and of course no one will be taken on the spring training trip who has not signed a contract.

In reference to that part of your letter pertaining to something being taken from the Club House, I have heard nothing regarding that up to this time and that matter can be adjusted with Manager Gleason after your arrival here in Chicago.

Trusting you have been spending a very pleasant winter, I remain,

Yours very truly
(Original signed by Mr. Comiskey)

Reg. Enc. (Referring to the enclosed contract for $7000 for one year, with the ten day clause in it.)

* * *

Savannah, Ga.
February 1, 1920

Mr. Chas. A. Comiskey,

Your letter and also contract Received and am returning the contract. You may think a thousand dollars is a liberal encreas. But I don't as I know what other players are getting that isent any Better player than I am, as I consider myself as good a Ballplayer as you have on the club, and as I stated to you Before I can make more money in the Billard Buisness then you offer me, as Mr. Sullivan and I just checked up and Did make more the past year with one place, and will open up another one soon. So if I Don't get ten thousand and a three year ironclad contract, I will not signe.

Joe Jackson
Congress Billard Parlor
17 Congress St.
Savannah, Ga.

*   *   *

(White Sox Letterhead)

Feb. 9, 1920

Mr. Joe Jackson
17 Congress St.
Savannah, Ga.

My dear Friend:

Your letter of recent date received and contents noted.

Of course, if you intend remaining in baseball, I consider myself in a good position to know just what this club can afford to offer in the way of a salary, but if you are putting yourself on the basis of retiring from baseball and entering the billard business, why of course I am no criterion as to what you are worth. Your future intentions as to what you are going to do rests absolutely with yourself, and you yourself must be the sole judge of that.

I am returning to you the contract which you sent, and the further condition that I am satisfied to make the enclosed contract read for the season of 1920, and 1921. I wish to know your final intentions at once, as I am making up the personnel of the club at this time preparatory to our departure for spring training.

With best wishes, I remain,

Yours very truly,
(Original signed by Mr. Comiskey)

*   *   *

Feb. 13, 1920
Savannah, Ga.

Mr. Chas. A. Comiskey:

Please find enclosed contract as I can't signe a contract for what you offer, and you must remember By the time I pay encome tax and live out of the Salrie you offer I dont have anything Left and as far as the Billard Buisness I have been in it for the Past two years and have Played for you for less money then any player on your club of my class of player, and I think I was very fair with you Last year, and if you dont think you can pay me what I am worth as a player I think it Best you trade or sell me as there ar other clubs that will.

And I will not signe a contract unless the ten Day clause is cut out and a three year contract.

Joe Jackson
17 Congress St.
Savannah, Ga.

* * *

(White Sox Letterhead)

Feb. 14, 1920

Mr. Joe Jackson
17 Congress St.
Savannah, Ga.

My dear Sir:

Your letter of Feb. 13 received, together with returned contract.

I note your statement that your billiard business will not interfere with your playing baseball. Up to the present time, have not received any offer to trade or buy your services from any club, and if we did receive such offer, I have not the slightest idea of trading or selling. Neither do I intend to enter into a contract with the ten-day clause eliminated.

The matter of the length of the contract is one for decision after the salary terms have been agreed upon. Kindly advise me your lowest playing terms for the season of 1920, and upon hearing from you will advise you immediately whether or not we can get together.

I note by the papers this morning that you are a hold out according to your own statement, even after you were asked to keep the matters of terms confidential.

With kindest regards, I remain,

Yours very truly,
(Original signed by Mr. Comiskey)

*   *   *

Savannah, Ga.
Feb. 18, 1920

Mr. Charles A. Comiskey:

Your Letter Received and note the contents. I wrote you before that I would play Ball for ten thousand and nothing Less, and I will not play for Less. I understand you have Raised some of the players without asking. I know of one you offered a $2300 Hundred raise that Didn't make any showing in the Series and I think my Past Record entitles me to what I ask and I don't think I am asking any more than I am worth as a player so will not sign for less.

Joe Jackson

Savannah. The player who was offered the $2,300 raise was Happy Felsch, one of the two men who met with Comiskey the morning after the Series to tell him what he knew.

Appendix C

Johnson, Landis Letters

The Cleveland Indians won the 1920 pennant by two games over the White Sox and Joe and his teammates were entitled to second place money. However, in the wake of the 1920 grand jury investigation, the shares of the indicted players were withheld. The criminal trial of the Black Sox took place in July 1921, and they were all found not guilty. Eight months later Joe had Katie write a letter to Ban Johnson, President of the American League, requesting his second-place money, which was approximately $700.

Chicago, March 21, 1922

Mr. Joe Jackson
409 East 49th Street
Savannah, Ga.

Dear Sir:

I have your letter of March 16th, and note the contents. My absence from Chicago delayed my replying to you at an earlier date.

Judge Landis is custodian of the money that, under ordinary conditions, would have been alloted to the Chicago players for finishing second in the championship race of 1920. As far as my knowledge runs, there has been no decision as to the disposition of this money. I will submit your communication to the Commissioner for his consideration.

I am—

Yours truly,
(Signed) B.B. Johnson

Two weeks later, Joe received a letter from Commissioner Landis. In light of the jury's verdict eight months earlier, it is one of the most bizarre documents in the entire Black Sox affair. What "crime" is Landis talking about?

BASEBALL

KENESAW M. LANDIS
COMMISSIONER
LESLIE M. O'CONNOR
SECRETARY-TREASURER

122 SOUTH MICHIGAN AVENUE
CHICAGO

April 6, 1922

Mr. Joe Jackson,
    409 E. 49th St.,
        Savannah, Ga.

Dear Sir:

President Johnson of the American League has forwarded me your letter to him, under date of March 16. *In view of the crime* in connection with the World's Series of 1919, of course the money about which you inquire cannot be paid to you. Neither can any club in organized baseball that had entered into a contract with you be permitted to carry out the contract. (Italics added).

Very truly yours,
(Signed) Kenesaw M. Landis
Commissioner

There's more to this than meets the eye. Landis, on the basis of a non-existent "crime," goes out of his way to rule Jackson's three-year contract with the White Sox null and void. This, of course, is a matter for the courts, not the Commissioner. Landis seems to be doing Comiskey a favor by telling Joe it would be futile to try to sue Comiskey for the back wages due him on that contract. Landis almost certainly knew when he wrote this letter that Attorney Ray Cannon had already begun a suit for Happy Felsch to recover the money due on his White Sox contract. Jackson learned of the suit a couple of weeks later when Cannon wrote to him at Felsch's request.

Appendix D

Landis Letters

THE LANDIS LETTERS

These letters were discovered in the mid-1980s in a trunk in the attic of the undertaker who buried Jackson. They clearly demonstrate two facts: 1.) Joe Jackson did make a request for a hearing regarding his banishment; 2.) Commissioner Landis first attempted to give Jackson a brush off, then placed him in a double-bind by demanding he make a "confession" of guilt as a precondition to receiving a hearing in which he could argue his innocence.

(These letters are reproduced by the kind permission of the Lester Irwin Collection.)

BASEBALL

KENESAW M. LANDIS   122 SOUTH MICHIGAN AVENUE
    COMMISSIONER˙   CHICAGO

LESLIE M. O'CONNOR
SECRETARY-TREASURER   June 20, 1923

REGISTERED MAIL, deliver only to addressee.

Mr. Joe Jackson
Bastrop, La.

Dear Sir:
I have received a letter dated June 12, purporting to come from you
and to bear your signature. In substance, it is an application for
reinstatement.

The signature thereto does not appear to be yours; therefore, beyond
this communication to you, no action will be taken thereon.

Very truly yours,
(Signed) Kenesaw M. Landis

*   *   *

*Undeterred by Landis's brush-off, Joe had Katie write another letter,
the contents of which may be imagined from Landis's second response.*

BASEBALL

KENESAW M. LANDIS   122 SOUTH MICHIGAN AVENUE
    COMMISSIONER   CHICAGO
LESLIE M. O'CONNOR
SECRETARY-TREASURER   July 16, 1923

Mr. Joe Jackson
Bastrop, La.

Dear Sir:
Your letter, which is dated 7-29, *(This must be a typo in the original,
6-29 is the only logical date)* came here in my absence and through an
error in forwarding, was delayed in coming to my attention.

Before I can pass on your application for reinstatement, it will be
necessary for you to forward to me for consideration in that connection, a full statement in detail of your conduct and connection with the
arrangement for the "throwing" of the World's Series of 1919. I feel I

should say to you that there will be no reinstatement of any player who had any connection therewith.

Very truly yours,
(Signed) Kenesaw M. Landis

Appendix E

Anonymous Telegram to Jackson

This anonymous telegram was sent to Jackson a few months after the suit was instituted against Comiskey. Jackson, we learn from Attorney Cannon's letters to him, already knew about the detectives sent to Savannah, but this telegram, from a person in a position to know, reveals that Comiskey uncovered nothing about Jackson he could use to undermine Jackson's case against him. Presumably, the detectives were looking for information to link Jackson to the 1919 fix.

WESTERN UNION TELEGRAM

RECEIVED AT
13X M 185 NL

CHICAGO ILL JUL 29 1923

JOE JACKSON
AMERICUS GA

COMMY SENT DICKS TO SAVANNAH TO SCARE YOU I AM IN POSITION TO KNOW BECAUSE I AM IN OFFICE WHERE REPORTS COME IN LAST REPORT WAS THEY HAD NOTHING ON YOU I ALWAYS FELT SORRY FOR YOU BOYS AND AM TIPPING YOU OFF TO GO RIGHT AFTER THIS FELLOW AS YOU HAVE GOT THE GOODS ON HIM AND THEY KNOW IT YOUR LAWYER IN MILWAUKEE JUST WON A BIG POINT AGAINST THEM AND THEY ARE SCARED TO DEATH THAT THE CASE WILL BE TRIED BEFORE A JURY KEEP YOUR MOUTH SHUT—(PLA?)Y BALL AND LISTEN TO YOUR LAW-YER AS HE IS CONSIDERED ONE OF THE (BEST IN ?) THE WEST IF ANYTHING ELSE COMES IN HERE I WILL KEEP IN TOUCH WITH YOU BY WIRE BUT YOU HAVE GOT THEM ON THE RUN NOW AND GIVE THEM A GOOD BEATING AND DONT LET THESE CHEAP DICKS SCARE YOU AS THEY HAVE GOT NOTHING ON YOU TO DATE AS I KNOW FROM REPORTS I HAVE SEEN AND THEY HAVE REPORTED THAT THEY ARE UNABLE TO GET ANYTHING ON YOU WILL WIRE LATER IF ANYTHING TURNS UP.

A FRIEND
905A JUL 30

Appendix 7

Jackson Testimony, Milawaukee 1924

Excerpts from Joe Jackson's Direct Examination in his 1924 suit against Comiskey. The questions are asked by his attorney, Ray Cannon.

Q: Did you have a talk with "Lefty" Williams one or two days after the World's Series was over?

A: I had a talk with Mr. Williams the night after the World's Series was over, that day.

Q: In Chicago?

A: Yes, sir.

Q: Where?

A: I think it was in the Warner Hotel.

Q: What talk did you have with Williams at that time?

A: Mr. Williams came in my room and held out a couple of envelopes and said, "Here, do you want one of these?" I said, "No, what is it?" He pushed it over to me again. I said,"Go on; what is it that you got?" He told me; "Why," he says "it is money." I says, "I don't want your money." He said it was part of what he got in a frame-up with some eastern gamblers and they had used my name.

Q: Who had used your name?

A: Cicotte and Gandil.

Q: And Williams?

A: And Williams.

Q: Did you give him permission to use your name?

A: No, sir.

Q: At any time?

A: No, sir.

Q: Did you know before that time that your name had been used by Williams with the gamblers?

A: Not up to that time, no sir.

Q: Or by Cicotte or Gandil?

A: Or by Cicotte or Gandil.

Q: What did you say to Williams then?

A: I told him they had a lot of nerve. I don't know just the word I used, but "Big bums" or something, to be out pulling that kind of stuff on me, knowing that it was the only way I had of making a livelihood.

Q: What else?

A: We had a few hot words there, and he was drinking, and I walked out of the room. As I was going I told him I was going down to see Comiskey about this in the morning. So the next morning I went down to Comiskey's office to see him and tell him all about it.

Q: What did you do when you got down there?

A: I got to the office there, and the front office door was always locked, and they got a solid window there, and when a ball-player wants to talk to Grabiner or Comiskey, you have to knock on the window.

Q: And they raise it up for you?

A: Yes sir.

Q: Did you knock on the window this day?

A: I knocked on the window this day.

Q: Who came to the window?

A: Harry Grabiner.

Q: He is the secretary of the defendant corporation?

A: Yes, sir.

Q: What did you say to Grabiner?

A: I told Grabiner I wanted to see Comiskey.

Q: What about?

A: He said Comiskey was busy and I couldn't see him, and I said, "It is important that I should see him, some information that I got out of Williams in regard to the World's Series", and he slammed the window down in my face and said, "Go on home, we know what you want."

Q: And did you see Comiskey at that time?

A: No, sir.

Q: Did you leave Chicago the next day for your home in Savannah?

A: Within the next day or two, I wouldn't say it was the next day.

* * *

Q: Mr. Jackson, I think we left off in your testimony last night at a place where you had returned to Savannah.

A: Yes, sir.

Q: And you had a letter—or you promised to write to Mr. Comiskey—is that it? Oh, you had a letter from Mr. Comiskey after you got down there?

A: Some two or three days after I got home, yes, sir.

Q: And did you reply to that letter?

A: My wife did.

Q: Did you offer to go to Chicago at any time and give him all the information you had concerning what you knew about the World Series?

At this point, Mr. Hudnall, Comiskey's lawyer, raised an objection which the Judge sustained and a long argument followed in which Cannon claimed the defendant had never responded to his request to produce certain letters which contained Jackson's offer. Hudnall denied the request had ever been made and the Judge finally asked him to produce them. Hudnall tried to hold back the letters because they documented Jackson's claim that he had offered to tell Comiskey in mid-November, 1919, what he knew about the fix. This information would reveal Comiskey's hypocritical public stance and his cover-up. The letters were ultimately produced and they are reproduced here in Appendix B.

Ray Cannon tried to return to the letters, but the Judge ruled they could not be discussed until they were produced. We do learn from this exchange, however, that Comiskey had also sent Jackson a telegram, another first, but since Jackson had not kept it, it too was not discussed. Cannon then turned to the episode of Harry Grabiner's visit to Savannah in February, 1920.

Q: And that was the first time that Mr. Grabiner had ever come to Savannah for the purpose of signing you up to a contract?

A: Yes, sir.

* * *

Q: And state whether or not it was usual or unusual for the secretary of the defendant corporation club to go all the way from Chicago to Savannah to sign up a player?

(Objection; sustained.)

* * *

Q: What was the first thing that you learned about Mr. Grabiner's presence in Savannah?

A: He called my house.

Q: On the telephone?

A: Yes, sir.

Q: Did he state where he was at that time?

A: He said he was in the Union Station, and he wanted me to come down there.

Q: What did you say to him?

A: I told him that we had been up practically all night at the hospital with my sister, and hadn't been home very long.

Q: What was the matter with your sister?

A: Appendicitis.

Q: Was she in the hospital at that time?

A: Yes, sir.

Q: And what did you do then?

A: Well, he kept pleading with me to come down there to see him,— that he wanted to get out of town, or something like that—and finally I agreed, and dressed and went down there.

Q: Down to the station?

A: Yes, sir.

Q: Did you meet him then?

A: Yes, sir.

Q: Where did you go then?

A: We got in the car and rode up some little side street there, or road, and into the main street of the city of Savannah.

Q: Now, what did you talk about when you got in the car?

A: Well, we first was talking about the condition of my sister, I was telling him about it. Then he began to talk contract, and I told him that under the present conditions I would rather he go on out of town, and we would take that up later—depending upon what the outcome might be of my sister.

Q: What did he say?

A: Well, about that time we were in the neighborhood of where the hospital was, and we drove up and got out and went in—him and I.

Q: To see your sister?

A: Yes, sir—and stayed in there some five or ten minutes, and went out.

Q: Then where did you go?

A: We was riding in the direction of where I live. He brought up the contract question again.

Q: Now, go on and tell everything that was said, Mr. Jackson, between you and Grabiner.

A: Grabiner, he—I repeated to him again that I would rather not talk contract right at that present time. He give me some excuse that he wanted to get it over with and get it signed, and I recalled his attention to them writing me to come to Chicago; and I said: "What's the matter with you people up there, anyway," I said, "that you didn't have me come up and give you that information that I knew?" "Oh, well," he says, "we made that investigation..."

Hudnall, apparently trying to prevent the information about Comiskey's investigation from being part of the record, raised another objection which led to another wrangle between the lawyers. When it was over, Cannon resumed his examination.

Q: Now, just start in where you left off, Mr. Jackson, and give us the entire conversation between you and Mr. Grabiner, everything that occurred.

A: Mr. Grabiner said that the Chicago White Sox had made an investigation, and they had the goods on three men—Cicotte, Gandil and Williams. "Though," he said, "we know Williams gave you $5,000, and we know also that you talked to Gandil and Cicotte in the East in regards to throwing the World Series." I told him, I said: "You are all wrong there; I have not talked to anybody on such subject." He said: "Well, just let it go at that," he says, "whether you did or whether you didn't," he says, "let's talk contract."

Q: What did you say about the $5,000 when he mentioned it to you?
A: I asked him: "What was I going to do with it? I expected to go back up there."
Q: Was there anything said by you to Grabiner about what took place at Comiskey's office the day after you got the $5,000?

Hudnall, trying to protect Comiskey, objects, but the Judge allows Jackson to answer.

Q: Give us all of the conversation.
A: I told him if he hadn't of been so mean on the morning after the World Series, I would have give him all of the information—or give Mr. Comiskey—if he hadn't of been so mean, and not let me talk to him and slammed the window in my face—that I would have give him all the information that morning.
Q: Now, what else was said, if anything, about your playing... *[Note. This might be a typo in the original, "paying" seems to make more sense in light of Jackson's answer.]*
A: Then I asked him: "What was I going to do with the money?" And he said I did the only sensible thing to do with it—that is, to keep it. "That bunch of bums"—that is the word he used, I think—"Why, keep it."—And we was riding along alone at that time right in front of my house—was was sitting right out in front of my house in the car. I wanted $10,000 a season; and he says: "Well, I tell you what I will do with you; I will give you a three year ironclad contract at $8,000 a season, instead of $10,000 at one. Now," he says, "you can take that, or we will kick you out of baseball." He said: "You know we can do pretty well as we please with ball players." I studied it over, and I thought I might as well take it. And he got the contract out, and I told him, I said: "You know, Harry, I can't read or write," I said, "now read that contract over to me." And he read the contract over to me. And I said: "Now, there is no ten-day clause in there." He said: "This is an old form of a contract; there is no ten-day clause in it." And I told him I would sign it.

As it turned out, there was a ten-day clause in the contract, (a copy of which Jackson never received) and Grabiner's misrepresentation of that fact was central to Jackson's suit against Comiskey. In his own testimony, Grabiner denied or challenged several aspects of Jackson's testimony, though neither he nor Comiskey could deny Jackson's visit to the White Sox office the morning after the World Series ended. It should be pointed out, however, that the Jury heard all the testimony and believed Jackson.

When Hudnall read part of the contract into the record, it revealed that Jackson's salary was actually "$7,000 per season and an additional sum at the rate of $1,000 per season, said additional sum being in consideration of the option herein reserved to the Club owner for the removal of this contract," referring to the so-called ten-day clause.

Appendix G

Civil Suit Verdict

This is the Special Verdict handed down by the jury in Joe's 1924 civil suit against Charles Comiskey, an "authentic copy" of which was inserted in one of the scrapbooks kept by Katie Jackson. Though it was overturned by the judge on the grounds that Jackson had perjured himself, the answers given in this verdict demonstrate the judgment rendered by a jury sworn to make their decision on all the facts presented at the trial. Apparently, after listening to the testimony, they believed that Jackson had been convinced by Austrian on September 28, 1920, to incriminate himself in the fix. If this is so, and the jury heard the discrepancies between Jackson's grand jury testimony and his testimony in their court room, it follows that they believed he was telling the truth in Milwaukee and had lied in Chicago. Furthermore, the verdict reflects their belief that Jackson's name had in fact been used with the gamblers without his permission.

STATE OF WISCONSIN   CIRCUIT COURT   MILWAUKEE COUNTY

Joe Jackson, Plaintiff
         vs.
American League Base Ball
Club of Chicago,
alias, Chicago American League
Base Ball Club, Defendant

Filed
Feb. 15, 1924
C.C. Maas, Clerk
Case No. 64772

Special Verdict

1. Did the Defendant offer the Plaintiff a sum of money sufficient to make the Plaintiff's share of the World Series receipts, equal to $5000, if the defendant's base ball club won the 1917 pennant?

ANSWER. YES.

2. If you answer Question number 1 "Yes," then answer this Question: Did the Plaintiff rely and act upon such information conveyed to him?

ANSWER. YES.

3. Did Grabiner, at the time the 1920 contract was signed, represent to the Plaintiff Jackson, that the contract did not contain a ten day clause?

ANSWER. YES.

4. If you answer Question number 3 "Yes," then answer this Question: Was the Plaintiff Jackson, induced to sign the 1920 contract in reliance upon such representation?

ANSWER. YES.

5. If you answer Question number 4 "Yes," then answer this Question: Did the Plaintiff Jackson, have a right to rely upon such representation?

ANSWER. YES.

6. Did the Plaintiff Jackson, unlawfully conspire with Gandil, Williams and other members of the White Sox Club, or any of them, to lose or "throw" any of the base ball games of the 1919 World's Series to the Cincinnati Baseball Club?

ANSWER. NO.

7. If you answer Question number 6 "Yes," then answer this Question:

Did the Defendant at the time the 1920 contract was signed by Mr. Comiskey about May 1st, 1920, know of the Plaintiff's participation in such conspiracy?

ANSWER. [LEFT BLANK, NO ANSWER RENDERED]

8. Did Williams give Jackson the $5000 before all the games in the 1919 World's Series had been played?

ANSWER. NO.

9. If you answer Question number 8 "No," then answer this Question: At the time Williams gave Jackson the $5000 did he tell Jackson that there had been an agreement between certain of the ball players on the White Sox team to lose or "throw" the games of the World's Series, and that the $5000 was his (Jackson's) share of the money received by the players for their part in the agreement?

ANSWER. NO.

10. If you answer Question number 3 "Yes," then answer this Question: What sum of money will fairly and reasonably compensate the Plaintiff for the defendant's failure to give Plaintiff a contract in accordance with Defendant's representation?

ANSWER. $16,711.04

* * *

Attached to Special verdict: "Certificate Number 9530 of authenticity of copy of Special Verdict, 16 February, 1924"

Signed by C.C. Maas, Clerk. Fee: Fifty cents.

Appendix H

Recent Support for Jackson

A SAMPLING OF RECENT SUPPORT FOR JOE JACKSON

SHOELESS JOE JACKSON CARRIES A LABEL
HE DOESN'T DESERVE

Joseph Jefferson Jackson was victimized by a profession which exploited both his talent to hit a baseball and his inability to read a book...

Here was a man hailed for his skill and mocked for his illiteracy, which is not to be confused with ignorance. He was despised for culpability in a scandal in which apparently he did not take part, the fixing of the 1919 World Series....

He was never called Shoeless Joe until after he was ostracized.

What numerous sports historians want him to be called now is a Hall of Famer. Shoeless Joe Jackson deserves nothing less.

Art Spander, *The Sporting News*, June 4, 1984

* * *

I'm of the unqualified opinion that Shoeless Joe Jackson was innocent of the charges that he conspired to fix the 1919 World Series and therefore deserves to be installed in the Hall of Fame.

Given the opportunity, I would vote for Jackson.

Art Spander, *The Sporting News*, May 29, 1989

* * *

Williams also acknowledged that he is "sympathetic" to the recent boomlet for Jackson's election to the Hall of Fame.

"I'm a little more compassionate now for Joe Jackson," (said Williams.) I know he took the money, but what a lot of people don't know is as soon as the World Series ended, he tried to give the money back."

Ted Williams, quoted by Jerome Holtzman in his "On Baseball" column, *The Chicago Tribune*, July 25, 1989.

* * *

TOO GOOD TO BE LEFT OUT

Shoeless Joe Jackson should get his foot in the Hall's door.

Excluding Joe Jackson for all these years strikes me as no mean injustice. Short of blatant attempts to undermine the integrity of the game—and I include cheating in that category—good play, rather than good character, ought to be the sole criterion for induction into the Hall of Fame. That's why loutish Ty Cobb is there. Jackson meets the standard too.

...Jackson was no villain; he was probably more an innocent victim or a scapegoat....In this country, when there is uncertainty, innocence is presumed, and in this instance there is reasonable doubt indeed. Besides, if a jury of his peers acquitted Jackson, shouldn't Hall of Fame electors heed them rather than Landis?...Until the day he died, Jackson fought to clear his name. The most persuasive argument in his favor is the way in which Jackson's plight has captured the American Imagination.... His story has been handed down through generations.... Baseball's most famous alleged criminal keeps emerging in books, plays and films as a symbol of good.... We can only speculate what indignities he might have inflicted upon American League pitching during the ensuing decade of lively balls... But of this I am confident: Someday Jackson will be enshrined in Cooperstown... I say to the custodians of baseball's honor roll, why wait?

Nicholas Dawidoff, *Sports Illustrated*, June 12, 1989.

Appendix 9

Affidavit In Re C. A. Comiskey II

Attorney David Carlson is a keen and knowledgeable observor of the Joe Jackson case. Upon meeting Charles A. Comiskey II in professional circumstances, he asked the grandson of the original owner of the White Sox what he thought of Jackson. Missing from the dry language of the affidavit is what actually happened. Mr. Comiskey said he believed Jackson was completely innocent because that had been the common wisdom when Jackson's name came up in Comiskey family conversation.

AFFIDAVIT

I, DAVID B. CARLSON, being first duly sworn on oath, depose and state as follows:

1. That I am an attorney, licensed to practice law in the State of Illinois for the last twenty-one (21) years.

2. That I am associated with the law firm of Rinella and Rinella, Ltd. at One North LaSalle Street, Suite 3400, Chicago, Illinois 60602.

3. That on the 26th day of February, 1986, at the law offices of Rinella and Rinella, Ltd., in the presence of Bernard B. Rinella, Charles A. Comiskey II, and Colleen Kelley, a daughter of Charles A. Comiskey II, I asked Charles A. Comiskey II whether or not Joe Jackson *had either conspired to throw or had attempted to throw any or all* of the games of the 1919 World Series to the Cincinnati Reds.

4. Charles A. Comiskey II responded to both questions *in the negative*.

FURTHER AFFIANT SAYETH NOT.

(Signed) David B. Carlson

SUBSCRIBED AND SWORN TO
before me this 18 day of
January, 1991.
Arlene Welbourne
Notary Public

An almost identical Affidavit was subscribed and sworn to by Bernard B. Rinella, the managing partner of the law firm.

Appendix J

Recent Commissioners' Responses

RECENT OFFICIAL MAJOR LEAGUE RESPONSES

Starting with Landis, baseball commissioners and other officials of organized baseball have received periodic requests to reinstate Jackson, or at least take another look at his situation, particularly in light of the exculpatory evidence that has become available since he was banished over seventy years ago. So far, no commissioner has done anything.

AMERICAN LEAGUE OF PROFESSIONAL BASEBALL CLUBS
280 Park Avenue, New York, N.Y. 10017

February 19, 1980
Our 80th Year.

(Letter in response to a fan's inquiry.)

Thank you for your letter about Joe Jackson. Perhaps you are right and that this matter should be reviewed. I am not sure. Right now, we have more immediate problems than we can handle, but perhaps at some not too distant future date the matter of a review could at least be considered. I have sent a copy of your letter to the Commissioner.

Sincerely,
L.S. MacPhail, Jr.
President.

* * *

BASEBALL
Office of the Commissioner

April 23, 1980

(Letter in response to a fan's inquiry about the status of the Joe Jackson case.)

The Shoeless Joe Jackson incident is dead forever. Baseball will never re-instate him because ignorance of the law is no excuse.

Joe knew about the fix and didn't report it—that in itself was a crime.

I can sympathize with your feelings about the matter but the decision will never be changed.

Thank You for your comments.

Sincerely yours,
Monte Irvin
Special Assistant to
the Commissioner

* * *

Office of the Commissioner
MAJOR LEAGUE BASEBALL

A. BARTLETT GIAMATTI
Commissioner

July 20, 1989

(Letter in response to a fan's inquiry.)

Thank you for sending me your letter and materials in support of your letter. I have said before and I will say to you, I am not going to play God with history. I am not going to become involved in whether Shoeless Joe Jackson should or should not be in the Hall of Fame. You are entitled to make whatever efforts you think you can, and I reserve the right to say what I have just said. Please do not expect me to take any further action in this matter.

With all best wishes.

Sincerely yours,
A. Bartlett Giamatti

* * *

Office of the Commissioner
MAJOR LEAGUE BASEBALL

FRANCIS T. VINCENT, JR.
Commissioner
September 13, 1991

(Letter in response to a fan's inquiry.)

Thank you for your recent letter and for the interest which you have expressed in Major League Baseball. Your comments regarding "Shoeless" Joe Jackson have been duly noted.

The circumstances surrounding Mr. Jackson being placed on the permanently ineligible list took place more than seventy years ago and I am not prepared to reconstruct them now.

As I have expressed on many occasions, I believe that baseball occupies a special place in American life. Consequently, I am always interested in knowing the views of the fans whose devotion to the game has made it a national institution.

Sincerely,
(Signed) Fay Vincent
Francis T. Vincent, Jr.

Appendix K

Katie Wynn Jackson's Will

We know that Lefty Williams threw down the $5000 and that eventually Joe picked it up. We know that Katie finally deposited it in their bank account in December, 1919. We also know that Joe asked Harry Grabiner what he should do with the money and Grabiner told him to keep it. But the question remains: what finally happened to the money? In view of Katie's Will, one could make the case that the tainted money, cleansed and amplified considerably, was put to a fine and humanitarian use.

KATIE JACKSON'S LAST WILL AND TESTAMENT
(From the *Greenville News*, November 15, 1959)

WIDOW OF SHOELESS JOE JACKSON
LEAVES ESTATE FOR CANCER, HEART

The widow of one of baseball's unforgettable characters, who set a World Series batting mark in 1919 that has never been excelled, has willed almost the entire estate left by her and her husband to the American Cancer Society and the American Heart Fund.

Mrs. Katherine (Katie) Wynn Jackson, widow of "Shoeless Joe" Jackson, stipulated in her will, filed in the Greenville County judge of probate office March 21, that $11,575.75 of the estate's funds be contributed to the American Cancer Society and that $11,575.76 be contributed to the American Heart Fund.

The famed "Shoeless Joe" died in December, 1951, of a heart ailment. Mrs. Jackson, his constant and devoted companion during the heights and depths of his baseball career, died last April 18. She had requested that no publicity be given to the bequests until six months after her death.

Jack M. Abbott, executor of the estate of Mrs. Jackson, disclosed the terms of the will Friday at the same time that he presented checks to Greenville officials of the cancer and heart fund societies at Greenville General Hospital....

The executor explained that Mrs. Jackson's estate amounted to "something over $30,000." The two bequests took the bulk of the estate and funeral expenses and payments of other obligations absorbed the rest.

Mr. Abbott, at Friday's informal gathering for the presentation of the checks, showed a copy of Mrs. Jackson's will.

It stipulated, in part, that:

"The following devise and bequeath of the rest, residue and remainder of my estate is made because of my desire and wish that additional research and study be made in certain fields of medicine.

"My late husband, Joe Jackson, was a victim of a heart ailment, and I suffer from another affliction. I am making this disposition of the balance of the property in my estate as a living memorial to my husband and myself."

The Greenville and state officials accepted the checks, and after clearance through attorneys, they will be sent to the headquarters of each association. The officials, surprised and grateful for the gift, said they were certain the money provided by Mrs. Jackson would be used wisely.

Mr. J. H. Walker (Greenville County president of the American Cancer Society) said, "The generosity shown by Mrs. Jackson truly reflects confidence that the shadows of cancer will one day be stamped out of the lives of men, women and children. Her thoughtfulness will be an inspiration to the scientists now engaged in cancer research. This is a very noble gift which was certainly inspired by her kind heart."

Appendix L

The Ted Williams — Bob Feller Petitions

Shoeless Joe is long gone, but not forgotten. Over the years many people have petitioned Organized Baseball to clear his name so he can be installed in the Baseball Hall of Fame. So far these efforts have been in vain. Now two of the modern game's greatest icons have come to the aid of their legendary predecessor. In 1998, Ted Williams and Bob Feller petitioned the Baseball Commissioner's Office and the Hall of Fame on Joe's behalf. Their plea, as spelled out below, is based on the argument that Jackson's "lifetime ban" from any participation in Organized Baseball ended when he died in 1951. Given the stature of Williams and Feller in the baseball universe, sooner or later these petitions will be answered. As we go to press with this edition, that answer has yet to arrive. Stay tuned.

D.G.

THE OFFICES OF THE ACTING COMMISSIONER OF MAJOR LEAGUE BASEBALL AND THE EXECUTIVE COMMITTEE OF MAJOR LEAGUE BASEBALL

IN THE MATTER OF:	)
	) A HEARING
JOSEPH JEFFERSON "SHOELESS JOE"	) IS REQUESTED
JACKSON, a Deceased Ballplayer;	)

THE PETITION OF TED WILLIAMS, AND BOB FELLER IN SUPPORT OF JOSEPH JEFFERSON "SHOELESS JOE" JACKSON

Here, on another fall afternoon
A Georgia millhand the kids called Shoeless Joe
Pegged a runner out at the plate on his knees
from against the far left-field stands.
And never played again...

...For Shoeless Joe is gone, long gone,
a long yellow grass blade between his teeth
and the bleacher-shadows behind him.

—Nelson Algren

Now Comes TED WILLIAMS, a former player for the Boston Franchise of the American League, and BOB FELLER, a former player for the Cleveland Franchise, individually, and also as class representatives of certain baseball fans and historians across the country (hereinafter "Scholars of the Game"), by their Counsel, Louis R. Hegeman, E. Michael Kelly, Nicholas J. Motherway, and Brian P. Shaughnessy, petitioning Major League Baseball regarding the records of a deceased ballplayer from the Dead Ball Era, JOSEPH JEFFERSON "SHOELESS JOE" JACKSON once a member of the Chicago Franchise of the American League, and a participant in the infamous Championship Series of 1919. In support of this Petition, TED WILLIAMS, and BOB FELLER show Major League Baseball the following:

NATURE OF THE ACTION

1. The Petitioners request that Major League Baseball, through the Offices of the Acting Commissioner of Baseball, the Honorable Alan Selig (hereinafter "The Commissioner"), and the Honorable Members of the Executive Committee of Major League Baseball (hereinafter "The Committee"), issue a declaration confirming that the above named player is no longer subject to any **current ineligible roster** or **current listing of ineligible "persons"** maintained by Major League Baseball.[1]

JURISDICTION AND VENUE

2. Major League Baseball, through the good offices of its Acting Commissioner, Mr. Bud Selig, and the Members of its Executive Committee, collectively hold all of the substantive powers of Major League Baseball, including all powers previously delegated to the Commissioners of Baseball. Among the powers regularly exercised by Major League Baseball is the inherent power to monitor, correct, and declare the entries found in the Records of the National Game. The exercise of this power, as the Commissioner and Committee know, has run the gamut from affixing or removing asterisks to certain records, to the placement or removal of the name of a living player or baseball executive on Major League Baseball's roster of ineligible persons.

3. The relief requested herein is of a ministerial nature, and involves a review of the current ineligible roster of Major League Baseball. Petitioners believe that upon reviewing the records and considering the issues raised herein, Major League Baseball will be able to issue a simple declaration that Joseph Jefferson "Shoeless Joe" Jackson, a player who died more than five decades ago, is no longer listed on a **current roster of ineligible persons** kept by Major League Baseball.[2] The scope and nature of the Relief requested by this

---

[1]In the unlikely event that Baseball might contend that Shoeless Joe, a deceased ballplayer, is somehow amenable to, or subject to, a current ineligible roster, Petitioners will show Major League Baseball why such listing entails a practical impossibility, and stands in derogation of honored tenets set forth in our Constitution, and Common Law, including concepts of Due Process; and perhaps most importantly, the stated policies of Major League Baseball (further detailed herein).

[2]On information and belief, Major League Baseball does not have written definitions or regulations setting forth the following terms: "Person," "ineligible roster,"

petition is clearly within the powers of Major League Baseball and can be granted readily and with little outlay of time or effort.

STANDING OF THE PETITIONER

4. The Petitioners, TED WILLIAMS, and BOB FELLER, players from the Modern Era, file this Petition on behalf of a deceased player from the Dead Ball Era who has no one to speak on his behalf, but also file on behalf of many fans, "scholars of the game," seeking a posthumous addendum to the "box score" of American Baseball History. Petitioners, by this petition, stand in as pinch hitters and late inning relief on behalf of "Shoeless Joe" Jackson, spiritual teammates in a flannel-clad fraternity who have stepped across the chalk lines and played their allotted innings, as part of a long progression known as "Baseball."

5. The Petitioners' standing is based on a continuous association with Major League Baseball dating from 1936 for Petitioner Feller, and 1939 for Petitioner Williams. The Petitioners' ties and service within the National Game have been continuous, save periods of service in the United States Marine Corps and United States Navy. Petitioner Feller had the privilege of playing 18 Championship Seasons for the Cleveland Franchise of the American League; Petitioner Williams had the privilege of playing 19 Championship Seasons for the Boston Franchise of the American League. The Petitioners, upon completing their playing days, have served Major League Baseball in a variety of capacities which include coach, manager, executive, and committee member for both Major League Baseball and the National Baseball Hall of Fame.

6. Petitioners have not met Mr. Jackson, and will gain no economic advantage or benefit by this petition. The Petitioners are motivated solely by objective considerations which include the integrity of the game, and the accurate preservation of a unique chapter of American Baseball History. Preservation in this case includes the honoring of individual records of accomplishment on the diamond,

---

"ineligible list," "permanent ineligible list," "eligible roster" or "eligible list." Further, on information and belief, Major League Baseball has no written rules or procedures for "restoration" to "eligibility" in the case of deceased ball players. Finally, on information and belief, Major League Baseball has never previously "restored" a deceased player.

which by any standard of excellence in any era, whether deadball or liveball, were remarkable. The opportunity to appropriately honor the records of Shoeless Joe is in danger of being lost as a result of a lack of advocates, dissembling procedural issues, and the perpetuation of distorted fact and harmful myth.

EXISTENCE OF A JUSTICIABLE ISSUE REQUIRING CLARIFICATION

7. This petition is filed because of a recurring issue raised in any discussion regarding the honoring of the deceased player. It is an issue which has engendered great debate, but fortuitously involves a topic which Major League Baseball can quickly resolve. As the Commissioner and Committee may recall, the National Baseball Hall of Fame, a private not-for-profit institution separate and apart from Major League Baseball, passed an amendment to the Rules of Election to the National Baseball Hall of Fame on February 4, 1991. The Rule known as Rule 6(E) states as follows:

"6(E) Any person on Baseball's ineligible list shall not be an eligible candidate." [3]

8. The Petitioners believe that the above Rule patently cannot apply to the deceased ballplayer, and has so informed the Hall of Fame (c.f. Ex "A" hereto): Shoeless Joe is no longer a "person" and has not been a "person" since the 1950s; and thus cannot be on Baseball's current ineligible list; cannot be "restored" to eligibility; and has completed his sentence and any period of ineligibility five decades ago. Moreover, the player's name was presumably removed by Major

---

[3]Rule 6(E) has from time to time been commonly referred to as the "Pete Rose Rule," but in the wake of the movies "Field of Dreams" and "Eight Men Out," also has been used as a de facto "Shoeless Joe Rule." The rule, as discussed in detail at other places in this Petition, cannot apply to the subject player as he died some 40 years prior to the passage of Rule 6(E), and even if ex post facto impediments are set aside, there remains the problem that the deceased player is no longer a "person" as required by Rule 6(E); and cannot be listed on any "ineligible" list as he completed his sentence in full, and should have automatically been stricken. Further, the frequently used concept of "restoration" cannot be used to "restore" a deceased player to any "eligible" roster, as there is no "eligible roster" in Major League Baseball. But even if there were "eligibility" and an "eligible roster," it would be impossible herein, as the Landis Ban dealt solely with eligibility to play Professional Baseball. That status cannot be achieved again—other than perhaps in a "Field of Dreams" in an Iowa cornfield under a harvest moon.

League Baseball from any ineligible list, or roster of suspended persons serving a sentence or ban, at the time the sentence was fully finished—in this case at the close of the player's natural life. Shoeless Joe Jackson died on December 5, 1951.

9.   Although Rule 6(E) clearly cannot apply for the reasons noted above, the Rule has, however created considerable confusion and as a result, has had a "chilling effect" on a process and procedure of a separate and very important institution—the National Baseball Hall of Fame. Moreover, the chilling effect and misapplication of Rule 6(E) has been abetted by an "Official Statement of Policy" on the Internet Website of the National Baseball Hall of Fame, which purports to set forth the ostensible **standing procedures** and **"restoration" procedures** required by Major League Baseball in "restoring" Joe Jackson, and thus theoretically clearing the first hurdle in any process directed towards the induction of Joe Jackson in the National Baseball Hall of Fame.[4] The Petitioners also have personal knowledge of the

---

[4]cf National Baseball Hall of Fame, Official Statement Regarding Pete Rose and Shoeless Joe Jackson: *www.com** Members Overview/Veterans Committee/Rules for Election/Rose & Jackson FAQ/Steal Home.* The above Internet announcement states that in order for Jackson to be eligible, an estate must apply to the Office of the Commissioner for reinstatement," ostensibly to regain his "eligibility." The statement is somewhat surprising as 1) Major League Baseball presumably determines its own procedures; (2) On information and belief, Major League Baseball has no procedures or rules for the "restoration" to the "eligibility" of deceased ball players, and therefore the Internet Website's "official policy" must be an extemporaneous determination, not a statement on behalf of Major League Baseball; (3) Further, on information and belief, Major League Baseball has no "eligible" roster that the players would be returned to, only a current listing of living persons that are suspended or "ineligible" from involvement in Baseball for set periods of years, or in certain instances, for life; (4) The requirement that only an estate can act on behalf of Jackson is, in essence, a procedural "poison pill," an artificial burden of great practical magnitude, as the player had no children; (5) An estate is not necessary and the requirement is artificial and vexatious, as the records and listing to be reviewed in connection with this Petition are not private property, they belong to Major League Baseball, and do not involve private rights or interests; (6) The requirement that only an estate can act seems to place the player in some sort of "limbo" awaiting action by an "estate"; an onerous and expensive form of redtape that masks the fact that the records sought are those of the National Game; (7) The concept obviously ignores the basic common law concept of sentencing, to wit: once a sentence is served in full, the period of suspension ends **automatically** by the inherent terms and duration of the sentence, without reference or need for subsequent procedures, petitions or filings by estates; (8) The deceased player is no longer under the jurisdiction of Baseball, and any concept such as "restoration," if logically possible,

above considerations serving as a bar to the placement of the name of Joe Jackson among the annual listing of 15 possible candidates for consideration by the Veterans' Committee of the National Baseball Hall of Fame, and would be most willing to recount them at length in any hearing in connection with this Petition.

10. In further support, the Petitioners would urge that the Commissioner and Committee take Notice of the many informed, respected baseball fans, "scholars of the game," including members of Committees of the National Baseball Hall of Fame, who believe that an open discussion should be had in the proper forum, the Committee Rooms of the Committee on Veterans of the National Baseball Hall of Fame—for purposes of considering whether, in fact, the career performance of Shoeless Joe Jackson, is worthy of induction into the National Baseball Hall of Fame.[5]

11. In considering the above issues, the Petitioners would draw the Commissioner and Committee's attention to certain key considerations which bear upon any decision rendered in response to this Petition:

A. Baseball, by this Petition, is requested to review its records, including the current roster of ineligible persons. This petition does not seek "restoration," a concept that is meaningless and impossible, as the players have served their sentences in full with dignity and cannot be "restored" to their former status as players. Further, and on information and belief, Major League Baseball has no regulations or rules for the "restoration" of deceased ballplayers, and has, in fact, never engaged in any procedure whereby a player is "restored";

B. Baseball is not being asked, pursuant to this Petition, to determine whether Shoeless Joe belongs in the Hall of Fame. As the Commissioner and Committee know well, that determination is properly within the jurisdiction of a Committee appointed by a Private Trust, and known as the Committee on Veterans of the National Baseball Hall of Fame. If the declaration requested herein is expeditiously issued, and Major League Baseball confirms that

---

would still, from a practical perspective, be meaningless, and from a theological standpoint, most incorrect.

[5]Whether a Player is ever inducted into the Hall of Fame is a separate issue which is properly placed in the hands of the Committee on Veterans, a Committee designated by the National Baseball Hall of Fame for purposes of deciding issues of the type raised herein.

Shoeless Joe is not listed on the roster of ineligible persons maintained by Major League Baseball, **it will greatly facilitate the Veterans' Committee taking up the issue of whether Shoeless Joe should be inducted into the Hall of Fame at its next meeting in March of 1998;**

C. Baseball is not being asked by this Petition to turn back the clock and retry the case, resolve disputed facts, or determine whether the player was guilty or innocent. The issue of guilt or innocence, although pertinent to the equities framing this Petition, is not a determining factor in connection with this petition. Shoeless Joe was sentenced and has served his sentence in full. The manner of sentencing, and the absence of due process, issues which are discussed herein, are set forth in the belief that they create **current equitable obligations** which Baseball should address out of fairness, and which involve facts which are not disputed and are of public record;

D. Judge Landis' service in saving the National Game is wholeheartedly acknowledged by this Petition. The Judge acted while others hesitated, and did so to insure the **survival of the National Game.** He entered harsh, "drum head" punishments in weathering a grave crisis, and thereby trammeled on the rights of at least two players. This fact is not mentioned herein to denigrate the memory of the Commissioner, and indeed his place and prominence in the History of the National Game is better served by an honest recounting, admitting relevant facts. The defensive "candy coated" interpretations which deny any faults become a parody, and distract the public from appreciating the true contributions of a great and resolute Commissioner who, along with Mr. Ruth.... saved Baseball[6];

E. Baseball is not being asked to engage in complicated historical analysis—the issues raised by this Petition are straightforward—**Baseball is merely asked to review its current records and acknowledge that the jurisdiction of Baseball over the deceased player ended at the time of his death in 1951,** some four decades before the passage of Rule 6(E) noted above;

F. Baseball is not being asked to make sweeping policy decisions,

---

[6]The Petitioners would also cite, in addition to the efforts of Judge Landis and the Bat of the "Bambino," another remarkable innovation, the introduction of a magic sphere, the "live" ball.

or engage in debate as to collateral issues or other suspended players. Further, this Petition is not tendered in the interest of making capital of recent news stories as to ex-players, living "persons" that are currently listed and serving a sentence on the "ineligible list" of Major League Baseball. The facts, issues, and relief sought by this petition are wholly different. The relief requested herein merely requires a checking of current records, and a declaration as to those **current listings of ineligible persons.** The relief requested herein, unlike certain pending requests for commutation of a sentence of ineligibility, does not require protracted debate, or the examination of policy issues, merely a ministerial inquiry—a task which should be completed in less than a business day;

G. **Baseball is being asked to recognize and shoulder certain obligations, which, based on equity and fairness, are owed to the memory of the deceased player:** Shoeless Joe lost his livelihood and brilliant career by virtue of a 10 minute statement issued by Commissioner Landis. The punishment was meted out within hours of a jury verdict which found the players "Not Guilty," and was carried out without any opportunity to be heard, without any findings as to the alleged guilty acts, without any opportunity to rebut the allegations or the sentence. In light of Baseball's avowed striving for "fairness," **an expedited statement that "Shoeless Joe" is no longer listed as "ineligible" would be a fitting footnote to the earlier denial of due process in 1921. Petitioners request that the National Game (and by separate correspondence, the Hall of Fame) set aside all procedural "red tape" and hasten the declaration prayed for herein, thereby extending but a modest courtesy and accommodation when compared with the courtesy and comity that has been accorded by Major League Baseball from time to time in the case of suspended Owners and Executives in terminating or shortening bans or suspensions— or restoring individuals.**

THE BACKGROUND FACTS AND KEY ISSUES– EXHIBIT "A" HERETO

12. Although the Commissioner and Committee are familiar with the background facts in connection with this Petition, the Petitioners have taken the liberty of incorporating a Memorandum written by

Counsel regarding the facts and issues presented herein, a Copy of which is made a part of this Petition and incorporated herein as Exhibit "A."

THE KEY ISSUES

13. If Judge Landis had made an investigation in 1921, and had reviewed the box score, and also had an opportunity to fully review the Grand Jury transcript (rumored to have been stolen from Court Records by Arnold Rothstein's counsel, Mr. Fallon), the Judge would have learned the following: (a) that Jackson received $5,000.00, from a teammate and friend, Lefty Williams, subsequently realized that he should not accept the money, and attempted to return the money, but was told by the club to..."keep it"; (b) **Jackson did nothing whatsoever in furtherance of any conspiracy to fix, and by his conduct on the field, clearly and effectively withdrew and distanced himself from the actions and conspiracy of others,** by playing brilliant baseball that included flawless fielding, and offensive statistics that easily led the Series and stood for many years.[7]

14. Because Baseball was fighting for survival, Judge Landis carried a ban that abrogated many basic tenets of our Constitution, Common Law, and subsequently annunciated policies of Baseball. The emergency is long past, the sentences fully served, yet Baseball appears to be continuing the deprivations exacted in 1921. The perception should be corrected for the following reasons:

A. Major League Baseball, in managing its records and policies, has at all times stressed the need **for honor, objectivity and fairness** because they are the records of our National Game, a duty which has been reiterated by Commissioners, including the late Commissioner Giammatti, who **stressed the "fidelity" of Baseball:**

I believe baseball is an important, enduring American institution. It must assert and aspire to the highest principles—of

---

[7]The scholars Donald Gropman, *Say it Ain't So Joe;* David Carlson, *Strike Four Joe Jackson, the Black Sox and 1919 World Series;* Irv Stein, *The Ginger Kid;* Elliot Asinov, *Eight Men Out;* and the late Bill Veeck, *The Hustlers Handbook;* have all produced wonderfully entertaining and scholarly histories as to the events herein. Their accounts of the Series and fix should be consulted at length by any scholar wishing to plumb the points and issues discussed in this Petition.

integrity, of professionalism, of performance, of fair play, within its rules. It will come as no surprise that, like an institution composed of human beings, this institution will not always fulfill its highest aspirations. I know of no earthly institution that does. But this one, because it is so much a part of our history as a people and because it has such a purchase on our national soul, has an obligation to the people for whom it is played—to its fans and well-wishers—to strive for excellence in all things and to promote the highest ideals.

B. In keeping with the standard of fidelity and need to strive for excellence, it should be noted that certain policies (including onerous standing procedures) are being attributed to Baseball and convey the unfortunate impression that Baseball is attempting to reach beyond this temporal setting, and control or further "punish" deceased players who have passed to . . . "the other side of the grass." Certainly the concept raises certain theological and related difficulties, as the concept would appear to assert a most ambitious concept of jurisdiction and punishment (somewhat suggestive of themes in Dante's *Inferno*). Petitioners believe that this unfortunate appearance is unintended by Baseball and would suggest that the relief requested herein has the ability to eradicate the above impression.

C. Baseball ceased to have any jurisdiction over the deceased player when he died, as decedent ceased to be a . . . "person" (c.f. Rule 6(E).[8] Any belated effort at urging that Joe Jackson is still on a permanent ineligible list would entail a form of after-the-fact, double punishment which is barred by all accepted concepts of common law. Moreover, it entails a tampering and altering with the sentence handed down by Judge Landis. The Judge banned Shoeless Joe from playing baseball during the remaining period of years that he was capable of playing, or at worst, during his lifetime. **Judge Landis did not bar or place Shoeless Joe on a list of ineligibility for perpetuity—he knew where his powers ended.**

D. If a permanent ineligible roster is being utilized as a procedural device to avoid what is apprehended by some to be an assault on the traditions of the National Game or the Baseball Hall

---

[8]C.f. Rule 6(E) of the National Baseball Hall of Fame as quoted herein on page 319, n.3.

of Fame, the continued listing of the deceased player, the use of "ineligible rosters," and onerous standing requirements are unnecessary: the National Baseball Hall of Fame has appointed a most independent body of very experienced members who have both the credentials and the prime duty of weighing the *bona fides* of various candidates. The committee has more than sufficient guidance (and protection) in other sections of the Rules of the Hall of Fame, including Rule 9 which states that ... **"Voting shall be based on the individual's record, ability, integrity, sportsmanship, character, and contribution to the game."** Most importantly, the members of the Committee have the experience, judgment, and love for the game which will insure that a competent and responsible determination will be made without need for long outdated ineligible lists and rosters, onerous standing requirements, and the effort at exercising jurisdiction over deceased players who fully served their sentences some 40 years ago.

E. Our Common Law, Constitution and legal traditions, while obviously not directly applicable to deceased players, set a benchmark for what is traditionally held to be fair and consistent with due process, and as such, provide a reference of the highest order. If the concepts are applied herein, it is apparent that the double jeopardy, the punishment of a person a second time (or as here, forever) is clearly a grave concern. In this case, Shoeless Joe served his sentence in full, and under concepts of due process and fair play that have evolved over hundreds of years in our Common Law and Constitution, the deceased player's name should have been stricken from any ineligible listing decades ago when he completed his sentence (1951). Any retention of his name on a subsequent listing or a current ineligible listing (which is Baseball's sole procedural mechanism for punishing "persons"), or any attempt at somehow banning or exerting "jurisdiction" over the player in perpetuity, entails twice placing the player in jeopardy for the same offense—and is **a blatant tampering with the sentence of Judge Landis, who, as noted above, knew the limits of his power.**

F. Any linking or tying this Petition on behalf of Shoeless Joe to the recent Petition on behalf of Pete Rose, either directly or indirectly, or taking this issue under advisement along with the Rose Petition, would, with all due respect, further deny due process to the memory and honoring of the deceased player: The key facts are wholly different, particularly the fact that Shoeless Joe fully paid his debt to Baseball. The relief requested herein is simple, and relates to the current listings of ineligible "persons" found in the current records of Baseball. No commutation of sentence, rehashing of salient facts or debates over the Goals and Philosophy of Major League Baseball are required. There is no linkage in the two cases, and given the disparity in issues, factual background, and the avowed policy of Major League Baseball as stated by the late Commissioner Giammatti, such linkage or tying would clearly be improper.

G. Major League Baseball can take Official Notice of its own disciplinary history, informal procedures, and certain logical considerations, as there are no written rules governing this situation:

(i) The ineligible roster of Major League Baseball has always served as the mechanism for punishing living suspended "persons"[9] (living beings) and should therefore contain only those names of "persons" that are being punished, during the period they are "punished" and "ineligible";

(ii) Once the punishment ends, and the players have died, a continued listing is "impossible," as the deceased players have ceased to be "persons" (and hopefully have passed on to the jurisdiction of a higher classification and League);

(iii) Once a sentence/suspension is served in full, one cannot logically continue to be listed on the roster or list of persons being punished—persons who are "ineligible";

(iv) Once a sentence is fully served, Baseball (for lack of better metaphor or analogy) has obligations analogous to a Warden, and an <u>automatic</u> duty to end the punishment on the anniversary and completion of the last day of the sentence. Here, Baseball had a duty to "free" Joe in 1951 and remove his name from any roster or listing of persons serving periods of punishment. The Petitioners are confident that the corrections were made long ago by deleting the name of Shoeless Joe.

---

[9]The Public understanding of the jurisdiction and candidates on the ineligible roster of Major League Baseball is succinctly reflected in the ubiquitous Rule 6(E) which speaks of "persons" listed on an ineligible roster. "Persons" are, on information and belief, not defined by Baseball, but are defined in *Webster's New World Dictionary* and *Webster's International Dictionary* as...."a human being...personality, self."

H. On the basis of the above, Joe Jackson having fully served his sentence and having ceased to be a "person" in 1951, cannot legitimately be listed on any current listing of "ineligible," suspended persons. Baseball can readily reach this conclusion and does not require any special or preliminary filing by an estate, or protracted internal policy debates. The issues at hand do not involve private rights and relate solely to the public record and public issues of Major League Baseball.

THE RECORDS OF BASEBALL

15. As the Commissioner and Committee know well, Baseball ultimately is a game of records. The keeping of the records and revisiting and correcting those records has always been the business of Baseball. What is requested herein is a ministerial checking of a set of records that hopefully were updated in the 1950s (but can still be updated if necessary), reflecting the status of the deceased player named in this petition. Again, Baseball is asked to merely acknowledge that the player fully served the allocated sentence and thus is no longer listed as a "person" on any current roster of ineligibility. Although a relatively innocuous undertaking, Petitioners believe that it will accomplish much in restoring historical equity to the treatment of the deceased player, and will fully comport with the standards announced by Commissioner Giammatti in discussing Baseball's records and procedures. In reviewing the removal of the Maris Asterisk from the season Home Run record, the Commissioner discussed an overall philosophy and need to be honest in reviewing records even if it sometimes bruised egos, including past heroes:

> "Baseball will always be indebted to Babe Ruth. He and Judge Kenesaw Landis were the two great men who helped save baseball. This does not in any way diminish the standing of Babe Ruth. He will always remain as a great baseball figure. But this should be done to maintain the fidelity of our records."

> The Chicago Tribune, September 5, 1991

16. Here, by analogy, it can be said that Baseball will always be indebted to Commissioner Landis. In granting this petition, Baseball will not dilute his standing in any way, as it merely acknowledges that the sentence the Judge imposed 76 years ago was dutifully served in

<u>full</u>, with dignity, and without rancor or criticism of the Commissioner or Major League Baseball.

THIS PETITION IS IN THE BEST INTEREST OF BASEBALL

17. The Petitioners are aware that there are substantial differences of opinion and very impassioned opponents on the issue of whether Shoeless Joe should go into the National Baseball Hall of Fame. The Petitioners believe that these differences are, in themselves, proof positive of a worthy issue: By granting the relief requested by this Petition and opening debate on the question of possible induction into the National Baseball Hall of Fame, the Commissioner and Committee would further honest, open debate by Scholars of the Game in a variety of public forums, including the Committees on Veterans of the Hall of Fame and the Society of American Baseball Researchers "SABR." Such action is certainly a much preferred and certainly more dignified alternative to the present situation, wherein action on the possible induction of Shoeless Joe appears to be muzzled, and wrapped up in a series of artificial restraints in the form of onerous standing requirements (i.e. the purported requirement that an estate act to restore the deceased ballplayer's name as a first and necessary step to induction). The purported standing requirement and other procedural "red tape," none of which is grounded or based on any written rules, leaves the public with an unfortunate perception of a National Game that is afraid of the issue, and seeks to exact further punishment, and continuing "jurisdiction" or control over the fate and honoring of a deceased ballplayer, long after he has **fully paid his debt to the National Game.**

* * * *

The Petitioners **WILLIAMS** and **FELLER,** collectively have over 100 years of experience in playing, managing, coaching and serving in various capacities in furtherance of Baseball. They have had the privilege of traveling the breadth of this country discussing the above issues with "scholars of the game." The sense of those discussions has resolved into three conclusions: (1) Major League Baseball, at a crucial time in its history, exacted a harsh punishment without due process, punishing Shoeless Joe for purported violations of an Unwritten Rule of questionable origin and purpose; (2) the ban was

entered without any consideration of wholly exculpatory and undisputed facts, including a box score which showed that only two
Chicago players played to win the 1919 World Series; (3) that the
punishment has been served in full, with dignity and grace.

Baseball should, in fairness, **make no further claim on Shoeless
Joe Jackson,** and should quickly affirm that Baseball's Jurisdiction
and the deceased player's "ineligibility" ended in 1951.

* * * *

WHEREFORE, on the basis of the above, the Petitioners TED
WILLIAMS, and BOB FELLER, respectfully call upon the Honor-
able Commissioner and the Members of the Executive Council of
Major League Baseball, to grant the following relief:

A) Issue a Declaration acknowledging that Joseph Jefferson
"Shoeless Joe" has fully served the sentence handed down by Judge
Kenesaw Mountain Landis on September 8, 1921;

B) Issue a Declaration confirming the fact that Joseph Jefferson
"Shoeless Joe" is not listed on any **current roster** or listing of
suspended persons or **"ineligible persons"**; and,

C) Issue any additional relief that the Commissioner and Executive Committee of Major League Baseball deem appropriate, and in
the Best Interests of our National Game.

The above Petition is respectfully submitted by the Petitioners for
purposes of furthering the best interests of our National Game. The
granting of the relief request herein will reflect the honor and dignity of
the National Game, and fairly address long debated and controversial
issues, thereby closing a Historic Chapter in American Folk History.

Respectfully,

"SHOELESS JOE" JACKSON

By:- *Ted Williams*
TED WILLIAMS

By:- *Bob Feller*
BOB FELLER

Dated: 1/14/98

330

Counsel for the Petitioners:

Louis R. Hegeman, Esq.
Gould & Ratner
222 North LaSalle Street,
Chicago, IL 60601
Tel: (312) 899-1630
Fax: (312) 236-3241

E. Michael Kelly, Esq.
Hinshaw & Culberson
222 North LaSalle Street, Suite
Chicago, IL 60601
Fax: (312) 704-3283

Nicholas J. Motherway. Esq.
Motherway & Glenn
100 W. Monroe, Street 200
Chicago, IL 60603
Tel: (312) 726-2699

Brian P. Shaughnessy Esq.
2100 Winchester, Suite 601
Wheaton, Il 60187
Tel: (630) 588-4122

THE NATIONAL BASEBALL HALL OF FAME AND MUSEUM
AND
THE OFFICE OF MAJOR LEAGUE BASEBALL

IN THE MATTER OF:)

)

JOSEPH JEFFERSON "SHOELESS JOE")
JACKSON, a Deceased Ballplayer;   )

MEMORANDUM REGARDING THE NOMINATION AND POSSIBLE INDUCTION OF "SHOELESS JOE" JACKSON IN THE NATIONAL BASEBALL HALL OF FAME

INTRODUCTION

TED WILLIAMS, a former player for the Boston Franchise of the American League, a member of the Baseball Hall of Fame, individually, and as a representative of baseball fans and historians across the country, hereinafter "Scholars of the Game," has asked Counsel: Louis R. Hegeman, E. Michael Kelly, Nicholas J. Motherway, and Brian P. Shaughnessy, to prepare a Memorandum to be filed with the **National Baseball Hall of Fame and the Office of Major League Baseball,** which addresses the relevant issues and procedures in connection with the nomination and potential election of the dominant hitter of the Dead Ball Era, JOSEPH JEFFERSON "SHOELESS JOE" JACKSON. Shoeless Joe last played Major League Baseball with the Chicago Franchise of the American League, and was banned in 1921 by Commissioner Kenesaw Mountain Landis.

I.

SCOPE OF THE MEMORANDUM

This Memo addresses three Issues: 1) Which Rules or Regulations govern nomination and voting in connection with a potential candidacy of "Shoeless Joe"; (2) What, if any, procedural requisites must be satisfied before "Shoeless Joe's" name can appear on a ballot of the Committee on Veterans; and finally, 3) Whether "Shoeless Joe"

Jackson is eligible for nomination and placement on the ballot of the Committee on Veterans for the year 1998?

II.

BACKGROUND FACTS

This Memorandum is directed towards certain facts, which are not disputed, are generally part of the public record, and which bear upon the Issues before the Committee on Veterans. The Committee, which is certainly familiar with many of the Facts, is asked to particularly focus upon the following:

1. Shoeless Joe was one of the infamous "Eight Men Out" who were banned by the First Commissioner of Baseball, Kenesaw Mountain Landis. Joe was banned in 1921, along with seven other players drawn from the line-up of the 1919 White Sox in connection with the "fix" of the 1919 World Series. The fix, the most famous sports scandal in history, rocked Baseball to its foundation and nearly brought the game down.

2. The fix of 1919 continues to captivate the public, at least in part because of classic literary and cinemagraphic connections: These include the opening of Fitzgerald's *The Great Gatsby,* Hollywood's *Eight Men Out,* "Shoeless Joe" in *Damn Yankees,* the right-handed-hitting Shoeless Joe in *Field of Dreams,* and many of the themes in *The Natural.*

3. Among Baseball fans, the captivation seems to be the result of the almost mythic prominence that has descended upon Shoeless Joe, the illiterate Southern mill hand, who, notwithstanding a deadball, beanball and the grand era of the "spitter," amassed the third highest average in history—.356. In the opinion of Mr. Ruth of New York, who modeled his swing after Shoeless Joe, Joe Jackson was..."the greatest hitter I ever saw," an opinion shared by knowledgeable observers.[1]

4. Ted Williams, having some experience in the above area of endeavor, although not in the era of the dead ball, and having done considerable hands-on research on the topic over several decades, as well as engaging in countless discussions and interviews of opponents and teammates of Jackson's, would concur with Mr. Algren that

---

[1] An opinion related by Babe Ruth to the Petitioner Williams.

Shoeless Joe Jackson was unique to the game, *"....the most natural man ever to wear spiked shoes, the canniest fielder, and the longest hitter..."—N. Algren.*

5. The continuing interest by Baseball Fans and Historians in the events of 1919 is undoubtedly fueled by the tension between brilliance and corruption that was the White Sox of 1919, the greatest collection of ballplayers prior to the 1927 Yankees. Perhaps fittingly, the team played in a somewhat surreal setting amidst the pens and slaughterhouses of Upton Sinclair's *The Jungle,* before boisterous fans drawn from the world of Farrell's Studs Lonigan, all within the confines of the Old Roman's "Baseball Palace of the World."

6. The Roster for the White Sox in the Autumn of 1919 was as follows: <u>Pitchers</u>: Claude "Lefty" Williams with 23 wins, Ed Cicotte with 29 wins, Dickie Kerr with 13 wins; <u>Catcher</u>: Ray Schalk; <u>1st Base</u>: Chick Gandil; <u>2nd Base</u>: Eddie Collins; <u>3rd Base</u>: Buck Weaver; <u>Shortstop</u>: Swede Risberg; <u>Left Field</u>: Joe Jackson; <u>Centerfield</u>: Happy Felsch; <u>Right Field</u>: Shano Collins.[2]

7. The 1919 White Sox's brilliance was tarnished by a series of internal flaws that would ultimately lead to the undoing of all but a few of the starting nine, and ironically, seem not unlike the ills that beset many current professional sport franchises: greed, cultural and educational disparities, and a recurring battle with ownership.

8. The cultural and educational divisions had, by the Fall of 1919, polarized the team into two camps: the "White" Sox, composed of college men such as Schalk, Collins and Kerr, who were protected from the ban, and a larger, rougher contingent, the "Black" Sox, a blue collar group that was ultimately banned to assuage the outraged public, a rough, rural contingent that had barely managed grade school, and in certain instances, as in the case of Shoeless Joe Jackson, were illiterate.

THE FIX OF 1919

9. There is no doubt as to the existence of a "fix" of the 1919 World Series which was participated in by certain members of the White Sox: the leaders Gandil and Risberg, and the other participants, Cicotte, Felsch, Williams and McMullin. There is no doubt that the fix included direct involvement by all of the above players at various

---

[2]Reichler, *The Baseball Encyclopedia.*

stages of the Series, including Felsch, Williams, and Cicotte. There is also no doubt that Risberg and Gandil dealt with and plotted a fix with two groups of gamblers, and perhaps as many as five groups of gamblers. The lineup on the gamblers' side included Bill "Sport" Sullivan, Hal Chase, and Arnold Rothstein (the "Bank"), who reportedly spent $350,000.00 to insure that the Fix of the 1919 Series was successful. There is certainly no doubt that at some point, the gamblers funneled money to Risberg and Gandil. But beyond the above basic facts, there are many significant gaps and considerable mystery as to how the fix was carried out on a game-by-game, inning-by-inning basis—and the micro analysis often leads to more confusion than truth?[3]

10. The players, unlike today's media-hungry stars, have thrown very little light on the above issues. Unlike their modern day successors, the Players of 1919 made no attempt to talk to the press, nor did they, on reflection, seek to "set the record straight." The players' unity in silence is a great irony—they were never a "team" while playing under the "Old Roman," but in the years following the fix of 1919, they closed ranks and maintained a collective silence that insured that many of the secrets of the fix of 1919 were carried to the..."other side of the grass"—including the ultimate question: which games were lost as a result of the fix, and which games were simply lost as a result of being outplayed.[4]

11. The mystery is compounded by the fact that the perpetrators of the fix on the White Sox: Risberg, Gandil, Cicotte, and Williams and

---

[3]Notwithstanding the myth and movies, there are many games that seem to have legitimately fallen to the verities of the game, and a Cincinnati pitching staff that had a 1.63 ERA in the World Series.

[4]It has always been theorized that there was a second group of fixers, a subtler group. This has led to a great deal of speculation, and a search for causal links. One set of events has to do with the reticence of the White Sox. The reticence of the Black Sox is understandable, but the hesitation of the players that were not indicted or banned, the White Sox, seems somewhat strange, and has been seized upon in essays by several experts that believe that the "fix" extended to members of the "White Sox" as well. They point to events, such as the all-night celebration that the White Sox threw the night the Black Sox were indicted by a Cook County Grand Jury—a curious form of conduct in response to the ill luck of a teammate—unless the group was rejoicing because the "noose" had missed them. See *Strike Four: Joe Jackson, the Black Sox, and 1919 World Series*, David B. Carlson, Chicago 1989; *Eight Men Out*, Eliot Asinof, New York, 1963; *The Golden Age of Baseball*, Harold Seymour, Oxford, 1971.

McMullen, were never a disciplined, coordinated group. The fixers literally had no idea of who, other than themselves, was playing below par in a given game. Risberg didn't know what Gandil was doing, and neither player knew for sure when Cicotte or Williams was not "bearing down." As a result there was a Chaplin-like bumbling and a confusion extending to the present day as to which games were lost as a result of honest efforts that fell short.[5]

12. The Box Score of the Championship Series of 1919 shows a record of performance that supports Commissioner Landis, with two conspicuous exceptions. Both camps, the "White Sox" and the "Black Sox" alike, had an abysmal series. Risberg had four errors and hit .080, while Felsch (a .300 hitter) hit .192, and Cicotte (a 29 game winner), and Williams (a 23 game winner) lost 5 games, made crucial errors and more than once cut off throws that might have prevented runs. Ironically, the non-fixers on the "White Sox" played as if they, too, were part of the shenanigans: Collins, the leader of the White Sox, made two crucial errors.

13. Only two players on the 1919 White Sox played each game of the Series to win: Shoeless Joe Jackson and Buck Weaver. They not only did not participate or abet the fix, but indeed, by their skill on the field, came close to overcoming the fix of their teammates. The two withdrew from the fix of the Black Sox by deed—and made their declaration with bat and glove. Both Jackson and Weaver set World Series records that lasted over the decades: Jackson was the only hitter on either side to hit a home run, and hit .357, the highest average on either side over a series that spanned eight games. His 12 hits established a record that stood until broken by Bobby Richardson in the 1964 World Series. He hit against a pitching staff that had a Series ERA of 1.63. Weaver hit .324, the second highest on the Sox team, and third highest average in the Series. Weaver and Jackson combined for a total of 23 hits, a record which was not broken until Messrs. Stargill and Gamer combined for 24 hits in the 1979 Series. Both players fielded .1000 with Jackson handling 17 chances flawlessly. Both players had key assists and putouts throughout the Series.[6] The box score testifies eloquently that they did not play to fix the World Series of 1919.

---

[5] *"The Year They Fixed the World Series,"* Kirby, ABA Journal, February 1988.
[6] *The Baseball Encyclopedia,* Reichler.

14. In addition to the Box Score, Major League Baseball has another source to look to regarding the winning efforts of Jackson and Weaver during the Series, the infamous Grand Jury Testimony. According to myth and movies, the Grand Jury Transcript seals the fate of Shoeless Joe.[7] Upon closer examination however, the document clearly trumpets the innocence of Shoeless Joe. Even a brief perusal shows a sobering image of a very candid, scared witness in an intimidating setting who testified honestly—particularly as to the various ways that he went about **playing to win in each game of the Series.** As a compendium, the sworn testimony underscores and supplies rock hard evidence that Shoeless Joe did nothing to fix the 1919 World Series:

(Testimony of Shoeless Joe before the Cook County Grand Jury September 28, 1920):

By Assistant State's Attorney Replogle to Shoeless Joe:

Q. Did you make any errors yourself that day?
A. No, Sir, not during the whole Series.
Q. Did you bat to win?
A. Yes.
Q. And run the best to win?
A. Yes, Sir.
Q. And field the best at the outfield to win?
A. I did.

   (Grand Jury testimony on page 9)

Q. Did you do anything to throw those games?
A. No, Sir.
Q. Any game in the series?
A. Not a one. I didn't have an error or a misplay.

   (Grand Jury Testimony on page 11)

---

[7]The Grand Jury testimony does show that Shoeless Joe pocketed $5,000.00 left in his hotel room at the Lexington Hotel by his teammate Claude Williams. He knew the money had sordid origins, but as his conduct and testimony show, he tried to return the money, and went out on the field and played flawless baseball setting records that lasted for decades. Further, Joe Jackson had no dealings with gamblers, did not bet on baseball or the World Series, and at worst, pocketed tainted money given to him by a teammate. On reflection he realized he should have refused, and attempted to return the money. Ultimately, he did nothing for the money and played an inspired Series.

PUBLIC OUTCRY AND THE APPOINTMENT OF A
COMMISSIONER

15. On the last day of the 1919 Series, Hugh Fullerton galvanized public opinion and started an inquiry that would ultimately lead to a criminal trial[8]:

Yesterday's, in all probability, is the last game that will be played in any World Series. If the club owners, and those who have the interest of the game at heart, have listened during the Series, they will call off the annual interleague contest...

> *The Chicago Herald and Examiner*
> October 12, 1919

16. The Fullerton article and the ensuing public outcry evolved into a national outrage resulting in two events:

A. A Grand Jury was convened in the Old Criminal Court Building on Hubbard Street in Chicago, and various players from the White Sox were called, including Lefty Williams, Ed Cicotte and Shoeless Joe Jackson. The ball players had been "volunteered" to go before the Grand Jury by the counsel for Ownership, Mr. Alfred Austrian, who at the time represented both the White Sox and the Cubs, and was clearly more intent on seeing the game and his client, the "Old Roman," Charles Comiskey, survive, rather than on the fate of a few hard-nosed, inarticulate players. As a result, the Players were not told that they could remain silent pursuant to the 5th Amendment. Mr. Austrian encouraged the players to "talk."

B. At about the time the Grand Jury was finishing its work, Major League Baseball appointed the First Commissioner of Baseball, Kenesaw Mountain Landis, a Federal Judge from the Northern District of Illinois. Judge Landis was the first and perhaps

---

[8]The Fullerton Article quoted above was but one of a series of articles on the Series. Fullerton had harangued about a fix long before the Series started. However, in a civil trial held in Milwaukee in 1924, Hugh Fullerton took the stand along with Charles Comiskey. The two admitted under oath that they could think of no instance during the 1919 Series wherein Joe Jackson had done anything to fix the Series, and admitted that he had played remarkably well.

the only true "Czar" of Baseball, a man free of any constraints, supervision, or authority—a stern, no-nonsense jurist famed for harsh sentencing and rigid standards in judging the conduct of the others.[9]

17. After the Grand Jury concluded its work, it indicted the eight "Black Sox," and thereafter the indicted players were placed on a suspended list, but they also received a written communication from their Club:

"If you are innocent of any wrongdoing, you and each of you will be reinstated."

18. As the facts show, that promise, notwithstanding a jury verdict wherein the players were found innocent, was never honored by Major League Baseball.[10]

THE TRIAL

19. In the fall of 1921, the eight Black Sox stood trial before Judge Hugo Friend. The players were acquitted by a jury on September 21, 1921—after two hours and forty minutes of deliberation. (A copy of the jury's verdict is attached hereto as Exhibit "A".)

THE BAN OF JUDGE LANDIS

20. The day after the Jury announced its "Not Guilty" verdict, the Eight Black Sox who had been acquitted were banned from Baseball by the new Commissioner Landis in his first official act. They became

---

[9]Judge Landis developed a reputation for sentencing which was harsh to the point that Appellate Courts had to step in and overturn the sentences because they exceeded the law or facts. The use of harsh sentences was particularly pronounced during World War I when he sentenced "Socialists" to hundreds of years only to find that upon review, the sentence had been either vacated entirely or significantly reduced. However, in his new position, there would no longer be a reviewing or Appellate body to serve as a judicial check and insure that the sentence fit the "crime".

[10]The representation, a promise (and obligation) made on behalf of Baseball, whether prudent or well founded, should have been binding on Baseball. The jury verdict was not fixed or tainted, although admittedly the home town jurors were biased. Baseball ignored its obligation, and history for the most part has glossed over the fact that Baseball ignored its promise. The common law recognizes a concept known as estoppel, which basically rests on equitable concepts, and here, arguably should have estopped the new Commissioner from punishing the players after the jury verdict was entered. Thus, the ban was entered in the face of a promise not to ban, and, of course, without any semblance of due process.

the infamous "Eight Men Out." Although they had been acquitted by a jury, and although the new Commissioner was familiar with the Rule of Law and was a Federal Judge sworn to uphold the Rule of Law (including the judgments of juries), the Commissioner handed down a sentence to each of the Eight Players that would effectively deny them the opportunity to play in the Major Leagues for the remainder of their careers. The players were dismissed without notice, without a hearing, and without an opportunity to rebut or answer the alleged charges, and without any finding whatsoever as to their culpability, or the rule or law which they were deemed to have violated.[11]

21. The ban by Commissioner Landis was a succinct public statement. It was the only action taken by the Commissioner in connection with the ban of Shoeless Joe and Buck. The entire "proceeding" took less than 10 minutes, and involved an announcement that made clear, if the text is read carefully, that the Commissioner was intent on keeping the National Game afloat at a time of grave crisis, and was willing to do so even if it meant the denial of due process and the ignoring of the Rule of Law. The pronouncement by a Judge after a Jury Verdict of "Not Guilty" is particularly surprising and makes clear that the ban was done much in the manner of an emergency "drumhead court martial." The text was surgical and succinct:

> *REGARDLESS OF THE VERDICT OF JURIES, no player who throws a ball game, no player that undertakes or promises to throw a ball game, no player that SITS IN CONFERENCE with a bunch of crooked players and gamblers where the ways and means of throwing a game are DISCUSSED and DOES NOT PROMPTLY TELL HIS CLUB about it, will ever play professional baseball!*

(Emphasis added.)

22. On information and belief, the above announcement was the only step taken by Judge Landis in connection with the sentencing of

---

[11]The manner of banning the players in 1921, without any semblance of due process contrasts starkly with the due process "overkill" which modern Baseball has embraced—as demonstrated in the Alomar-Umpire incident, and the elaborate due process hearings accorded George Steinbrenner and Pete Rose.

Weaver and Jackson, and no further findings, orders, listings of ineligibility or instructions were entered by Judge Landis.[12]

23. The sentence by Judge Landis, quoted above, lists several forms of conduct which were punishable by the ban. However, in another marked deviation from traditional judicial practices, Judge Landis made no attempt to delineate the individual conduct that was being punished, or make findings as to individual conduct. As a result, and based on the facts that are undisputed, it would appear that there was only one theory of culpability that could be assigned to the two players: the failure to tell the club about the fix. As is discussed below, it would appear that many were guilty of not telling the club, but ultimately were excused and went unpunished. Indeed, whether a failure to... "tell the Club," given the circumstances, was a crime, misdemeanor, infraction, or even a punishable offense will be left to the reader. As Jackson and Weaver did not play to fix, but played to win, did not bet on baseball, and had no dealings with the gamblers, this third category, a catch-all and unwritten rule, is the only possible basis for their ban.[13]

24. The requirement that a player tell his club was not a published rule of Baseball, and was obviously treated by the new Commissioner as some form of unwritten moral imperative by which the players were automatically bound.[14] In relying on that, the Commissioner, perhaps,

---

[12]The language of the sentence is imprecise; it has generally been construed to cover the life of the players, but on closer reading allows for another reasonable interpretation tied to the focus of the punishment: the playing of major league baseball. If that focus is used, it is apparent that the sentence is shorter, a <u>sentence of years</u>—an indeterminate period of years spanning the period wherein the players would be capable of playing baseball with sufficient skill and competence to play at a professional level. Under the latter interpretation, the players" sentences would most certainly have been completed by 1935. If the sentence is given its most common interpretation, a life-sentence, it ended in the '50s—December 5, 1951 for Joe Jackson and January 31, 1956 for Buck Weaver.

[13]As the Grand Jury Testimony shows, Jackson attempted to return the money, but was told by the Secretary of the Club... "to keep it." It was not illegal to keep the money. From a moral standpoint, however, the pocketing of the money was clearly a grave moral lapse. Jackson apparently quickly realized the lapse and acted to report the fix, tried to tell his club, did nothing for the money and tried to return the money. Further, his efforts on the field showed a consistent effort to overcome the fix by a remarkable performance, which came close to defeating the fix and set World Series records which lasted for decades.

[14]Another less charitable critique would perhaps conclude that the players were

overlooked another equally strong **moral imperative of the age:** one to which the players accorded great deference. The players of 1919 lived in an era that had not yet heard the message of Mr. Miller and Mr. Fehr, had not been introduced to sports agents and lavish shoe contracts—and did not realize that they could charge for their signatures—they signed for free. They were, in many ways, uniquely talented indentured employees, ill-educated and naive—but they certainly had a well defined code of conduct which honored some concepts that lamentably have been forgotten in a game that was, at its inception, a "team sport" based on common and respected bonds. As part of that bond, a simple code was maintained, and people learned as part of that code that it was wrong to betray a confidence—to snitch. In a sense, the Series of 1919, and the events leading to the appointment of the first Commissioner, set the stage for the clash between the unwritten moral imperatives from the World of Judge Landis, versus the unwritten Code and moral imperatives of the working man, the man on the street. The Judge and "his law" prevailed.

25. The sentence of the Commissioner, based on a failure to tell the club of the fix, is perhaps most interesting if viewed from the perspective of who was ultimately banned—and who was <u>excused</u> from the requirement to "tell his club." There appears to have been a selective or, perhaps more accurately, a double standard, used in determining which players had.... "failed to tell the club." Clearly, the Second Baseman Collins, who stood between Gandil and Risberg inning after inning for several years, and but a short distance from the mound in an 8-game series, knew of the fix (according to the papers, every citizen on the South Side over 8 years of age knew of the fix), yet Collins did not... "tell his club." Nor did Ray Schalk...who had opportunity to "tell his club." Schalk had caught Cicotte and Williams, and knew their skills and weaknesses—and was well aware of their "stuff." As an experienced catcher, he certainly knew when the pitchers were not bearing down. Ray Schalk issued a statement to the press after the Series (admittedly in support of his teammates) stating that there was no fix and that fact was apparent to anyone who had watched the Series. Both Schalk and Collins, college men,

---

convicted of a "crime," based on a law which did not exist. The concept of a life sentence for failing to tell the club about facts appearing daily in the papers is, in many ways, the "Catch 22" of the Landis era.

avoided the ban, and are now, because of their skills, justly enshrined in the Hall of Fame.

26. Shoeless Joe did not enjoy the above collegial benefice, and was banned at the height of his career. He never donned the uniform or crossed the chalk lines of a Major League Stadium to play a Major League Baseball Game again. **Shoeless Joe Jackson served his full sentence without any reduction of time, although he had behaved admirably, and had never commented negatively about Major League Baseball, or Commissioner Landis.** Joe Jackson died on December 5, 1951.

27. Shoeless Joe was interviewed in 1942 in connection with an article for the *Sporting News*. Joe told Scoop Latimar, the author of the article and an editor of the *Greenville News* (the same writer to first use the nickname "Shoeless Joe" in the press), that he was innocent, and had played to win:

> *"Regardless of what anyone says, I'm innocent of any wrongdoing. I gave baseball all I had. The Supreme Being is the only one to whom I've got to answer...and I have this consolation...the Good Lord knows I am innocent of any wrongdoing."*

28. The magnitude of the loss felt by Shoeless Joe, who was at the zenith of his career when the ban was issued, can only be speculated upon—but certainly we gain a sense of the enormity from the essay, "The Green Fields of the Mind" by the late Commissioner Giammatti—an essay which deals with but a single season, but by analogy gives poignant insight into a lifetime loss:

> *The game begins in the spring, when everything else begins again, and it blossoms in the summer, filling the afternoons and evenings, and then as soon as the chill rains come, it stops and leaves you to face the fall alone. You count on it, rely on it to buffer the passage of time, to keep the memory of sunshine and high skies alive, and then just when the days are all twilight, when you need it most, it stops...and summer is gone.*

29. The "Fix" of 1919 was the product of a scheme devised by two Black Sox players, Swede Risberg and Chick Gandil, who acted in concert with the Pitchers Cicotte and Williams and perhaps ultimately as many as five groups of gamblers, including "Sleepy" Bill Burns,

Joseph "Sport" Sullivan, Abe Attel, Billy Maharg, and the infamous Arnold Rothstein, who bankrolled the fix. The players were banned for life without hearing. None of the gamblers were ever convicted or punished in any way, and no investigation of the Fix was ever initiated by Major League Baseball, although there were many issues and contradictions left unresolved after the ban.[15]

THE BAN THAT SAVED BASEBALL

30. This Memorandum would be remiss if it did not acknowledge that Commissioner Landis, in banning certain of the Black Sox, acted decisively at a time of emergency amidst grave conditions which threatened to bring down the game. Judge Landis, in addressing the emergency and ultimately saving Major League Baseball, moved quickly and efficiently, but in doing so, sacrificed careers and due process. In the case of Joe Jackson (and Buck Weaver) it appears that he unfortunately ignored the one "witness" that would have provided immutable truth—the box score.

31. The Box Score shows that Joe Jackson hit and fielded in a manner that resulted in records that stood for decades. It is perhaps the most eloquent argument and proof that can be made on his behalf.

THE KEY ISSUES

32. Judge Landis did not hold an investigation of the fix prior to banning Joe Jackson. If Judge Landis had made an investigation in 1921, and reviewed the box score, and had an opportunity to fully review the Grand Jury transcript (rumored stolen from Court Records by Arnold Rothstein's counsel, Mr. Fallon), the Judge would have learned the following: (a) that Shoeless Joe received $5,000.00 from a teammate and friend, Lefty Williams, subsequently realized that he

---

[15]As an addendum it should be noted that, although the players were banned forever for fixing games, fraternizing with gamblers, or "not telling their club," Commissioner Landis utilized a different standard when it came to dealing with Owners' conduct in the same era. Indeed, the most egregious Villain of the Black Sox Series, Arnold Rothstein, the gambler who bankrolled and managed the fix and invested $350,000 in seeing that it worked, was often seen, in years after the ban, attending games as the regular guest in the Club Box of the New York Giants. Judge Landis knew of his presence and did not punish the Giants—a most puzzling moral flip-flop given the Fix of 1919, Rothstein's involvement and obvious propensity to tamper with the outcome of World Championships.

should not accept the money, and attempted to return the money, but was told by the Club to... "keep it"; (b) there is no evidence that Jackson did anything whatsoever in **furtherance of any conspiracy to fix, and by his conduct on the field, clearly and effectively withdrew and distanced himself from the actions and conspiracy of others,** by playing brilliant baseball that included flawless fielding, and offensive statistics that easily led the Series and stood for many years."[16]

33. Because Baseball was fighting for survival, Judge Landis imposed a ban that abrogated many basic tenets of our Constitution, Common Law, and subsequently annunciated policies of Baseball. The emergency is long past, the sentences fully served, yet Baseball appears to be continuing the deprivations exacted in 1921. The perception should be corrected for the following reasons:

A. The National Game, which to the public is personified by two Institutions, Major League Baseball and the National Baseball Hall of Fame,[17] which have a need as the Fiduciaries of the National Game to insure that **honor, objectivity and fairness** are the guiding principles in all dealings relating to the National Game, a sentiment eloquently set down by the late Commissioner Giammatti, who **stressed the "fidelity" of Baseball:**

I believe baseball is an important, enduring American institution. It must assert and aspire to the highest principles—of integrity, of professionalism, of performance, of fair play, within its rules. It will come as no surprise that, like an institution composed of human beings, this institution will not always fulfill its highest aspirations. I know of no earthly institution that does. But this one, because it is so much a part of our history as a people and because it has such a purchase on our national soul, has an

---

[16]The scholars Donald Gropman, *Say it Ain't So Joe;* David Carlson, *Strike Four: Joe Jackson, the Black Sox and 1919 World Series;* Irv Stein, *The Ginger Kid;* Elliot Asinov, *Eight Men Out;* and the late Bill Veeck, *The Hustlers Handbook;* have all produced wonderfully entertaining and scholarly histories as to the events herein. Their accounts of the Series and fix should be consulted at length by any scholar wishing to plumb the points and issues discussed in this Memorandum.

[17]"Baseball" appears to be used by the Public in a generic sense, and although the National Baseball Hall of Fame is a wholly separate entity from Major League Baseball, the public perception is often an amorphous entity known and referred to as "Baseball."

obligation to the people for whom it is played—to its fans and well-wishers—to strive for excellence in all things and to promote the highest ideals.

B. In keeping with the standard of fidelity and need to strive for excellence, it should be noted that certain "policies" are being asserted, which are not part of the Rules for Election, and are not based on any duly promulgated Rules. They include the recent statements asserting that an estate must act on behalf of Shoeless Joe for purposes of "restoration" before Major League Baseball. These unwritten statements, because they are at odds with the duly promulgated Rules for Election, convey the unfortunate impression that "Baseball, and in this case, the Hall of Fame, in its Internet Policy (attached as Exhibit "B"), is attempting to reach beyond this temporal setting, requiring various punitive undertakings which have the *de facto* effect of exerting further control, jurisdiction, and a sentence in perpetuity, which in effect continues to "punish" deceased players who have passed to . . . "the other side of the grass."

C. Joe Jackson, as noted above, died without heirs, and thus the purported requirement that an estate act on behalf of Shoeless Joe is, in effect, a procedural "poison pill," an unreasonable burden based on nonexistent Rules which would entail an unnecessary, fruitless task, which does not involve private rights or property. The subject or focus of any effort regarding Shoeless Joe involves public records, which belong to Baseball and the Fans, and are not the private property or domain of any estate. There is no "estate" requirement set forth in the "Rules of Election" of the National Baseball Hall of Fame. To prolong the "sentence" of Jackson based on a nonexistent Rule, stands in derogation of the "fairness" urged by Commissioner Giammatti, and also obviously raises some rather interesting theological difficulties—as does a concept of a sentence in perpetuity and the *de facto* punishment of deceased players (somewhat suggestive of themes in Dante's *Inferno*). This unfortunate result is clearly unintended by the Hall of Fame. The listing of Shoeless Joe Jackson on the Ballot will quickly and efficiently eradicate any such impression.

D. Any Jurisdiction over the remembrance, honoring, and possible induction of Joe Jackson lies solely with the National Baseball Hall of Fame, and no other entity. Major League Baseball ceased to have jurisdiction over Shoeless Joe as of the date of his death. This point has great import in considering Rule 6 of the *Rules For Election,* and particularly Rule 6(E) (discussed in detail below). On the date of Jackson's death, he ceased to be a "person," c.f. Rule 6(E).[18] Further, any belated argument in defense of the Statement of Policy in the Web Site noted earlier, urging that Jackson must be "restored" or is somehow still under the jurisdiction of Major League Baseball, ignores the Rules For Election, and entails a form of after-the-fact, double punishment which is barred by all accepted concepts of Common Law "fairness." Moreover, the requirement that an <u>estate</u> seek restoration entails a tampering of the Hall of Fame and an altering of the sentence handed down by Judge Landis. The Judge banned the players from playing baseball during the remaining period of years that they were capable of playing, or at worst, during their lifetime. **Judge Landis did not bar or place the two players on a list of ineligibility for perpetuity—he knew where his powers ended.**

E. If a "restoration" and "permanent ineligible roster" is utilized as a procedural device to avoid what is apprehended by some to be an assault on the traditions of the National Game or the Baseball Hall of Fame, it is an errant endeavor. The continued listing of the players on an "ineligible list," onerous standing requirements and petitions by estates, and reliance on Rules which are nonexistent and certainly not found in the Rules for Election by the Committee on Veterans, are wholly unnecessary. The National Baseball Hall of Fame has appointed a most independent body of very experienced members that have the credentials and experience necessary to weigh the *bona fides* of various candidates. The committee has more than sufficient guidance (and protection) in the true Rules of the Hall of Fame, including Rule 9 which states, **"Voting shall be based on the individual's record, ability, integrity, sportsmanship, character, and contribution to the game."** If the Committee, in its wisdom and after considering all of the facts, is against the induction, it can simply refrain from supporting the nomination by vote. The Members of the Committee on Veterans have the experience, judgment, and love for the

---

[18]C.f. Rule 6(E) of the National Baseball Hall of Fame as quoted herein on page 319, n.3.

Game which will insure that a competent and responsible determination is made without need for outdated "ineligible" lists, onerous standing requirements, and other "Official Statements" which are not found in the governing procedures of the "Rules For Election" of the Hall of Fame.

F. Our Common Law, Constitution and legal traditions, while obviously not directly applicable to deceased players, set a benchmark for what is traditionally held to be fair and consistent with due process. If the above concepts are applied herein, it is apparent that the double jeopardy, the punishment of a person a second time (or forever) is clearly a grave concern. In this case, a player served the stipulated sentence in full. Under all concepts of due process and fair play that have evolved in our Common Law and Constitution, Joe Jackson's name (along with Buck Weaver's) should have been stricken from any ineligible listing decades ago when he completed his sentence in 1951. Any retention of their names on a subsequent listing or a current listing (which is Baseball's sole procedural mechanism for punishing "persons"), or any attempt at somehow banning or exerting "jurisdiction" over deceased players in perpetuity, entails twice placing the players in jeopardy for the same offense—and is **a blatant tampering with the sentence of Judge Landis, who, as noted above, knew the limits of his power.**

G. Any linking of the nomination of Shoeless Joe to the recent Petition before Major League Baseball by Pete Rose, either directly or indirectly, or concern as to possibly setting a precedent or link to the Rose situation, is neither appropriate nor supported by the facts and law. The key facts are wholly different, particularly the fact that Shoeless Joe fully paid his debt to Baseball. Pete Rose is still serving a sentence, and is a "person" that is governed by a completely different set of "Rules of Election."

H. The National Baseball Hall of Fame and the Committee on Veterans can take Notice of the Following Facts which, because of the applicability of the "person" requirement under Rule 6(E), are surplusage, but should also perhaps be noted as they also further demonstrate that Shoeless Joe cannot legitimately be listed on any current ineligible roster of Major League Baseball:

(i) The ineligible roster of Major League Baseball has always served as the mechanism for punishing living suspended "persons"[19] (living beings) and should therefore contain only those names of "persons" that are being punished, during the period they are "punished" and "ineligible";

(ii) There is no instance in the History of the Game wherein Baseball placed or maintained the name of a deceased player on an ineligible roster;

(iii) Once the players' punishment and period of ineligibility ends, and certainly after a player has died, a continued listing as "ineligible" is an impossibility as the deceased players have ceased to be "persons" (and hopefully have passed on to the jurisdiction of a higher classification and League);

(iv) Once a sentence/suspension is served in full, one cannot logically or ethically continue to be listed on a punishment roster (and thus further punished). To allow for further listing as "ineligible" is a continuation of punishment, and in this case would entail a continuous punishment of some 75 years, including some 41 years after the death of Shoeless Joe, a sentence never intended by Judge Landis. Baseball would not allow this to happen and clearly would not allow a sentence beyond the sentence handed down by Judge Landis;

(v) Once a sentence is fully served, Baseball (for lack of a better metaphor or analogy) has obligations analogous to a Warden, and an automatic duty to end the punishment on the completion of the last day of the sentence. Here, Baseball had a duty to "free" Joe in 1951 from any roster or listing of persons serving periods of punishment.

I. On the basis of the above, Joe Jackson, having fully served his sentence and died on December 5, 1951, ceased to be a "person" in 1951 and cannot be listed on any current listing of "ineligible," suspended persons maintained by Major League Baseball, as that would mean that he is still suspended and thus punished after death—and well after his sentence and punishment had expired.

---

[19]The Public understanding of the jurisdiction and candidates on the ineligible roster of Major League Baseball is succinctly reflected in the ubiquitous Rule 6(E) which speaks of "persons" listed on an eligible roster. "Persons" are, on information and belief, not defined by Baseball, but are defined in *Webster's New World Dictionary* and *Webster's International Dictionary* as. . . . "a human being. . . . personality, self."

J. It has been suggested that a private estate must file a petition with baseball to initiate any action on behalf of Shoeless Joe. The Committee can find no Rule requiring any such procedure in the *Rules for Election,* and further would note that any such process of petition for restoration would be a fruitless venture, as the records and issues at stake relate solely to the public records of Major League Baseball and do not involve private rights or property, the proper and traditional purpose for appointing an estate.

III.

APPLICABLE RULES AND PROCEDURES

Rules of the National Baseball Hall of Fame:

The National Baseball Hall of Fame has codified two sets of rules governing election to the National Baseball Hall of Fame. There is but one set of Rules for Elections administered and voted upon by the Baseball Writers Association, and a second very specific set of Rules governing the **Committee on Veterans.** The Rules are from time to time supplemented and amended. As noted above, the Rules which apply in this setting, a copy of which has been attached hereto as attachment "C," are **the sole set of Rules governing the actions of the Committee on Veterans.**

Even a brief perusal of the *Rules for Election* makes clear that the Rules are a complete, independent and comprehensive set of rules. The Rules begin with a statement as to the correct name of the Committee in Rule 1 and 2, and end at Rule 12 with a set of Rules regarding amendment. The Rules deal with all phases of the nomination and voting process including: eligibility, nomination, and election procedures, as well as various committees, appointments of members, and qualities to be considered in evaluating candidates.

All of the *Rules for Election* are <u>written,</u> there is **no reference or incorporation or reference to any other oral or unwritten polices, custom or usage. Further, there are no ties, connections, or references with the rules of any other organization save Rule 6 E which is discussed herein.** The referenced Rules are complete, self standing, and all steps for election are found within the four corners of the *Rules For Election.* The *Rules For Election* are not tied or dependent to any other entity nor do they depend upon, or require that any requisite acts be carried out by any other institution, entity or individual as a pre-requisite. (There is, within Rule 6(E), a certain reference to an ineligible list in the case of living candidates— "persons"; but the use of the term "persons" patently does not apply in the instant case.)

The Rules of Election of the Nominating Committee are the Sole Rules governing Nomination and Election by the Committee on Veterans.

A. General Qualifications in the Rules for Election–Rule 6:

The qualifications needed by a Nominee are set forth in Rule 6. Shoeless Joe Jackson (1890–1951), played Major League Baseball from 1908 to 1920 and thus satisfies the ten year requirements of Rule 6(A). Shoeless Joe played before 1945 and therefore is not impeded by the 60% Rule in 6(A).

B. Rule 6(E): The So-Called "Pete Rose Rule":

The Committee will recall that the Rules were amended in 1991 to include the so-called Pete Rose Rule. The Rule succinctly states... *"(E) any person on Baseball's Ineligible List shall not be an eligible candidate."* The Rule patently does not apply because the decedent Jackson is not a "person" as defined by all commonly used Dictionaries. Further, the word is used in all common parlance to describe a living being and this is the plain unambiguous meaning and usage of the term.

In addition, and as discussed at length above in paragraph 33 and its various sub-parts, Shoeless Joe could not properly be listed on a current "ineligible" list of Major League Baseball. This latter point is again noted for historic reasons, as the Rule patently does not apply because of the initial impediment—the fact that Shoeless Joe is not a "person," having died some 46 years ago on December 5, 1951.

C. Rule 9—Voting:

The Rule states that.... *"voting shall be based on the individuals record, ability, integrity, sportsmanship, character and contribution to the game."*

The above Rule and standards are directed to the Committee on Veterans sitting *en banque* in formal review at an annual meeting.

This issue clearly falls within the dominion of the Committee as a whole. The Committee will hopefully consider the discussion set forth above, as well as other presentations made before the full Committee. There will undoubtedly be some discussion in connection with the issues of integrity and character which will center upon the demeanor, dignity and humility displayed by Jackson in the face of a lifetime ban for a "crime" which did not exist, and which he had not violated. His actions at worst showed a naive judgement in associating with certain members of his team, and a brief period of greed. His conduct as discussed above certainly did not show any association with gamblers, betting on the series. As to the fix, the box score speaks volumes, as does the Grand Jury testimony quoted earlier herein, and makes clear that Shoeless Joe renounced any conspiracy or fix by his conduct and most demonstrable forms of communication, his bat and glove. The efforts and results are perhaps the most eloquent body of testimony for Shoeless Joe, and very difficult to argue around—people engaged in fixes do not field flawlessly, hit .357 against stellar pitching, and set World Series records that stand for decades. This is also shown in the Grand Jury testimony which is set out above.

As to the Requirements dealing with Shoeless Joe's "Contributions to the Game" (Rule 10), we believe that the evidence is overwhelming. While only Cobb and Hornsby have higher lifetime averages, most knowledgeable hitters and scholars of the game believe that Shoeless Joe was the dominant hitter of the deadball era and perhaps the greatest hitter of all time.

Rules of Major League Baseball:

Major League Baseball has no Written Rules of Procedures dealing with or allowing for the listing of deceased ballplayers, or the continued listing of a deceased player on any ineligible list after a sentence has been fully served. Baseball has no Written Rules or Procedures for the "restoration" of deceased ball players, and has not previously "restored" a deceased ballplayer at any time in the past. Finally, Major League Baseball has no Rules or Procedures dealing with the nomination or induction of deceased players in the National Baseball Hall of Fame.

CONCLUSION

The Committee on Veterans of the Hall of Fame has the only set of Rules relating to the possible election of Shoeless Joe Jackson to the National Baseball Hall of Fame. The Rules are known as the *Rules For Election of the Committee on Veterans*. They are the sole Rules governing the procedures for nomination and voting on candidates for the National Baseball Hall of Fame. The Rules do not have any provisions which would bar the nomination of Shoeless Joe Jackson. In particular, Shoeless Joe is not barred by Rule 6(E) of the Rules for Election because said Rule only relates to living candidates, "persons" that are listed as ineligible (and serving a sentence imposed by Major League Baseball).

Major League Baseball has no Written Rules or Procedures which would appear to bear upon the subject issues. Shoeless Joe Jackson completed his sentence in 1951 and thus paid his debt to the National Game in Full.

Joseph Jefferson "Shoeless Joe" can be listed as a nominee for the next meeting of the Committee on Veterans. Many Fans and Students of the Game believe said nomination will reflect the honor and dignity of the National Game and Hall of Fame, and fairly address long debated and controversial issues, thereby closing a Historic Chapter in American Folk History.

Respectfully,

**THE CHICAGO LEGAL COMMITTEE
IN RE: JOSEPH JEFFERSON
"SHOELESS JOE" JACKSON**

Louis R. Hegeman, Chairman
Gould & Ratner
222 North LaSalle Street,
Chicago, IL 60601
Tel: (312) 899-1630
Fax: (312) 236-3241

Nicholas J. Motherway, Esq.
Motherway & Glenn
100 W. Monroe, Street 200
Chicago, IL 60603
Tel: (312) 726-2699

E. Michael Kelly, Esq.
Hinshaw & Culbertson
222 North LaSalle Street, Suite
Chicago, IL 60601
Fax:(312) 704-3283

Brian P. Shaughnessy Esq.
2100 Winchester, Suite 601
Wheaton, IL 60187
Tel: (630) 588-4122

CERTIFICATE OF SERVICE

The undersigned, one of the Attorneys for the Petitioners, hereby certifies that that true originals of the forgoing Petition, duly signed by the Petitioners Ted Williams and Bob Feller, were duly served upon the **Commissioner of Baseball, the Honorable Alan Selig,** and Upon the **Members of the Executive Committee of Major League Baseball** by placing sealed envelopes, with all postage prepaid, in the mail slot of the United States Mail located at 222 N. La Salle, Chicago, 60601 on January 16th, 1998 and addressed as follows:

By Certified Mail Return Receipt:

The Honorable Alan Selig,
Acting Commissioner, Major League Baseball
350 Park Avenue
New York, New York 10022

By Certified Mail Return Receipt:

The Executive Committee of Major League Baseball
350 Park Avenue
New York, New York 10022

I hereby certify that the above envelopes were so deposited and the above information is correct.

Louis R. Hegeman, One of the
Attorneys for the Petitioner

January 16, 1998.

Sources

The materials on which this book is based came from dozens of people in conversation with the author, and from a wide range of printed matter.

Microfilms of some of the newspapers that covered Joe's career were scanned almost day by day. The most useful of these newspapers, to all of which I am grateful for their kind permission to quote passages in this book, were the *Greenville News*, *Savannah Press*, *New Orleans Times Picayune*, and the *Cleveland Plain Dealer*.

The most useful periodicals were: *Baseball Magazine*, *Collier's*, *Everybody's*, *Harper's Weekly*, *Literary Digest*, *McClure's*, *The Nation*, *New Republic*, *North American Review*, *Saturday Evening Post*, *Scribner's Monthly*, *Sport Magazine*, *Sports Illustrated*, and *True*.

The following list is a combination of books that provided background information and books that focused more closely on Joe Jackson and his world.

Algren, Nelson. "The Swede Was A Hard Guy," in *The Last Carousel*. New York, 1973.

Allen, Frederick Lewis. *The Big Change*. New York, 1952.

———. *Only Yesterday*. New York, 1931.

Asinof, Eliot. *Eight Men Out: The Black Sox and the 1919 World Series*. New York, 1963.

Axelson, G. W. *"Commy": The Life Story of Charles A. Comiskey*. Chicago, 1919.

Baseball Encyclopedia, The. Toronto, 1969.

Baseball's One For The Book: The Sporting News. St. Louis, 1967.

Beard, Charles A. and Mary R. *The Rise of American Civilization*. New York, 1930.

Brown, Warren. *The Chicago White Sox.* New York, 1952.

Cleveland, Charles B. *The Great Baseball Managers.* New York, 1950.

Cobb, Ty, with Al Stump. *My Life In Baseball: The True Record.* New York, 1961.

Coffin, Tristram P. *The Old Ball Game: Baseball In Folklore and Fiction.* New York, 1971.

Creamer, Robert W. *Babe: The Legend Comes To Life.* New York, 1974.

Danzig, Allison, and Reichler, Joe. *The History Of Baseball.* Englewood Cliffs, N.J., 1959.

Daley, Arthur. *Inside Baseball.* New York, 1950.

————. *Sports of The Times.* New York, 1959.

Dickey, Glenn. *The Great No-Hitters.* Radnor, Pa., 1976.

Farrell, James T. *My Baseball Diary.* New York, 1957.

Fishwick, Marshall. *The Hero, American Style.* New York, 1969.

Fowler, Gene. *The Great Mouthpiece: A Life Story of William J. Fallon.* New York, 1931.

Haywood, William D. *Bill Haywood's Book: The Autobiography of William D. Haywood.* New York, 1929.

Hodges, Russ. *Baseball Complete.* New York, 1952.

Holtzman, Jerome. *No Cheering in the Press Box.* New York, 1974.

Katcher, Leo. *The Big Bankroll: The Life and Times of Arnold Rothstein.* New York, 1959.

Lardner, Ring. *You Know Me Al.* New York, 1914.

Leuchtenburg, William E. *The Perils of Prosperity 1914–1932.* Chicago, 1958.

Lieb, Frederick G. *The Baseball Story.* New York, 1950.

————. *The Boston Red Sox.* New York, 1947.

————. *Connie Mack: Grand Old Man of Baseball.* New York, 1945.

Liebling, A. J. *The Press.* New York, 1961.

Link, Arthur S. *American Epoch: A History of the United States Since the 1890's*. New York, 1955.

Longstreet, Stephen. *Chicago*. New York, 1973.

Lord, Walter. *The Good Years: From 1900 to the First World War*. New York, 1960.

Luhrs, Victor. *The Great Baseball Mystery — The 1919 World Series*. New York, 1966.

Malamud, Bernard. *The Natural*. New York, 1952.

Martin, Milward W. *Twelve Full Ounces*. New York, 1962.

McCallum, John D. *The Tiger Wore Spikes*. New York, 1956.

———. *Ty Cobb*. New York, 1975.

Mott, Frank Luther. *American Journalism*. New York, 1949.

Peterson, Harold. *The Man Who Invented Baseball*. New York, 1973.

Pettitt, George A. *Prisoners of Culture*. New York, 1970.

Potwin, Marjorie A. *Cotton Mill People of the Piedmont*. New York, 1927.

Rice, Grantland. *The Tumult and the Shouting*. New York, 1954.

Ritter, Lawrence S. *The Glory of Their Times*. New York, 1966.

Robertson, Ben. *Red Hills And Cotton: An Up Country Memory*. New York, 1942.

Schacht, Al. *My Own Particular Screwball*. New York, 1955.

Seymour, Harold. *Baseball: The Early Years*. New York, 1960.

———. *Baseball: The Golden Years*. New York, 1971.

Shoemaker, Robert H. *The Best In Baseball*. New York, 1949.

Shumway, Harry. *I Go South: An Unprejudiced Visit to a Group of Cotton Mills*. Boston, 1930.

South Carolina: A Guide To The Palmetto State (U.S. W.P.A. Writers' Program). New York, 1941.

Spaulding's Official Baseball Guide: 1920. New York, 1920.

Spink, J. G. Taylor. *Judge Landis and Twenty-Five Years of Baseball*. New York, 1947.

Van Vorst, Bessie. *The Woman Who Toils*. New York, 1903.

Veek, Bill, with Ed Linn. *The Hustler's Handbook*. New York, 1965.

Voigt, David Quentin. *American Baseball: From Gentleman's Sport to the Commissioner System*. Norman, Oklahoma, 1966.

Walker, Stanley. *City Editor*. New York, 1934.

Walton, Perry. *The Story of Textiles*. New York, 1925.

Ward, John W. *Red, White, and Blue: Men, Books and Ideas in American Culture*. New York, 1969.